POSITIONED

Strategic Workforce Planning
That Gets the Right Person in the Right Job

Dan L. Ward
and Rob Tripp with Bill Maki

⋏AMACOM

American Management Association

New York • Atlanta • Brussels • Chicago • Mexico City • San Francisco
Shanghai • Tokyo • Toronto • Washington, D.C.

Bulk discounts available. For details visit:
www.amacombooks.org/go/specialsales
Or contact special sales:
Phone: 800-250-5308
Email: specialsls@amanet.org
View all the AMACOM titles at: www.amacombooks.org
American Management Association: www.amanet.org

This publication is designed to provide accurate and authoritative information in regard to the subject matter covered. It is sold with the understanding that the publisher is not engaged in rendering legal, accounting, or other professional service. If legal advice or other expert assistance is required, the services of a competent professional person should be sought.

Library of Congress Cataloging-in-Publication Data

Ward, Dan L.
    Positioned : strategic workforce planning that gets the right person in the right job /
Dan L. Ward and Rob Tripp, with Bill Maki.
        p.   cm.
    Includes index.
    ISBN-13: 978-0-8144-3247-1
    ISBN-10: 0-8144-3247-6
    1. Manpower planning.   2. Personnel management.   3. Strategic planning.   I. Tripp, Rob.
    II. Maki, Bill.   III. Title.

    HF5549.5.M3W37   2013
    658.3'01—dc23

                                                                            2012040290

About AMA

American Management Association (www.amanet.org) is a world leader in talent development, advancing the skills of individuals to drive business success. Our mission is to support the goals of individuals and organizations through a complete range of products and services, including classroom and virtual seminars, webcasts, webinars, podcasts, conferences, corporate and government solutions, business books, and research. AMA's approach to improving performance combines experiential learning—learning through doing—with opportunities for ongoing professional growth at every step of one's career journey.

Printing number
10   9   8   7   6   5   4   3   2   1

Contents

Preface

Rob Tripp and Dan L. Ward with Bill Maki

THIS BOOK IS ABOUT the variety of tools, techniques, and processes collectively known as Strategic Workforce Planning (SWP.) It is about getting people resources when and where you need them and doing it efficiently and effectively. SWP is a fundamental requirement for survival as an organization. When done well, it provides competitive advantage. When done poorly, it results in a breakdown of the alignment between objectives and execution.

The authors of the individual pieces you will find in this book were selected because they are among the best in the world as shown by their actual performance or their record of effective research and analysis on workforce-related topics. The book is divided into four primary sections. The first provides a historical perspective on the evolution of the field, the second provides firsthand accounts from some of the people currently practicing in the field, the third drills down into analytics that have emerged as the field has matured, and the fourth takes a look at future directions for this type of work.

In the 1970s, the U.S. Department of Labor provided Manpower Institution Grants to a number of universities to promote study of improved workforce analysis. Dan Ward was one of the products of an applied economics graduate program developed under this funding, with a strong focus on econometric modeling and applying cost measurement techniques to social sciences. "We measured everything that we could measure and counted everything we could count and created forecasts, projections, and simulations," he says.

Rob Tripp came to this field from a different direction. With a Ph.D. in statistics, he was hired right out of graduate school into the U.S. auto industry, where he built complex models to simulate the impact of business actions on the hourly workforce, supporting strategic business planning and union contract negotiations.

Many traditional human resources colleagues were envious of the successes of these people, who were bringing a quantitative approach to workforce issues. These new workforce planners always seemed to be able to get funding for their proposals, while most traditional HR projects were rejected. The reason was simple. These trained workforce planners came to the table armed with "hard" data and spoke the language of business: numbers. It was a heady period for the early workforce planning professionals. We made forecasts of turnover and projected recruiting and staffing numbers—building beautiful models and scenarios that drove action plans.

Over the years, we began to realize that while these tools were critical, they were not sufficient in and of themselves. We regularly hear truisms such as "What gets measured gets done. What gets rewarded gets repeated." We realized that performance metrics can drive behavior but not always the desired behavior. Ineffective or misguided planning can take an organization down the wrong path. There can be serious unintended and unrecognized consequences of a well-executed but poorly conceived plan.

In his presentations, John Boudreau uses a slide that says "Not everything that can be counted counts and not everything that counts can be counted." Our solutions need to blend comprehensive data with social, behavioral, and cultural insights to be truly effective in the long run. Truly effective Strategic Workforce Planning is more than an exercise to run the numbers: It is ultimately a disciplined conversation about talent, especially strategically critical talent, and it puts the metrics, projections, forecasts, and scenarios in a total organizational context and ensures that the discrete parts are aligned against a truly strategic perspective.

DEDICATION

It would be impossible o list all the people who have provided assistance in the creation of this book, but we would like to specifically thank our wives and children for their continuing support while their fathers toiled many nights, weekends, and vacation days to nurture an idea to become this finished work. Thank you for bearing with us.

Also in particular, we want to recognize two workforce planning friends who continually provided sage advice, counsel, and sometimes just an argument when our not yet fully baked ideas needed refinement.

Thomas P. Bechet was a friend, colleague, and coeditor for us in *Best Practices in Human Resource Forecasting and Modeling,* the collection we did for HRPS in 1994. Tom passed away in 2008, but his influence continues.

Bill Maki started the journey with us for this book but had to pull out as a result of a health situation. We pray for his full recovery and look forward to his return and reengagement in future workforce planning topics.

SECTION 1

Historical Perspective

Dan L. Ward

THIS FIRST SECTION OFFERS insight into earlier practices in Strategic Workforce Planning (SWP). In 1969, **James W. Walker** authored "Forecasting Manpower Needs" in the *Harvard Business Review*, which created quite a stir when senior executives were introduced to the concept. In the 1970s, he founded the Human Resource Planning Society, now known as HR People & Strategy (HRPS). We asked Jim to write the first chapter of this book because no one is more qualified to talk about how this field gained its prominence over the past forty years. His chapter, "The Origins of Workforce Planning," allows the reader a chance to sit beside Jim as he describes the professionalization of our field.

Borrowing the title from an old George Gershwin song, "How Long Has This Been Going On?" is my own sometimes lighthearted but sincerely heartfelt look at the ascent of SWP. Our tools and techniques have evolved. We continually refine our terminology, but the fact remains that humans have always been concerned with the fundamental concepts of SWP, even if our tools and terminology have become sophisticated only in more recent years. We can claim this is a brand-new field and define it carefully to support that claim, or we can recognize clues that it may actually date back to recognized community construction projects that began 13,000 years in the past. One can accept or reject the historical time line offered in this chapter, but I am personally proud to be practicing in a career field that can simultaneously be portrayed as both one of the world's oldest *and* youngest career specialties.

Alex G. Manganaris's "The Evolution of Strategic Workforce Planning Within Government Agencies" offers another opportunity to sit alongside someone who was there during some of the most significant SWP efforts of past decades. SWP seems to flow in and out of favor in a cyclical fashion within private industry, but it has been steadily applied within many government agencies.

Dan L. Ward is the associate department head for the MITRE team providing support to the U.S. government on workforce strategy and human capital topics. In this role, he leads advisory support for workforce planning, organization design, people strategy, and change management activities. Dan has provided advice and counsel to a variety of U.S. government agencies.

Ward earned his bachelor's degree in social science and his master's in workforce economics from the University of North Texas. Prior to joining MITRE in 2006, he held senior level roles in HR, knowledge management, and strategic planning at GTE, Texaco, and EDS. One-third of the Fortune 100 companies have sought his counsel on advanced people strategies.

He started his career as a management scientist with Western Electric, developing workforce simulation studies. His cost-benefit studies on alternate staffing strategies have been cited in *Fortune*, *BusinessWeek*, the *Wall Street Journal*, and the Work in America Institute, among others. He is an award-winning photographer and has published three photography books, the latest being *Tribute*, a photo-haiku study of Civil War memorials.

Bill Maki was an equal partner with Dan and Rob at the beginning of this book project. He was one of the earliest members of the Human Resource Planning Society and a past president of the group. With a bachelor's degree in mathematics from the University of Washington and a master's in statistics and operations research from Oregon State University, Bill was one of the pacesetters for workforce forecasting and modeling. He retired after thirty-nine years with Weyerhaeuser and continues to write and speak on workforce planning related topics. Bill helped design the layout of this book and suggested some of the contributors. Due to a health problem, he relinquished his editing role on the book but continued to provide advice, counsel, and moral support to Dan and Rob.

The Origins of Workforce Planning

James W. Walker

AS EARLY AS 1890, in *Principles of Economics*, economist Alfred Marshall was calling for the analysis and planning for labor needs in organizations. As a founder of neoclassic economics, he brought supply and demand, marginal utility, and costs of production into a coherent whole.

However, while I was conducting research as a graduate student in the 1960s, I found few advances in research or practice in what was then called manpower planning over the decades that followed the publication of Marshall's book. Military organizations, defense contractors, and oil companies managed their high talent staffing rigorously, but most business organizations focused on their talent requirements in a limited way (e.g., management replacement planning, short-term recruitment needs forecasting, productivity analysis driving staffing requirements). Few academicians were interested.

I was drawn to the subject through my consulting-research relationship with American Oil Company (Amoco) from 1966 to 1969. I worked with the company's organization and manpower development division on a series of projects. What fascinated me most was the company's desire to implement more effective, more creative manpower planning and development processes.

EARLY STATE OF THE ART

While an assistant professor at Indiana University, I focused on manpower planning. I wrote a series of articles and papers, which in turn opened new doors to corporations for research. In 1969, I authored an article in the *Harvard Business Review* entitled "Forecasting Manpower Needs," in which I described steps that researchers had taken toward improved models for manpower forecasting and planning, and made a call for advances. I wrote, "Although many managers are trying to do something about manpower planning, few of them are talking about it."

The article aimed to increase awareness of research and practices at the time, when—of course—forecasts had to be created on mainframe computers. Models typically relied upon historical data, but some experimented with simulations where more realistic parameters could be used. Also, models focused on particular organizational units or functions where greater specificity was possible. Examples were described that:

▶ Created projections of manpower needs for a company for each of ten years in the future (a manufacturing company)

▶ Focused on particular questions such as recruiting needs (State Farm Insurance, Schaefer Brewing)

▶ Projected talent requirements taking into account productivity patterns (Professor Eric Vetter)

At American Oil and many other companies at the time, manpower plans were limited to staffing levels and costs, projected in three-year rolling plans, with adjustments each year. Longer-term business plans focused on financials and capital requirements.

On the supply side, I wrote that "computers have come of age." The Air Force, Army, and Navy all were using "automated personnel data systems" for planning, assignments, and development. These were large systems tracking demographics, assignments, training, and other variables, as well as analysis of retention, progression, and cost-effectiveness of alternative staffing patterns. Because of the large scale and unique characteristics, these models did not transfer easily to the private sector. Aerospace companies were among those that designed systems along the same principles. AT&T developed its famed Interactive Flow Simulator (IFS), which permitted analysis of movement and an ability to guide future planning for its million-plus employee base. In many companies, modeling was spurred by affirmative action planning needs.

In the article, I also discussed replacement and succession plans—essentially plans for the top talent segment of an organization. I called for more emphasis on succession planning in order to facilitate development planning for individuals rather than merely naming replacements for specific managerial positions. An example given was a leadership program at Xerox covering 1,200 employees with a focus on a top talent subset of fifty with executive potential.

EARLY RESEARCH AND PRACTICES

In 1967, Eric Vetter, professor at Tulane University, published *Manpower Planning for High Talent Personnel*, the first book-length discussion of manpower planning techniques for business organizations. He reported the results of his doctoral dissertation research, surveying practices in a variety of companies, many of them aerospace and engineering-focused organizations. Vetter identified four steps in a process of manpower planning: (1) data collection and analysis resulting in manpower inventories and forecasts, (2) determination of goals and problem solutions, (3) implementation of plans and programs, and (4) program control and evaluation.

Once I moved to San Diego in 1969, I learned more about industry practices as a guest at meetings of the Southern California Aerospace Manpower Council, an informal consortium of the major organizations including McDonnell Douglas, Lockheed, North American Rockwell, TRW Systems Group, and the Jet Propulsion Laboratory. Some of those in the council represented the personnel function; others were from program planning functions with workforce planning responsibilities. For example, Rockwell's B-1 bomber program required complex manpower plans with different skills moving onto and off the program

In 1972, Elmer H. Burack and I edited a book, *Manpower Planning and Programming,* that contained thirty-two reprinted articles and original papers on manpower forecasting and models, information systems, and programming, with authors from GE, Standard Oil Indiana, North American Rockwell, TRW, Inland Steel, McKinsey, and such universities as Harvard, MIT, the University of Minnesota, and schools in the United Kingdom.

A year before the book appeared, I had joined Towers Perrin as practice leader of the firm's manpower planning and development practice. We conducted surveys on manpower planning practices and worked to advance the state of the art and practice. Some of the more interesting projects included development of:

▶ Early processes for defining and addressing the human resources implications of business unit plans, including staffing gaps and changes required for business success.

▶ A quantitative process for optimizing officer staffing in a major bank, within retail, corporate, international, and other divisions. It featured a sophisticated process of matching time devoted to particular activities and related results achieved, yielding guidelines for deploying officer talent to achieve business outcomes.

▶ An occupational taxonomy in a forest products company to provide a relevant framework for manpower forecasting and planning and for facilitating deployment of talent among jobs within families with similar characteristics. This is a precursor to today's workforce segmentation initiatives.

▶ A process in a pharmaceutical company requiring unit-by-unit planning of staffing levels based on managers' estimates of time devoted by staff and its relation to business outcomes (past and desired future).

▶ Rationalization of staffing in each and every division of a major international development bank, entailing detailed self-reporting of time allocation to functional tasks and unit-level analysis justification of proposed future staffing based on the findings related to unit mission/objectives.

Not all of these approaches evolved into practices common in business organizations, but they addressed the organizations' needs and often introduced new approaches to the challenges posed.

ORIGINS OF THE HUMAN RESOURCE PLANNING SOCIETY

By 1976, a few colleagues and I thought it would be fruitful to formalize a network of professionals in academia, business, and government to share experiences and insights on the subject and, more specifically, to host an annual conference, conduct workshops, and publish a journal. These colleagues were from such companies as Weyerhaeuser, Bankers Trust, International Paper, J.C. Penney, Mobil Oil, General Motors, Lockheed, Gulf Oil, and AT&T; academicians who had contributed to the subject area; and leaders of the Manpower Analysis and Planning Society (MAPS) in Washington, D.C., a group of federal agency representatives doing manpower planning. Following a charter conference in 1978 in Atlanta (attracting 225 attendees), the Human Resource Planning Society (HRPS) became a prominent "niche" organization appealing to the more "strategic thinkers" in the human resources profession. "Human resources" and "workforce" replaced "manpower" or "personnel" as the preferred terms of reference. Recently, HRPS redefined what its letters mean, becoming HR People & Strategy. The world turns.

HR PLANNING AND STRATEGY

In 1980, McGraw-Hill published my textbook *Human Resource Planning*. The second edition was renamed *Human Resource Strategy* to reflect the increasing emphasis on alignment with business strategy and priorities.

In the 1980s, we experienced a variety of emphases, including environmental scanning, benchmarking/best practice surveys, career (and career path) planning, succession planning ("executive workforce planning"), and metrics (which moved to center stage for a number of years). At the high talent level, companies emulated the General Electric (Jack Welch) practice of planning by sorting employees into ABC categories and focusing attention on the persons with the highest performance and potential. McKinsey declared a war for talent and pressed for more diligent talent management by employers.

With the advancing of computer applications, more sophisticated and more customized forecasting and planning became common. Tom Bechet, my colleague at Towers Perrin and later a partner in The Walker Group, worked with many companies in developing forecasting models within organizations. He championed a focus on issues that models need to address rather than large-scale, broad-based approaches. He championed simple desktop spreadsheet applications, using data downloaded from mainframe systems.

HRPS invested funds in sponsored research for many years and hosted an annual research consortium each summer, with research papers presented by both academicians and practitioners. They were fruitful and enjoyable networking events. My colleague Karl Price edited the papers for publication as a book each year. This helped engage academicians and encouraged research in the field. Also, HRPS published many journal articles and a book on manpower planning (edited by Tom Bechet, Rob Tripp, and Dan Ward).

REFLECTIONS

In a field where the primary professional association in the 1960s was the American Society of Personnel Administration, our endeavors were strikingly different from the norm. During these early years, large companies created staff positions to create and lead the planning efforts—within HR or elsewhere (sales, finance, manufacturing). Human resource planning was an emerging professional niche. Over time, however, responsibility for planning shifted to unit line and HR executives, enabled by new online analytic tools and databases and supported (even nudged) by staff or consultants.

One thing I've learned, however, is that best practices rarely stick. All too often, new generations of talent rediscover human resource planning and reinvent tools to meet their particular needs. As a consultant, I worked with some companies several times in my career, each time with different clients on the team. When organizations restructure or merge with others, past practices or systems often do not survive, and needs are perceived to be new and different. Nearly half of the many companies I consulted for over the decades no longer exist today (e.g., Gulf Oil, Digital Equipment, Texaco, Manufacturers Hanover) or have the same names but are entirely different entities with new management (e.g., IBM, AT&T, John Hancock, Chase).

Such organizational change, together with new generations in management, helps stimulate consideration of new, better approaches and innovation. However, progress is uneven. Consulting firms and software vendors help provide continuity and gradually advance the state of the art and practice. However, they often keep their approaches proprietary, making it difficult to build the professional body of knowledge and, in turn, peer evaluation and improvement. Their clients instead are more prone to sharing their experience and knowledge in their own forums and interest groups. Knowledge is shared more through networking and less through the seminars, conferences, and publications relied on in the early years.

My good fortune was being invited to work with American Oil long ago, and I embraced a field just waiting to develop. Those early years and decades following were very exciting.

James W. Walker is a consultant, speaker, and author on human resource strategy and contemporary workforce management issues. Jim and his colleagues worked together for fifteen years as The Walker Group, a management consulting firm based in Phoenix and later in San Diego. Before that, for fifteen years, he was a vice president and director of the human resources consulting practice at Towers Perrin, based in New York, for fifteen years.

Jim is author of the award-winning text *Human Resource Planning*, regarded as seminal in the field of strategic human resources management. He is an author or editor of nine other books and many professional articles. He was founder of the Human Resource Planning Society and has been active in many professional activities. His most recent book is *Work Wanted*, a book on the choices that baby boomer professionals and managers face as they challenge myths of aging, work, and retirement (2009).

He earned a B.S. in accounting from Millikin University, then an M.A. in labor and management and a Ph.D. in business administration from The University of Iowa. Upon graduation, Jim was an assistant professor of management at Indiana University and San Diego State University. From 1979 to 1981, on leave from Towers Perrin, he was associate professor of management at Arizona State University.

Jim currently lives in La Jolla, California, and enjoys occasional consulting and speaking, tempered with local community activities. He is president of 939 Coast Management Association, a role that challenges the best skills he acquired in his many years of consulting. He welcomes contacts at walkerjamesw@gmail.com, Facebook, or Linkedin.

How Long Has This Been Going On?

Dan L. Ward

STRATEGIC WORKFORCE PLANNING (SWP) is really about survival—having properly qualified people when and where you need them to achieve or sustain a desired outcome. This need to bring assurance to the future is fundamental to human nature. Families and tribes have a survival instinct to continue the family or tribe. Chiefs, shamans, hunters, farmers, artisans, and craftspeople all develop techniques to pass down their legacy from one person to the next to ensure the continuity of the "tribe."

The largest early artificial structures thus far discovered are a series of twenty circular stone structures in Eastern Anatolia, Turkey, called Göbekli Tepe. Göbekli Tepe was created by people who were believed to be nomadic hunters. The discovery of these large "public works construction projects" has challenged assumptions about how early these types of community activities began in human culture. Radiocarbon dating confirms that construction began around 11,000 BC and continued over 3,000 years. It would be incredibly naïve to imagine that these buildings were constructed by people who spanned the Mesolithic and Neolithic ages without some sort of rudimentary planning. (I hope some reader will tackle this topic for dissertation research!)

As communities grew, the risks from not passing on their inhabitants' legacy also became more intense. The more you have, the more you have to lose. The preservation of culture and heritage became more complex. As humans, we became increasingly sophisticated in our tools and techniques to preserve our way of life. Strategic Workforce Planning evolved as part of this path of creating tools and processes to ensure the continuation of a way of life, whether it is centered around a tribe, a community, a society, or Joe-Bob's Well Drilling Service.

Societies sometimes exhibit behavior that can be likened to schools of fish, swimming *en masse* in one direction, then another. A management theory becomes popular and organizations race to be the first to adopt the latest fad. Management is a competitive sport, and managers seek new tools and techniques that will enable their team or organization to be more effective—to continually improve and to be better this year than last.

This, of course, leads the consulting world to always seek a new differentiator—a product or service that will fill managers' desire to improve. Old techniques may be polished or burnished, repackaged, and sold in their new and improved version. Slight variations can provide substantial, if temporary, advantage as fundamentals are fine-tuned and retuned to specific circumstances. Skeptics may gloss over the differences and call them buzzwords, but if simple benchmarking and copying were sufficient to ensure success, there would be few failures.

If your e-mail in-box looks like mine, you receive a variety of promotional literature every day. Vendors want to sell you tools and techniques that will make your life better. (My brother once told me he received an ad for software that would "cut his workload in half." He ordered two copies, but sadly, neither copy provided the promised workload reduction. He has to work just as hard and is out the cost of the software.)

For those of us who have been in this line of work for more than three decades, it has been surprising to see the number of people who currently take credit for having "invented the concept of Strategic Workforce Planning." It is not unusual to see claims that are along the lines of "up until now, no one has ever conceived of or successfully executed workforce planning." Sometimes, these claims include appropriate caveats that allow them to be factual within a specific context (e.g., "the first time workforce planning was ever done *exclusively using Excel 2010 and PowerPoint*"). Workforce planning actually has a long and robust history. The tools have evolved and many process variations exist, but the underlying fundamental has existed since the beginning of human culture: *We think about the future in order to anticipate our needs and reduce our risks.*

One challenge we must acknowledge at the very beginning is that we deal in an area characterized by ambiguity. Workforce planning is *not* accounting. We do not have anything like GAAP (Generally Accepted Accounting Principles) or a common definition of terms such as ROI (return on investment) as financial managers do. There are few if any standard terms with *universal* agreement on the part of workforce planners. This lack of commonly accepted definitions and processes has made our field more chaotic than necessary, but it is what it is.

In the late 1960s and early 1970s, a variety of academics and researchers, such as Bill Pyle and Eric Flamholtz, attempted to establish formal definitions under the discipline they called Human Resource Accounting (HRA). Some companies attempted to identify and even amortize their investments in people, but the general consensus of the period was that the payoff was not worth the effort. In more recent years, SHRM (Society for Human Resource Management) has tried to standardize definitions for HR as a field with some common approaches underscored by the certification processes. Much progress has been made, but there is still a lack of consistency in workforce planning terminology.

Up until the 1970s, much of the work in this area was referred to as *manpower planning*. "Manpower" as a term was trademarked by the company Manpower Inc. (Manpower Inc. allegedly requested that the U.S. Department of Labor rename its Manpower Administration. The Labor Department apparently complied. In 1975, the Manpower Administration became the Employment and Training Administration.) My graduate degree program in Manpower Economics from the Manpower and Industrial Relations Institute at North Texas became Applied Economics.

Eric Vetter published the most commonly quoted definition of manpower planning: "getting the right people at the right place at the right time." It does not appear to have been in print prior to his book, published in 1967. His full definition is very comprehensive:

> The process by which management determines how the organization should move from its current manpower position to its desired manpower position. Through planning, management strives to have the right number and the right kinds of people, at the right places, at the right time, doing things which result in both the organization and the individual receiving maximum long-run benefit.
>
> It is a four-phased process. The first phase involves the gathering and analysis of data through manpower inventories and forecasts. The second phase consists of establishing manpower objectives and policies and gaining top management approval of these. The third phase involves designing and implementing plans and action programs in areas such as recruiting, training, and promotion to enable the organization to achieve its manpower objectives. The fourth phase is concerned with control and evaluation of manpower plans and programs to facilitate progress toward manpower objectives.[1]

By the late 1970s and early 1980s, numerous articles and several books had been published with some shared better practices. The majority of processes in print had the common elements shown in Figure 1: Analyze the current supply, project what will remain of those resources in the future, prepare a future demand forecast, compare the supply and demand to identify gaps or surpluses, develop plans to deal with those gaps or surpluses, and execute the plans. I developed my first version of Figure 1 for a Human Resource Planning Society conference in 1980, and it was already a mature concept at that time.

Two decades earlier, a group of federal agency employees in the Washington, D.C., area began meeting over lunch to share techniques for more effective manpower planning. The informal group quickly expanded to include academicians

JRE 1. COMMON ELEMENTS OF BEST PRACTICE MANPOWER PLANNING PROCESSES.

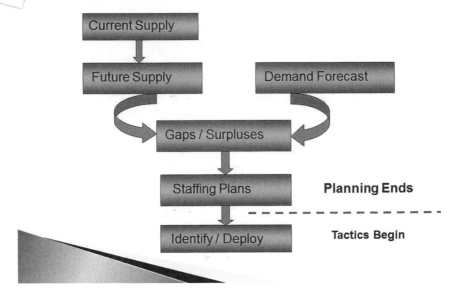

and businesspeople. By 1966, they became more formal in their meetings and called themselves the Manpower Analysis and Planning Society (MAPS). The founders included Morton Ettelstein, who led manpower planning at the Environmental Protection Agency (EPA), and Dick Niehaus, who led workforce research and planning activities for the Department of the Navy.

James Walker participated in several MAPS meetings as an invited guest, including a 1976 study of workforce planning practices jointly sponsored by MAPS and the Scientific Workforce Commission (now called the Commission for Professionals in Science and Technology). Jim, who was then leading the HR planning practice at Towers Perrin, took the concept of MAPS back home to New York City. He pulled together a small group of people—strategy leaders from Fortune 100 companies—who agreed to create a national version of MAPS. The New York group began meeting in 1977 and officially kicked off as the Human Resource Planning Society (HRPS) in 1978. According to Jim, MAPS was the prototype for HRPS and became the first HRPS affiliate.

The MAPS group continued as an expanded discussion group of functional experts, but they never created a formal structure. After several of the key members retired, no one took over the effort of organizing regular meetings, and the group faded away. By the mid-1980s, there was no regularly sponsored venue in the D.C. area for people strategists to get together. In the late 1980s, the group was reestablished as the Human Resource Leadership Forum, which continues as an HRPS affiliate with more than 200 active members from D.C.-area employers.

Today, there are twenty HRPS affiliates in North America and similar organizations aligned with HRPS in Europe, Asia, and South America.

Jim Walker was in the forefront of moving HR from personnel administration to people strategy and HRP (human resource planning). His founding of HRPS in 1978 has been recognized as one of the ten most critical events in the evolution of HR. The migration from manpower planning (MPP) to human resource planning was much more than semantics. MPP was often done in a vacuum. HRP put people planning into that larger context, as shown in the common elements in Figure 2.

HRP was usually strongly joined to a business planning process. Business planning has also been in and out of favor. Jack Welch wiped out the strategic planning department at General Electric and replaced it with strategic marketing. HRP disappeared with it.

Workforce planning surfaced as an alternative—not quite as "integrated" as HRP was, but reminding us that we always need to "get the right people" and do it in the context of the organization's infrastructure.

Scenario planning began playing a more critical part in the discussion. Instead of planning for a specific strategy, we looked at vectors. We asked more strategic alignment questions, such as: *How do we better prepare to respond to those things we cannot possibly predict with any accuracy? What are the implications of internal and external factors?* This was similar to HRP, but not necessarily formally linked with a business plan, as seen in Figure 3.

Due to the lack of integration, workforce planning fell short. Strategic Workforce Planning began emerging and resurfaced some HRP issues. A workforce plan

FIGURE 2. THE EVOLUTION OF SWP, WITH A CONCENTRATION ON HUMAN RESOURCE PLANNING.

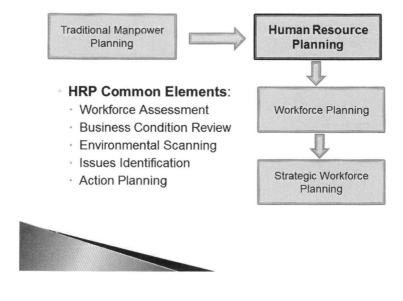

FIGURE 3. THE EVOLUTION OF SWP WITH A CONCENTRATION ON WORKFORCE PLANNING.

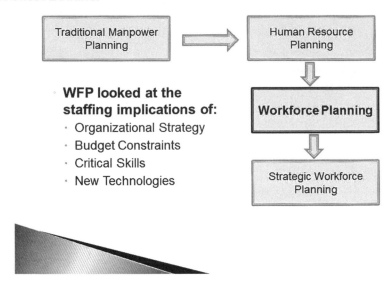

cannot stand alone. It has to exist in context. Some new elements also crept in, with popular phrases including *outsourcing* and *core competencies*. The planner was now asking questions, such as:

➤ Who does the work?

➤ Does it have to be an employee?

➤ Does it make sense to outsource noncritical aspects of the work?

➤ Does it make sense to outsource even critical aspects if someone else can do them better?

➤ How do you plan in a matrixed environment?

➤ What are the pros and cons of virtual organizations?

Strategic Workforce Planning (see Figure 4) is our hot buzzword these days. *It will not be the last one applied to our field.* Ideas evolve and terminology drifts. In *Gödel, Escher, Bach: An Eternal Golden Braid,* Douglas Hofstadter proposes that ideas compete just as vigorously as living creatures compete. It really is a matter of survival. Sometimes the drift in terminology reflects a true evolution of thinking and/or process. Other times, it may be more cosmetic than real and merely reflect a need for vendors to differentiate their products.

At Texaco, we created *The Texaco Guide to Strategic Workforce Planning* in 1994. It was not SWP the way we are thinking about it now, but it was very close. The title may have been slightly ahead of its time, but the common mind-set among expe-

FIGURE 4. THE EVOLUTION OF SWP WITH A CONCENTRATION ON STRATEGIC WORKFORCE PLANNING.

rienced practitioners was that individuals exist within a larger talent context. A plan is no stronger than its weakest component.

We have all seen great plans, beautiful products that sit on a shelf. Was it really a great plan if it was not used? Scenarios are not supposed to be exact forecasts, but aren't *plans* supposed to provide effective guidance?

Eleven thousand years ago, our SWP ancestors developed a process to get people in the right place at the right time to quarry large limestone blocks, move them to a destination, and stack them in large stone circles, decorated with stone art carvings in such a way as to produce permanent stone structures at Göbekli Tepe. We can only guess how it was done, as these events predated written instruction, but it seems reasonable to think the process was pretty simple, with people drafted as needed. If we accept this site as the first enduring evidence of some sort of rudimentary workforce planning, Figure 5 shows a theoretical historical time line of key points of evolution.

Five thousand years ago, a construction project was even more grandiose than at Göbekli Tepe, as heavy stones were shipped many miles and stacked in precise ways to form pyramids. The written records do not describe the workforce planning techniques involved, but we are aware that staff recruiting techniques were fairly harsh, involving wars and slavery. Management techniques were also apparently pretty abrupt, with beatings and executions routinely used as a motivational technique.

Today, we have to work a little harder to get the people we need. Skills and competencies are more diverse than they used to be. Motivation is a little more

FIGURE 5. A HISTORICAL TIME LINE OF KEY EVENTS IN STRATEGIC WORKFORCE PLANNING.

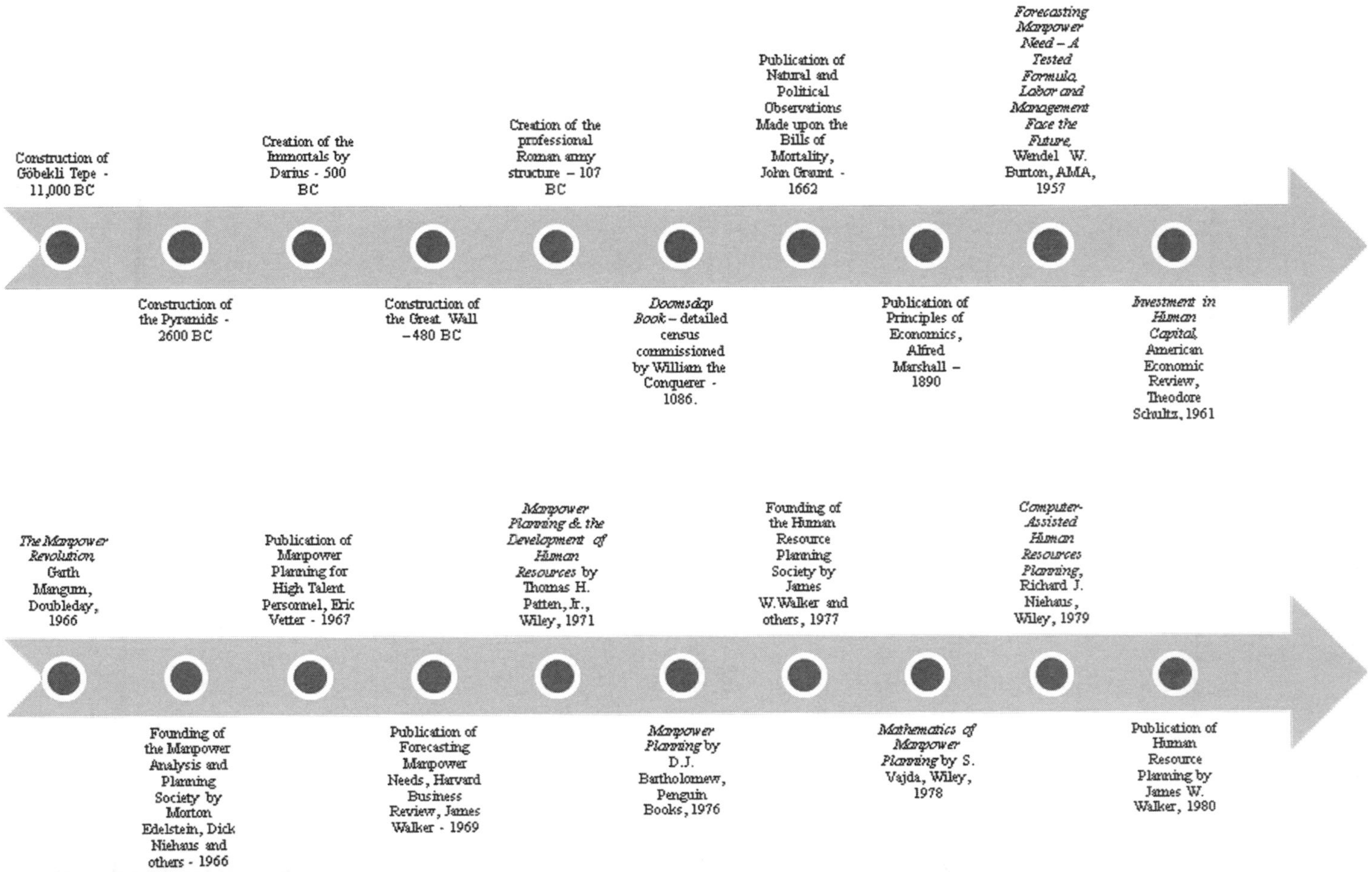

Construction of Göbekli Tepe - 11,000 BC

Construction of the Pyramids - 2600 BC

Creation of the Immortals by Darius - 500 BC

Construction of the Great Wall −480 BC

Creation of the professional Roman army structure − 107 BC

Doomsday Book - detailed census commissioned by William the Conqueror - 1086.

Publication of Natural and Political Observations Made upon the Bills of Mortality, John Graunt - 1662

Publication of Principles of Economics, Alfred Marshall − 1890

Forecasting Manpower Need − A Tested Formula Labor and Management Face the Future Wendel W. Burton, AMA, 1957

Investment in Human Capital American Economic Review, Theodore Schultz, 1961

The Manpower Revolution Garth Mangum, Doubleday, 1966

Founding of the Manpower Analysis and Planning Society by Morton Edelstein, Dick Niehaus and others - 1966

Publication of Manpower Planning for High Talent Personnel, Eric Vetter - 1967

Publication of *Forecasting Manpower Needs*, Harvard Business Review, James Walker - 1969

Manpower Planning & the Development of Human Resources by Thomas H. Patten, Jr., Wiley, 1971

Manpower Planning by D.J. Bartholomew, Penguin Books, 1976

Founding of the Human Resource Planning Society by James W. Walker and others, 1977

Mathematics of Manpower Planning by S. Vajda, Wiley, 1978

Computer-Assisted Human Resources Planning, Richard J. Niehaus, Wiley, 1979

Publication of *Human Resource Planning* by James W. Walker, 1980 challenging—we no longer use whips or swords in the workplace. Employees have a lot more freedom to walk away from work they do not enjoy.

Today's projects involve a wider range of skills than cutting stone into blocks, moving blocks from the quarry to the worksite, and stacking blocks in a precise way to get the final shape we want. The job descriptions are usually pretty complex today. Moreover, the definition continues to evolve, as shown in this version, from Wikipedia:

> *Strategic Workforce Planning* is the framework applied for Workforce Planning and Workforce Development, where the links between corporate and strategic objectives and their associated workforce implications are demonstrated.

We can be sure the field will continue to evolve. Terminology will change. Sometimes, it will be a distinction without a difference, but occasionally, we will see breakthroughs that could be game changers. As workforce strategists, we can choose to be on the cutting edge, or by default, we will end up on the cutting floor.

Reference

1. Eric W. Vetter, *Manpower Planning for High Talent Personnel* (Ann Arbor: University of Michigan, 1967), p. 15.

The Evolution of Strategic Workforce Planning Within Government Agencies

Alex G. Manganaris

CRISIS OR DRAMATIC CHANGE seems to bring out the best in us. Yet good planning helps mitigate the potential of a crisis occurring and makes it easier to respond to rapid change. In my career, stretching from the Army Research Institute for the Behavioral and Social Sciences to the Office of the Director of National Intelligence, with a variety of stops in between, workforce analysis and planning has been my central career focus. The "in-betweens" have involved budgeting often associated with labor or workforce utilization.

In this chapter, I would like to share some of my experiences and get a few points across:

▶ The differences and interrelationships between workforce analysis and workforce planning

▶ How "small analyses" can be big contributors to organizational decision making

▶ How major changes driven by legislation often create the best opportunities to contribute

▶ That people pay attention when the budget is involved

WORKFORCE ANALYSIS AND WORKFORCE PLANNING

Workforce analysis develops analytical relationships found in the workforce supply (faces) and methods to estimate future demand (spaces).

▶ *Workforce supply.* A good example related to the supply, or faces, is an *attrition rate* or *turnover rate*. These are two different and related measures. There is much discussion that can result from debating the difference between these two measures (let's substitute *loss rate* from one time period to the next). Suffice it to say there is a host of quantitative work in this area. For example, we can develop an estimate of what percent of a retirement-eligible cohort will retire over the next year, two years, or five years. Dominant methodologies are logit regression analysis and observable statistics.

▶ *Workforce demand.* What do we need in the future? This can be expressed in positions or full-time equivalents (FTEs), and there are distinct differences between the two. Workforce demand is the bigger challenge and is often constrained by budgetary limits, political constraints, and uncertainty. How many air traffic controllers do we need in five years? How many Middle East analysts do we need? Is there new technology that may change any relationships between workload and positions needed to satisfy that demand? This is often the area that receives the least attention and yet is the most challenging.

Workforce planning brings together the supply and demand pieces. The goal is to have supply meet demand at a future point in time. Current gaps between supply and demand are good to know about but difficult to react to. My second example below provides an object example of the complete process of workforce planning while I was at the Internal Revenue Service (IRS).

EXAMPLES OF WORKFORCE PLANNING AND ANALYSIS
Example 1. Short-Term/Quick Analysis: U.S. Air Force

In the early 1990s during a period of cutbacks, two major commands of the U.S. Air Force faced funding shortfalls in regard to civilian pay dollars. These funding shortfalls would cause major reductions in force (involuntary separations) in the civil service workforce that were not based on any workload reductions (reduced demand). These two commands were characterized by having a large civilian workforce proportionally compared to military personnel. Military personnel were managed centrally and governed by congressionally authorized end-strength levels, so this was not part of the challenge. Civilian personnel are funded from a variety of appropriations, but operations and maintenance (O&M) accounts make up the dominant funding source. Unlike the military pay appropriations, O&M funding (and civilian funding in general) is fungible, so that it can be spent on labor or nonlabor. The two heavily civilian commands were hit disproportionately hard since funding levels were heavily constrained at the time.

The personnel directorate (faces) was asked to see what could be done working with the "requirements shop," or manpower (spaces). A simple spreadsheet analysis demonstrated that the two commands were right to worry about funding.

Based on a month-to-month analysis, controlling for functional transfers and expected attrition, these two commands would run out of funding even with a draconian hiring freeze in place. Simply put, they could not shed people fast enough. (This does not address workload concerns, only the affordability of the workforce, or supply.) Other commands had slack based on their current onboard levels and expected utilization of the civilian pay dollars. Often, commands set funding levels below what was needed for all the approved positions. The two large civilian commands planned to use 100 percent of their labor dollars on paying civilian personnel. The other commands funded about 85 to 95 percent of their civilian "authorizations." For the most part, civilian pay was mostly funded out of appropriated O&M dollars, and these funds are fungible to meet other needs. Incremental budget reductions associated with the "peace dividend" were often allocated to the O&M account. For the other commands, dollars allocated for civil service pay were used for other purposes (e.g., fixing runways or infrastructure improvements) or could absorb reductions.

The spreadsheet I developed projected the expected workforce level at the end of the fiscal year. Using the average strength and average FTE costs, it showed that the two civilian commands would be forced to lay off hundreds of workers, while other commands had "excess" civilian pay funding. This would be a tough story to explain to Congress and a tougher sell to the career civil service and labor unions. The results of my analysis were briefed to the Air Force Council, which was chaired by the vice chief of staff of the Air Force. The decisions were made to reallocate manpower spaces and associated funding from a number of commands to the two large commands facing shortages.

This was not a very sophisticated analysis. No complex methodology was applied. The simplicity of it was the selling point, with the analysis using available data and attrition estimates and providing a format that people could easily understand. It was easy to brief and demonstrate and also involved allocation of resources and potential layoffs. It helped avert an emerging crisis.

Example 2. Major Restructuring: Internal Revenue Service

In 1998, Congress passed the Restructuring and Reform Act, commonly known as RRA 98. A critical part of the restructuring was changing the Internal Revenue Service (IRS) from a geographically based organization (e.g., Northeast Region, Midstates Region) to a business line–based organization (e.g., Wage and Investment, Large and Mid-Size Business, Tax Exempt and Government Entities). With changes in technology, it did not make sense to have a number of regional IRS entities when you could have a national focus on specific business lines, such as individual filers, small business organizations, or tax-exempt organizations.

When I arrived in March 1999, design teams of IRS employees and contractors were at work building the new requirements structure, or, as they liked to call it, an organizational "footprint." While the design of the footprint was not done in a vacuum, independent of the current workforce distribution, it was still necessary to examine or test what the implications were to the current workforce. What was needed was a way to estimate how we could take the current workforce deployed throughout the country and align the workers to the new organization.

I was fortunate to have a talented in-house analyst named Ed Harris and contract support. We received the requirements footprint from the design teams. The footprint provided information on the number of positions that would be required by occupation, pay grade, business unit, and location. This was then compared to the current personnel supply. We had the personnel data file and knew the inventory of people (current employees), and we could structure the inventory in the same format as the footprint.

With this in mind, we needed an algorithm to initially match the faces to the spaces, and the easiest way to do this was a cost minimization network linear program. I believe we set the cost of a direct match to one (so if you had a grade 12 revenue agent in New York and a grade 12 revenue agent space in New York, it was a direct match). We played with some of the matching rules. For example, if an occupational title (e.g., revenue agent, criminal investigator) was in the correct location but one grade off, we set a higher cost but made the near match a reasonable possibility.

Non-matches received a high cost. From here, we were able to analyze the areas where the footprint was not aligned with the workforce supply. There were two uses for this information. First, we could inform the commissioner of the "misalignments" of spaces and faces. Second, when we identified that there were key occupations—say, revenue agents or revenue officers—that did not align, this caused us to question the new design. These were mission-critical occupations, and we needed all of them that we had. Some of these results became new information that the design team used to adjust the footprint.

Once the footprint became reasonable, we had a secondary routine that examined the unplaced supply (those people not being matched) and estimated the impact of applying congressionally authorized voluntary early retirement authority and variable separation incentive payments. Together, these are commonly referred to as VERA/VSIP. The secondary analysis used estimates derived from work I had done previously during the Department of Defense drawdown with Dr. Pat Mackin from SAG Corporation.[1]

In the end, this process tested the new organizational design and provided estimates of possible impact to operations and people. For example, we were able to forecast the possible cost to VERA/VSIP and areas where there would be potential personnel shortfalls. After we stood up the new organizations, our estimates, especially at the aggregate, proved to be very accurate.

Example 3. Policy Guidance and Expectations

The Intelligence Reform and Terrorism Prevention Act (IRTPA) of 2004 led to many changes in the intelligence community (IC), most notably the creation of the Office of the Director of National Intelligence (ODNI). The overall goal was to improve collaboration and integration across the IC agencies and make major changes in existing agency roles. Resident within the new structure was a strong focus on human capital and workforce planning.

I decided that when working to aid the integration of a community, the focus is on providing policies and a framework that conforms to the Office of Management and Budget, the Office of Personnel Management, congressional direction, and best business practices. In my role at the ODNI, I set out to examine the needs of the community and see what initial steps had been taken. What I learned was that IC workforce planning before my arrival was centered around an IC-specific computer model that required uniform data inputs for all IC agencies. This was difficult, since the community is drawn from six different cabinet-level departments and seventeen different agencies, including the DNI organization itself. In addition, it would be onerous to determine how to ensure a level of compliance that provides uniform measures without strict uniformity. We needed an alternative approach.

Running in parallel at the same time was the President's Management Agenda (PMA) of George W. Bush, of which workforce planning was a key element. I was able to use this as a unifying policy. The Assistant Director for National Intelligence (ADNI) for Human Capital, had pushed the idea of Civilian Employment Plans, which would later be named Human Capital Employment Plans (HCEPs). By carefully defining the parameters and structure of these plans, coordinated with agency representatives of the IC, we were able to identify a "sweet spot" of HCEP requirements that could be met by most IC organizations. Also, these plans provided prima facie evidence of workforce planning capability. For some organizations, this was easy; for others, it was a stretch.

Subsequently, in the administration of President Barack Obama, there was a push to do "multisector" workforce planning. This involves looking at the contingent workforce of support contractors. My office had already organized and made routine the "core contract personnel inventory" for the IC in response to congressional concerns of an overuse of contract personnel. This inventory focused on contract personnel augmenting the work of U.S. government personnel. These contingent employees usually were in level of effort (LOE) contracts. (We distinguished between those contract personnel delivering a definable product or commercial service with core personnel who responded to day-to-day tasks. Those "inherently governmental" decisions were reserved for U.S. government personnel in accordance with the law irrespective of contract personnel type.) So we had a jump-start on looking at the total labor contributions of the civilian, military, and contingent workforces. All sectors need to be considered in order to really address the key workforce planning questions: What do we have now? What do we need in the future? And how do we shape what we have now to meet future needs?

A key final point is based on my career and experience. Having spent most of my non–human capital time in budget and finance, I understood that there was often a disconnect between dollar resources and human resources. We pushed for workforce representation in the congressional budget justifications that accompanied the president's budget. We had very open-minded leadership within the office of the IC CFO. A strong linkage is needed between dollar resources and human resources in order to have organizations provide sufficient focus on the importance of workforce planning. The workforce you need does not appear the day the funding appears for the positions. Senior analysts, mathematicians, and senior managers are developed over a number of years.

Summary of the Three Examples

The first example provided here shows that unexpected events present opportunities to contribute. To be prepared as an organizational asset, a continual and energized workforce analysis and planning function is necessary to allow a swift analytic response. The doorway to influence the decision-making process is open only briefly. You will notice in all three examples that there was (to borrow from John P. Kotter's *Leading Change*) "a sense of urgency." In the second and third examples, specific legislation was driving the importance and legitimacy of these efforts. Such opportunities come along in the workforce planner's career occasionally and often provide the best opportunity to contribute. But the opportunity closes quickly, and you need to be invited to the table (or the meetings!) in order to fully contribute.

The greater challenge in workforce planning is in the more stable periods. At these times, workforce planners need to have a functioning capability to analyze trends and develop the necessary coefficients (attrition rates, buyout take-rates) or tools (models) to better deal with emerging issues. But most important, you need to be engaged in the discussion and ready to add value as the next crisis emerges.

Finally, the greatest challenge for workforce planners is estimating future requirements (spaces). It is difficult to have leadership focus on the "to be" workforce since we are often focused on the current exigency. For some organizations, this is easier than for others, especially if the organizations have obvious workload measures (e.g., phone calls per hour) and good projections of future demands (e.g., 30 percent increases in phone calls over the next three years). It is far more challenging when the workload is less defined (e.g., analytic reports). But in the end, it is the planning that is important. As General Dwight Eisenhower in his role as commander of D-Day in World War II noted: Plans are nothing, but planning is everything.

This article reflects the opinions of the author and not necessarily his employers.

Reference

1. Alex Manganaris and Patrick C. Mackin, "Separation Incentives and Early Retirement: DoD Civilians." Paper presented at the 71st annual international conference of the Western Economics Association, San Francisco, June 1996.

Alex G. Manganaris is currently chief of Workforce Planning within the Office of the Assistant Director of National Intelligence for Human Capital. Prior to that, Alex worked as a senior manager in the IRS's CFO, responsible for budget execution and systems and analysis that provided labor forecasting from 2003 to 2006. Alex also was director for Strategic Workforce Planning at the IRS (1999–2003). Alex has a variety of work experience primarily as an operation research analyst in workforce planning and analysis within Office of the Secretary of Defense (1992–1999), HQ U.S. Air Force (1989–1992), Grumman Corporation–Procurement Finance (1987–1989), Congressional Budget Office–Defense Analyst (1985–1987), and the U.S. Army Research Institute for the Behavioral and Social Sciences (1983–1985).

Alex is a graduate of the W. Averill Harriman College for Policy Analysis and Public Management at the SUNY Stony Brook (MS 1983) and has a degree in sociology from SUNY Stony Brook (BA 1979). He is married to Nina Manganaris and has three "almost" grown children (Sam, Emma, and Marina). His interests include baseball, motorcycles (not Harleys), and playing the guitar (not all that well).

SECTION 2

Current Practices

Rob Tripp

IT HAS BEEN SAID that if you line up thirty workforce planners, you will get thirty different definitions of the term! You will see some of that in the following chapters by several leading practitioners of the art and science of Strategic Workforce Planning. But at its core, SWP is about workforce demand, workforce supply, understanding the gaps, and taking actions to address those gaps—all embedded in the business, economic, demographic, cultural, technological, and political context of our increasingly complex world. So just to add to the list of definitions, here's mine (SWP definition number 31):

> Strategic Workforce Planning is a disciplined business process that ensures that current decisions and actions impacting the workforce are aligned with the strategic needs of the enterprise.

Although I don't think we're yet to the place where workforce planning can be considered a separate profession or even a specific academic discipline, the field has grown during the last few years to the point where:

► There are many articles on SWP available just a few clicks away (some are pretty good, too!).

► A small number of books about SWP are available. (If you're just getting started, I strongly recommend Tom Bechet's *Strategic Staffing*.)

► You can take a class in SWP and even become a certified Strategic Workforce Planner.

▶ There are several SWP conferences, consortia, roundtables, and other informal and/or formal workforce planning associations.

▶ A number of the large HR consulting firms have active and experienced workforce planning practices that help companies implement SWP as a business process.

▶ There are several high-quality commercial workforce planning software packages from both mainline and boutique vendors.

▶ With a bit of effort, you can develop your own network of SWP peers through more than one social media site.

As you read the following chapters on workforce planning, you will get a feel for some of the breadth of approaches as well as the struggles needed to mature this work in various public and private organizations.

Robert D. Motion of Raytheon, in "It's Not Just Data: Workforce Planning and Change Management," has described the "burning platform" that led Raytheon to develop an effective SWP process, the company's learnings along the way, and how the process and those learnings have better positioned Raytheon for the future. His chapter is a really nice "how to do it" summary.

Boeing has found its own way to SWP and in so doing is now a recognized company leader. Everything has been "homegrown" and absolutely focused on meeting the needs of the business. **Dianna Peterson** and **Tina Krieger**'s contribution, "Strategic Workforce Planning at Boeing," is the result of an interview conducted by Amy Sund and Rick Smith with Dianna and Tina. Boeing's burning platform was around its concern for future technical talent and what is called the STEM (science, technology, engineering, and math) education pipeline, and the company has developed tools and processes to help answer the questions about its future talent supply.

In "The Role of WFP in Mergers and Acquisitions," **Mary Boudreaux Carroll** has provided a nice summary of her work in mergers and acquisitions, partly through her experience as HP acquired EDS in 2008.

In "Workforce Planning: Does It Hurt Enough to Begin?" **David Howerton**, who also experienced the HP acquisition of EDS, gives us a glimpse of how EDS's workforce planning efforts grew out of its pain points and ultimately led to EDS's integrated workforce management processes.

Our third contributor from EDS, **Jeff Buchmiller**, in "When Workforce Planning Worlds Collide," sees the workforce planner as an architect whose workforce planning framework spans core HR and business and finance activities and brings them together.

China is different. **Naomi Stanford**'s "Workforce Planning in China" tells of the enormous challenges faced by HR managers dealing with rapid growth and changes in the ability of global enterprises to compete for talent. She provides a nice summary of key opportunities and actions in the face of great uncertainty.

China is not the only expanding economy: In "Workforce Strategies for High-Growth Markets," **James David Eyring** and **Alison Romney Eyring** share their learning about the challenges of the BRICs and other expanding economies. (*BRIC* refers to Brazil, Russia, India, and China; the term is often shorthand for many rapidly growing economies.) They offer some tools and insights to help us address those challenges.

As **Marta Brito Perez** tells us in "Strategic Workforce Planning in the Federal Government: A Work in Progress," robust workforce planning has become essential to the success of the federal government. Her work with the National Cancer Institute's Center for Global Health is a story of engagement with multiple stakeholders to develop a robust SWP process that will be a model for other government agencies. Additional case study material for this article is in the electronic version.

The workforce challenges in government are both similar to and different from those in private industry. In her chapter, "Strategic Workforce Planning: Vital Tips for Professionals in the Public Sector," **Rachel Bangasser** points out that SWP in the public sector is similar to but also different from that in the private sector, and she shares her learnings about SWP from her experience in state-level government.

In "Do as I Say, Not as I Do!" **Laura Chalkley**—also in the public sector—ties workforce and succession planning together with individual and organization development, areas of major HR concern that are not always fully integrated into SWP.

In "SWP: A Rigorous Simulation Optimization Approach," **Marco Better, Fred Glover**, **Dave Sutherland**, and **Manuel Laguna** have shown an intriguing approach that they believe provides a realistic way to find the best balance among the various "levers" we have available to reduce or eliminate demand versus supply workforce gaps. They do this by drawing on many years of experience in applying mathematical optimization techniques to many business problems. To quote their conclusion, "we believe no other approach to Strategic Workforce Planning can achieve the same level of accuracy at such granularity and with more confidence in the predicted outcomes." Although their contribution is more technically detailed and analytically advanced than the other chapters in this book, their approach may exactly meet your needs.

Peter Howes is one of the most experienced workforce planning professionals in the business today. As the founder of Infohrm, originally a stand-alone consulting and software company that is now part of the SuccessFactors system, his experience is long and deep. His starting point is to think of SWP as a risk mitigation process. Peter's contribution, "Wisdom on Workforce Planning," takes you into the foundations and basic components of SWP and provides a high-level summary of key aspects of effective SWP practices and integration with HR and business strategy.

Sometimes the best teachings are personal. **Dan Hilbert**'s piece, "Pioneering New Business Frontiers: Unaware of What 'Shouldn't' Be Done," contains a personal account of his journey from finance to SWP. He tells how a strong focus on business outcomes, along with a willingness to "step out of the box," took him from scratch to founding OrcaEyes and now being one of the leading SWP consultants in the field today. I hugely enjoyed the read and am sure you will, too.

As noted in the beginning of this section, you will see a variety of approaches and processes, clearly showing that "not one size fits all." Dig in, enjoy the read, have a silent debate with the authors, and write up SWP definition number 32. Maybe you can even write your own chapter!

Rob Tripp is a workforce planning manager at Ford Motor Company, where he has been engaged in numerous workforce planning and workforce analytics activities in support of business needs, from building forecasting models and bringing the power of statistics to workforce issues to telling compelling stories about the future based on data. Prior to joining Ford, Rob worked at General Motors, where he developed and used various workforce planning models that simulated workforce actions involving the hourly workforce, including models that simulated complexities of the contracts with unions and served as "what-if" tools in response to both contract negotiations and business strategic planning.

Rob, Dan Ward, and the late Tom Bechet coedited *Human Resource Forecasting and Modeling*, published by the Human Resource Planning Society in 1994, and one of HRPS's most popular titles for some time.

Rob's longtime appreciation for the work of Hari Seldon led him to pursue and earn his Ph.D. in statistics at Virginia Tech. Rob is married to Lucinda Tripp and is father of two incredible sons. They live in Redford, Michigan. Rob's answer to midlife crisis is learning to play the highland bagpipes.

It's Not Just Data: Workforce Planning and Change Management

Robert D. Motion

INTRODUCTION

"If you don't know where you are going, any road will get you there."
—Lewis Carroll

THE CONVENTIONAL WISDOM is that workforce planning is all about numbers. If you can create the right models and analytics, then all things come into place. What follows is the story of implementing workforce planning successfully in a Fortune 100 defense contractor and how we learned that numbers are only part of the answer. The fundamentals of change management are even more crucial for success than the numbers themselves. An analyst can create the prettiest charts in the world, but they don't do any good if the decision makers aren't willing to buy into the premise and then act on their findings.

THE BURNING PLATFORM

In June 2008, our company was bidding on an unprecedented amount of international work. As our leaders looked at the business forecast, there was a lack of confidence that we had a clear understanding of the resource requirements and preparedness to meet those requirements. I was asked to lead a small team to figure out if we were prepared. We were given a deadline of thirty days to develop an international workforce plan for the company. We went right to work, initiating the usual call for data from each of our six businesses to understand our needs. As we began to analyze the data, it became eminently clear that we had our work cut out for us: There was no real consistency in the data, how it was collected, what it was saying, or even in the baseline terminology being used. Even more puzzling was the fact that many of our contacts simply couldn't figure out how to predict or even forecast their requirements: "too complicated," "too many variables," and "everything always changes anyway" were common responses to our queries. Simply put, we were facing "garbage in—garbage out"; we had an answer, but we did not trust it. After reporting these findings, our SVP of HR gave us a new directive: "Now that you know what you don't know, go figure this out." And so began my introduction to workforce planning and what would become the next three years of my life.

GETTING STARTED

Before starting our journey, it was critical to have alignment with our sponsors on where to focus to make sure that the solution we designed appropriately met the needs of our customer. We recognized that workforce planning can mean different things to different people, so common language was critical for gaining traction and scoping a solution. When we started in late 2008, the understanding of workforce planning varied greatly across the organization. In fact, if you had gathered thirty people in a conference room and asked them to define workforce planning, you would have gotten thirty different answers. As such, we spent about six months benchmarking both inside the company and externally to baseline our understanding of current practices and definitions in this space.

There are two basic definitions of workforce planning: Strategic Workforce Planning and Operational Workforce Planning. Similar to the strategic and financial planning processes in a company, the two worlds of Strategic Workforce Planning and Operational Workforce Planning are distinct activities that ultimately tie together, but their focus, methodologies, use, and timing may differ:

▶   *Strategic Workforce Planning* aligns with the strategic planning process and identifies the critical skills and talent needed to meet the business's five-year strategic plan. SWP aligns talent decisions with business strategy, financial forecasts, technology roadmaps, and trend analyses of internal and external talent.

▶   *Operational Workforce Planning* aligns with the AOP (annual operating plan) and facilitates day-to-day operations by identifying headcount and staffing requirements to meet program needs based on forecast business activity and required number of employees. Plans identify talent shortages that will impact the business within the next eighteen months. (Note: Some organizations would also add a third definition, *Workforce Management*, that involves immediate staffing needs. We consider this part of Operational Workforce Planning for our purposes.)

Our company historically focused on Operational Workforce Planning, and the process largely rested in the ownership of engineering. We had current practices in pockets that ensured the identification and fulfillment of our workforce needs. In contrast, our HR and senior leadership teams were more concerned about the long-term talent needs of the company, and there were currently no processes in place to understand what we needed to look like from a talent perspective in the long-term future or where to focus to get there.

External HR circles were also beginning to pay attention to SWP. Publications such as *Beyond HR* by John W. Boudreau and Peter M. Ramstad helped promote workforce planning by introducing concepts such as pivotal roles and supply chain frameworks for talent. Conferences started to focus on workforce planning, and a number of boutique consultancies emerged to address the area. In short, the confluence of industry trends and internal needs helped focus our direction.

We also learned through our benchmarking from other companies that had successfully implemented workforce planning that there were a number of common critical success factors:

▶ Executive sponsorship to help drive endorsement and participation
▶ Relevance to the business: tying workforce planning to significant business issues and existing planning processes
▶ Strategic investments in resources, education, and tools
▶ Establishing a workforce planning center of excellence with dedicated resources in the business
▶ Recognition of workforce planning as the path to building strategic HR capabilities
▶ Common tools, metrics, and reporting
▶ A structure whereby HR owns the process and the business owns the plan— just like financial planning and analysis

We proposed a solution that adhered to these tenets. We also purposely focused on developing a robust process instead of identifying and implementing an IT solution. Our rationale for this was threefold:

1. Without a process to scope the problem and provide for consistent inputs, we would be left with "garbage in—garbage out."
2. Previous attempts at workforce planning had failed when the conversation revolved around technology.
3. A proof of concept would be needed to convince leadership that this was feasible (especially workforce modeling) and worthy of investment.

Our research also revealed four capabilities critical for success in workforce planning. These were:

▶   *Business (data) analysis.* Understands how to use and interpret qualitative and quantitative information

▶   *Business acumen.* Understands the business context and strategy

▶   *Partnering skills.* Understands how to advise management

▶   *Change management.* Enables the organization to implement change effectively

While HR business partners traditionally excel at partnering and change management, business acumen and data analysis skills vary across the organization. Because of its emphasis on using data to align talent with the business strategy, workforce planning requires excellence in these areas. As a result, we would place a substantial amount of effort in developing a solid foundation based on immersion learning to ensure sufficient capability in the organization.

WHY SHOULD WE DO THIS? IDENTIFYING THE BUSINESS CASE

In partnership with HR leadership, we developed a vision and business case for what we wanted to accomplish. We wanted workforce planning to:

▶   Be proactive and predictive, aligning talent resources with business strategy

▶   Focus on the critical talent needed to meet our business strategy

▶   Help us foresee our workforce needs ahead of demand

▶   Identify strategic talent vulnerabilities and create plans to mitigate risk

▶   Utilize knowledge of internal and external talent markets

▶   Direct talent investment decisions in an integrated manner

▶   Help us manage our talent resources across the enterprise

▶   Allow us to make smart decisions about when to fill talent gaps via acquisition versus development

The benefit to us was tangible: To help us grow in the direction of our business strategy, we needed a workforce planning process. Without it, we would inhibit our readiness to grow by not having the talent needed at the right time.

WORKFORCE PLANNING FOUNDATION

Before implementing a workforce planning process, it was important to prepare the organization through stakeholder engagement, organizational readiness assessment, team selection, analytics, and training. This would ensure the foundational understanding and support necessary to successfully execute the process.

Change Management

We employed a multipronged approach based on our internal change management model to do this:

➤ *Executive sponsorship*. Our sponsor would be the SVP of human resources.

➤ *Scoping for success*. We intentionally scoped workforce planning utilizing an incremental change approach. Rather than try to do everything at once, we would focus on one area of the workforce that would allow us to execute successfully while having an immediate impact. For us, this was focusing on a portion of the workforce—the critical talent needed to execute our business strategy. We also chose to pilot the process in two businesses before launching at an enterprise level. As such, we were able to test the process as designed and bring tangible results back to our stakeholders.

➤ *Stakeholder mapping*. This was concerned with understanding the various stakeholders involved in workforce planning, their relative degree of support or resistance, and strategies to address concerns and enlist support.

➤ *Socialization*. Meeting individually with leaders involved in the process prior to launch allowed all to review the concept and address concerns.

➤ *Risk assessment*. Here, we carefully outlined risks associated with the initiative and developed actions to mitigate risk.

Team Selection and Governance

Over the course of two years, we established a cross-business team responsible for executing workforce planning:

➤ *Workforce planning center of excellence*. We had already established a center of excellence (COE) within corporate HR that had historically conducted workforce analytics. This team was rechartered as our Enterprise Workforce Planning Team in 2009, and it became the hub for designing the infrastructure (models, analytics, templates, tools) and processes for the workforce planning process.

➤ *External partnership*. We worked closely with an external partner throughout this process. We found that a third party helped establish credibility for our approach and that we could use an "outside voice" as a change agent when needed. We were then able to leverage this external experience in the development of our process and training. Perhaps most important, an external perspective helped provide balanced feedback to enhance our methods.

▶   *Pilot team.* During the pilot, the COE worked with a small, agile team of HR partners in our two pilot businesses. We were then each responsible for the relationships necessary to execute the process.

▶   *Enterprise Workforce Planning Team.* After presenting the results of the pilot to the HR leadership team, we asked for part-time resources from each of our businesses: a lead and an analyst. The lead would be responsible for change leadership and execution of the process in the business, while the analyst would assist with execution and work with the COE to provide the supporting data and analysis necessary for workforce planning. We also enlisted partners from our peer functions in HR to ensure that we aligned with and complemented current processes.

Our governance model was consistent with our research findings. The business would own the plan, while HR would facilitate the process. In similar fashion, the corporate entity would facilitate the process for the enterprise, while each business would be responsible for its execution. At the business level, the Workforce Planning Team facilitates the process with support from HR, with ownership ultimately residing in the business.

Learning

We developed and implemented learning for HR practitioners and team members to ensure a common understanding of the objectives, terminology, tools, methodology, analytics, and outputs of workforce planning. This included two and a half days of immersion learning for our workforce planning leads and analysts, as well as a half day of learning for HR business partners and other stakeholders involved in helping execute the process. The core team then continued to hold regular teleconferences to ensure continued alignment throughout the year.

THE WORKFORCE PLANNING PROCESS

Workforce planning is fundamentally a gap analysis process. In its essence, it involves understanding what the workforce needs to look like in the future to meet the business's needs, understanding the dynamics of the workforce today, and then assessing the gap between the desired "to be" state and the current state. As such, the workforce planning process at a high level looks like this:

1.   Understand the business strategy.
2.   Assess current workforce capability.
3.   Model the future workforce.
4.   Analyze and validate the talent gap.

5. Build the strategic workforce plan.
6. Monitor and adjust.

Understand the Business Strategy

Workforce planning starts with understanding the business strategy and the underlying talent implications to paint a picture of a desired future state of the business. This is the basic background that the workforce planning team needs to then diagnose the next steps. It requires a thoughtful and proactive partnership with the strategy and finance groups to ensure a clear understanding of the business drivers that will ultimately direct selection of talent needs. One must identify where the business is headed in terms of markets, products, geographies, and the high-level talent implications of the strategy. It is helpful to understand any related quantifiable data—such as growth rates, sales, and margins expectations—as these will be helpful for modeling.

Assess Current Workforce Capability

The next step of the process involves developing an understanding of the current workforce and its alignment with the business strategy. To do this, we conducted a series of facilitated discussions with business leadership to segment roles in the workforce according to their criticality to business objectives. Specifically, we wanted to understand the roles that are absolutely critical to achieving the long-term strategy. We chose to use an interview approach because it helped assess the current state and generate alignment within the organization. The interview was designed with a specific protocol of ten questions to ensure that the conversation achieved its intended outcome.

While the interview results themselves were powerful, it was important to add a quantitative element to these discussions. One lesson learned in our process was that this was much easier said than done, as the roles identified by business leaders did not match the job titles in our HRIS (human resources information system). To address this challenge, we mapped each role, identifying current incumbents via algorithms and roster validation, so we could create a robust current state depiction of the workforce. This included total headcount, historical attrition rates, retirement vulnerability, diversity, and other demographics.

The Unit for Planning: Roles. Planning in our company is done at the role level. This was also an important context to set as it helps establish a consistent context for conversation, analytics, and action. Here is how we explain it:

▶ *Role* is a defined set of tasks, dependencies, and responsibilities that can be assigned to an individual. It is a job, or "what you do," (e.g., systems engineer).

▶ *Competency* is the knowledge, skills, attitudes, and behaviors (KSABs) most critical to performance excellence in a specific role.

▶ *Skill* is a trainable ability that an individual performs in order to accomplish work.

▶ *Capability* is the ability to perform or execute a specific course of action, and it is the sum of expertise and capacity.

Here's a simple analogy: An astronaut is at essence an individual who explores space. That role may require certain competencies, such as leadership. It may also require certain skills and capabilities—repair and diagnostics, moon walking, space operations, information synthesis, and flexibility/adaptability. Customers won't need to know "How many people with moon walking do we need?" Instead, they need to know "How many astronauts do we need? Can we fulfill the mission?" You plan for the role, and then fulfill/drill down to the capability as needed.

This distinction is critical for making analysis feasible, as an individual usually performs one role (primarily) and on occasion a handful of roles on a part-time or collateral basis. In contrast, each individual can have hundreds of competencies and capabilities, creating an exponential combination of possibilities that ultimately become unmanageable for planning purposes. For example, I remember when one organization of about 8,000 employees was proud when it reduced its inventory of skills to a mere 3,400 skills. The logic plays that each position and employee becomes a "unicorn": Everyone is unique and there is nothing in common across the company. In contrast, we learned that the same organization had a couple hundred roles, which allows for the application of predictive modeling tools and analytics while providing sufficient detail to generate action.

Prioritization Through Workforce Segmentation. Workforce segmentation is a tool that can be used to help prioritize talent investments. Segmentation has long been used in marketing circles and other disciplines to identify the most impactful customers, products, or investments. In a similar fashion, different roles of the workforce impact the business in different manners. By evaluating them with a lens of criticality to the business, one can identify opportunities where the need for investment and the potential returns are proportionately greater. The segments we chose were as follows:

▶ *Strategic roles* are critical to creating long-term advantage. They are the game changers that the organization by definition needs to achieve its future state; it cannot get there without them. They are generally critical to overall business strategies related to entering new markets, new products, or new services. They provide market differentiation, foster innovation, and support next-generation products.

▶ *Key roles* are critical to delivering results within the current fiscal year. They are critical to immediate business priorities, driving existing products, programs, services, and markets. Current business results are at risk if we don't have these roles. They directly impact revenue and/or execution of work/programs. They are the "hair on fire" positions that keep hiring managers and recruiters up at night if they are not filled immediately.

▶ *Core roles* are foundational to running the business. This may be a skilled workforce, but it can cross industries, doesn't drive new value, and often serves as a support function to the organization. Companies may choose to have it as employee versus outsourcing.

▶ *Transitional roles* are not critical to business strategies and may be opportunities for reinvestment. They may be attached to end-of-lifecycle products or old generation technology, or they may not be critical to business differentiation.

Model the Future Workforce

"All models are wrong. Some are useful."—George Box

Perhaps the greatest power in workforce planning is its ability to lend a quantitative element to understanding a potential future state of the workforce. Merging quantitative intelligence with qualitative feedback drives alignment and ultimately action. This involves the creation of supply models, demand models, and scenarios that will be used to create overall talent investment strategies and action plans. The qualitative lens allows for focus on a general area, and quantitative data then adds specifics. Instead of saying that we "need more capture experts," models allow leaders to see precisely how many capture experts would be needed given a series of assumptions.

That being said, the intent of modeling is often misunderstood. We often create the expectation that modeling can predict the future; rather, it creates a view of a possible future given a series of assumptions. A good analogy can be found in weather forecasting. We tend to complain that "the weatherman didn't know what he was doing because the high today was 95° instead of 92°." In reality, the weather forecast was generally accurate that it would be hot and sunny, and the guidance was sufficient for us to know whether or not to wear shorts today and if we needed an umbrella. When you look at it in this context, the weatherman actually did pretty well.

There will always be outliers, but modeling can provide sufficient direction that is instrumental for making decisions. Why is modeling such a powerful tool for workforce planning? Especially in volatile environments, a robust model can help us bound uncertainty. By the simple virtue of going from an overwhelming sense of the unknown to a range of possibilities, the conversation with leaders can change from "I don't know what we need" to "we have a potential gap of fifty-five to seventy-five engineers."

When developing our workforce planning model, it was critical that it addressed the needs of our customers. Based on the scope of our initiative, we had to:

► Assess supply, demand, and gap over a three-year horizon
► Focus on a particular role based on our segmentation results
► Allow for multiple scenarios, or "what-if" analysis

To enhance credibility, we developed our workforce models by leveraging a number of tried-and-true methods that have been applied in other disciplines:

► *Financial modeling.* Applying revenue forecasting methods to people, both in terms of headcount and cost
► *Regression analysis.* Analyzing multiple factors to determine those that best explained movement in talent, especially voluntary attrition and retirements
► *Monte Carlo simulation.* Running mathematical scenarios of business demand to determine and visualize the probability of talent needs for a particular role
► *Systems theory.* Understanding the unique variables in the talent system and how they connect together to impact supply and demand
► *Segmentation.* Prioritizing needs and follow-up analysis based on impact to the business

While the development of this model involved complex analysis, algorithms, and computations, we strove to balance precision with simplicity. We needed an end product that could be used by HR business partners with their leaders. It also had to be easy to navigate and simple to understand. We ultimately developed a simple Excel-based front end that showed a forecast gap for a particular role. It visualized the current headcount, showed potential demand for the next three years, supply for the same period, and the resulting gap. The model had three slides that could be adjusted to produce different scenarios based on business demand, retirement vulnerability, and voluntary attrition drivers.

Finally, we partnered with internal subject matter experts in engineering and finance in the creation and review of our models. This was not just important for honing the model, but the endorsement of these experts provided credibility of these models with customers.

Analyze and Validate the Talent Gap

Given that we employed a bottom-up process, it was important to combine and analyze our current state data and predictive models to determine a potential course of action. This involves understanding what the data is telling us and then getting alignment from leadership and subject matter experts on talent gaps and areas of focus. To help with this analysis, we developed a comprehensive decision support guide for our HR business partners and workforce planning practitioners. This provided a list of probing questions and potential solutions for driving to a final solution:

- ➤ What do we know about the current workforce?
- ➤ Is there a gap, do we believe it, and are we willing to invest to close the gap?
- ➤ What is driving the gap: replacements or growth?
- ➤ What does the incumbent workforce tell us about risks (retirement, attrition, knowledge management, etc.)?
- ➤ What do we know about the internal and external talent markets to close the gap?
- ➤ Is the talent available externally? Is it specific to location/geography? Is it specific to an industry or competitor? What is the time and cost to acquire?
- ➤ What does the internal talent market look like? Do we have this capability today? Do we have internal development programs in place to fill the gap? What are the cost and time frame for development?

Build the Strategic Workforce Plan

Once the gaps have been analyzed and validated, the team then rolls up the results to create a robust action plan to close the gaps and design talent investment strategies for the next thirty-six months. This often involves multiple stakeholders, especially in large, complex organizations. It needs to involve the owner of the role in the business, the HR business partners, and experts/input from other HR specialties such as talent acquisition, talent development, learning, and compensation. From there, the team can come up with a balanced recommendation that if implemented will ensure mitigation of talent risks, alignment of the talent base with the strategy, and closing of any workforce gaps.

The Power of Synergy. Because our company consists of businesses with separate P&Ls, we deployed this process independently within each business. After completion of these discussions, the business workforce planning teams affinitized the results to see which roles were most critical to their business. We then came together as an enterprise team and identified five roles that were critical to the company. By providing real data that we had roles that were common priorities across multiple businesses, we provided a strong business case for enterprise investments. To date, our talent development and learning organization has used these results to focus its efforts on developing enterprise-level talent pools to support these roles, and our talent acquisition organization is looking at opportunities for joint sourcing efforts.

Monitor and Adjust

Workforce planning is a continual, cyclical process. As such, it is important to monitor the action plan to ensure accountability within the organization and allow for adjustment wherever necessary to align to changing business needs. This includes creating a scorecard to measure progress and then designing regular check-in points to assess whether or not adjustments to the plan need to be made. Scorecards will vary by company depending on the scope of their workforce planning efforts. They should, however, be straightforward, be easy to interpret, and include useful metrics that drive the intended behaviors of the plan.

KEY LEARNINGS

Throughout this experience, the team came away with a number of key learnings:

▶ The workforce planning process (especially business leader interviews) created "buzz." Leaders are now more actively thinking about workforce issues linked to business strategy.

▶ The HR community embraced the value of workforce planning and the concept of segmentation.

▶ There was widespread enthusiasm and support for HR to lead this process.

▶ Structured qualitative data gathering and sophisticated modeling add business value and compel action.

▶ HR business partners need to have strong capabilities in business acumen, business analysis, partnering, and change management.

▶ Training the HR community is a "must have" for establishing a strong foundation and building speed.

CONCLUSION

We are now in our third workforce planning cycle as an enterprise. When we started our workforce planning initiative in 2009, I was told that it would take at least five years to reach full maturity. Although I was skeptical at the time, this advice could not have been truer. We have progressed by leaps and bounds since we started, but there is still a world of opportunity in the realm of workforce planning. Workforce planning is a growing and evolving discipline, and there will always be new business challenges to address, models to explore, and opportunities to partner and influence action. The journey was not easy, but it has been worth every second.

Bob Motion became Director of Enterprise Workforce Planning at Raytheon Company. in September 2011. He joined the company in 2003 and held positions in talent acquisition, where he developed strategies, workforce analytics, and competitive intelligence to support talent acquisition objectives. Raytheon is a Waltham, MA-based technology and innovation leader specializing in defense, homeland security, and other government markets throughout the world. It employs 72,000 people worldwide.

In his current position, Motion is responsible for all activities related to workforce planning and positioning the workforce to align with the company's business strategy. He is responsible for the annual strategic workforce planning process across Raytheon's six businesses, which enables the segmentation, identification, prioritization, and planning for talent needs. This includes leadership of a cross-business team; thought leadership of workforce planning practices; championship and integration of workforce planning across the business; and overseeing the development of supporting infrastructure,. In addition, his team provides strategic analysis of workforce composition, talent needs, growth strategy/contract wins, and the talent market to create strategies for developing and retaining the our talent base.

Prior to joining Raytheon, Bob was a management consultant specializing in data analytics and information technology for PricewaterhouseCoopers and Armeta Solutions.

Motion holds a bachelor's degree from the University of Texas at Austin, where he graduated with special honors and majors in Plan II, government, and history. He also holds an MBA from the Cox School of Business at Southern Methodist University. He resides in Allen, Texas, with his wife and two sons.

Strategic Workforce Planning at Boeing

Dianna Peterson and Tina Krieger

based on interview by Richard L. Smith and Amy Sund, Ford Motor Company

THE BOEING COMPANY has long been seen as a leader in workforce planning. In fact, the organization's approach to Strategic Workforce Planning has led Boeing to be named an American Productivity and Quality Center's (APQC) "Best Practice" company. Subsequently, Boeing Strategic Workforce Planning leaders receive many external requests for consulting in this field. The following interview, conducted with Boeing's Dianna Peterson (senior director, Strategic Workforce Planning) and Tina Krieger (senior workforce planning strategist) gives the reader some insight into Boeing's journey. We discuss their successes, their challenges, and some lessons learned along the way. First, we'll review their approach to workforce planning.

First things first: One classic definition of workforce planning is that it is a process for making sure the organization has the right number of people, in the right jobs, with the right skills at the right time to accomplish current and future business plans. How does Boeing define workforce planning?

A classic definition has been created by Boeing, which is to ensure we have the right mix of skills and talent to successfully execute our current and future business strategies. We've developed a workforce planning approach designed to maximize Boeing's ability to effectively meet current and future business objectives. This approach is an intentional framework to aid in business decisions by generating insights and deeper understandings of workforce implications to business plans. The outcome of utilizing this workforce planning approach is a long-range people plan (LRPP).

Our definition is based upon the systematic approach that is available for use across the company, which leads to the identification of gaps as well as recommended solutions to mitigate these gaps. These recommended solutions become your people strategies. Our approach, and associated tools, creates an environment that encourages the right dialogue as well as provides robust, in-depth analysis.

Traditionally, the workforce planning process works like a gap analysis: Estimates of the organization's future demand for talent are compared to the projected internal supply of talent to identify surpluses and shortages. Is this a key element of your process? If so, can you give us an idea of how Boeing's workforce planning process does gap analysis?

While gap analysis is a big part of our process, our approach focuses on having the right conversation with business leaders. In fact, we have developed questions designed to help leaders critically think about their workforce; questions such as which skills make or break your business strategy? What is the culture of your workforce? Where does your skill pipeline reside?

As many are aware, we have internally developed a number of tools to support our analysis efforts. For instance, our HR dashboard provides an excellent view of the internal complexion of Boeing's skills, which is a key to understanding our internal skill availability. Additionally, we have developed a skills planning system that allows managers the ability to plan their skill requirements five years into the future. In addition to understanding our internal supply/demand, we also broaden our view to include the external supply/demand for these same skills.

We have also developed a future workforce modeling tool; we use this tool to supplement our business-based workforce projections by modeling potential effects on our workforce. In this tool, we consider factors such as internal skills management policies and practices, external economic conditions, along with hiring and attrition rates. This enables us to develop a more robust view of potential workforce trends and be better prepared to mitigate potential workforce-related risks.

Boeing's workforce planning process has a focus on the organization's "talent philosophy." What is the company's talent philosophy and what is its role in the workforce planning process?

The talent philosophy element of our framework is designed to help leaders recognize and understand their organization's culture. For this element, it is necessary to identify critical/strategic skills that are imperative to ensuring the success of your business strategy. There should also be dialogue relative to the leader's philosophy around talent. For instance, at Boeing, the company embraces lifelong learning, which is part of our company's management model and one of our talent philosophies. As you have discussions with leaders, you might discover that the culture within the organization needs to be addressed as part of the people plan.

Workforce planning can be done with greater or lesser degrees of central control. For example, it is possible to centrally define and control the workforce planning process. Alternatively, a central team can create tools, processes, and techniques and assist the units as they do their own workforce planning. In the latter case, the central role is training and facilitation rather than managing and control. How would you describe Boeing's approach?

We try to take an enterprise approach to SWP, in which our staffing needs are informed by our business and finance plans. We have created several tools, including but not limited to a web-based guidebook, training modules, and virtual communities of practice, specifically developed to serve Boeing organizations in their workforce planning efforts. These tools have been designed to be utilized by leaders company-wide; however, many leaders and HR generalists continue to feel more comfortable involving us to facilitate their Strategic Workforce Planning discussions.

Our approach is very scalable and easily adapted for any organizational size. As such, SWP occurs at various levels of the organization. For instance, part of our infrastructure includes functional skill teams that focus their workforce planning efforts on specific skills, which leads to identifying gaps in specific talent domains. Skill leaders develop networks that provide them the ability to leverage skills across units.

Workforce planning is integral to the business planning process. To make that integration work, partnerships are critical. Can you tell us about the importance of establishing partnerships with key stakeholders (like business development, finance, etc.), and how you have done that?

In developing our process we quickly recognized the value of engaging internal business partners. Consequently, we have formed many unique and diverse partnerships. We work closely with finance and strategy to better understand our five-year business plan and its implications on our future workforce requirements. We also collaborate with our international organization to identify global talent needs. We are currently working with our modeling and simulation group. This group is typically involved in product development; however, they approached us about the potential use of a workforce modeling tool designed uniquely for our SWP use. We have also recognized a great opportunity to integrate workforce planning and risk management. The risk management organization provides us with visibility of all identified human capital risks as a result of their internal auditing processes. These internal company partnerships (see Figure 1) have contributed to the maturity of our workforce planning approach, resulting in a very holistic SWP effort.

Most companies have a long-range finance plan, and a long-range business plan, but often there is no direct link to a long-range plan for people. Can you explain how Boeing links its long-range people plan directly to its finance and business plans, and why that is important?

It was recognized within Boeing that both a long-range business plan/long-range financial plan and the need to enhance our long-range people plan exists. We seek to

FIGURE 1. STRATEGIC PARTNERSHIPS.

encourage that workforce planning discussions occur concurrent with business and finance planning conversations. Clearly, the outcome of strategic workforce planning is a solid workforce plan (or long-range people plan) based on the organization's strategic business plan, budgetary resources, and skill requirements. We recommend that our approach be used and leveraged to maximize the organization's ability to meet current and future business objectives. Dynamic analysis of the internal and external workforce provides the opportunity to identify potential challenges/opportunities, make decisions based on information, and drive action that will enhance organizational performance.

Boeing is a large global company. Tell us a bit about Boeing's perspective on workforce planning as a global enterprise. Is workforce planning at Boeing global? If so, how do you balance the challenge of aligning the planning process globally with allowing regions and units autonomy to customize their approach?

The foundation for our approach has been to develop and deliver tools, training, and consultation across the enterprise. Our SWP approach provides a framework designed to promote the right conversation and support business decisions by generating a deeper understanding of workforce implications to business plans. The framework serves as a systematic approach that will drive people strategies. The aim of this proactive approach is to encourage effective dialogue with leaders, develop a model to pro-

vide visibility of future workforce data, perform data analysis, and make recommendations for improvement designed to bring value directly back to the enterprise. However, this approach is not mandatory for use across the company. Consequently, we have deployed more of a grassroots effort that continues to grow and is employed by an increasing number of organizations.

Enough about *how* you do it, let's talk about how *well* you do it. Boeing has received a fair amount of internal and external recognition for its approach to workforce planning. Can you tell us how you're being recognized for your work?

Actually, recognition initially came from outside the company. Although our approach to workforce planning has been designed with a "keep it simple" focus, it does include a certain amount of cultural change. Consequently, some within the company have struggled to embrace our approach and have some level of difficulty realizing the value these products and services bring to the company. Thankfully, more and more organizations are committed to using our approach and recognize its value.

Our first recognition of any significance occurred in 2009. The American Productivity and Quality Center (APQC) solicited our participation in one of their benchmarking studies. As part of APQC's benchmarking, we were one of fourteen companies asked to go through their rigorous interview process. Ultimately, we were identified as one of six companies named as a "Best Practice" company in the emerging field of Strategic Workforce Planning. It's worthy to note that some of our most meaningful recognition came from conversations with the external companies who were involved in this study. Several of the participating company members commented, "You've kept it so simple; I can get my head and hands around it." Two or three companies asked if we planned to patent our materials because they wanted to buy them. We took their advice and have since licensed our web-based guidebook and curriculum to two medical companies.

From an external perspective, we are sought to deliver our course material, provide presentations at various conferences and were recently asked to colead The Conference Board's newly formed Strategic Workforce Planning Council. Our model has been recognized by PLS, a consulting firm that offers courses in various topics. PLS requested we teach our course to an external group of people, including some Boeing personnel. The course we delivered through PLS was also accredited by SHRM. We continue to have opportunities to deliver our course to executives and leaders within, and outside, of Boeing. Overall it has been accepted as a tool to help build HR capabilities in the discipline of Strategic Workforce Planning.

Although external recognition has been more common, there has been increased appreciation for our approach throughout the company. For example, we once presented data related to Quality of Hire of new employees coming from specific universities. After the presentation, one executive said, "I can't believe an HR organization did this work." This leader's comment was an encouraging signal to us that we were simultaneously maturing and delivering meaningful insights to our company leaders.

As a company with six years doing workforce planning and a recognized leader in this area, is there anything you have learned over the years that you would have paid dearly to know when you were just getting started?

One of our greatest learnings was we should not have expected the HR community to immediately understand the value and utility of our SWP approach. Recently, a consultant shared that 50 percent of the organization will never get it, 25 percent might get it, and 25 percent may not. Our reality is that there is great truth to this statement, and, as part of our experience, we have learned that the use of common language across the organization is imperative. It is crucial that we define and use the same terms if the whole organization is going to understand what we are doing in this area of expertise.

Having a sponsor or champion at the right level was another key learning. For us, support for SWP was on and off at times, but once we gained the support of one or two key leaders in the HR leadership team, things progressed in a positive fashion.

One of the challenges of workforce planning is managing the complexity of the organization's need for talent. Some companies have created a workforce planning process that collapses of its own weight—too many talent groups, too much detail. To what extent do you focus or limit your approach? For example, do you concentrate on a limited number of critical talent groups? Are there any activities that are aligned with or support workforce planning?

Based upon extensive internal and external research, we recognized this issue early in the process. In fact, we actually began our initiative on the heels of a failed attempt at workforce planning within one of our internal organizations. The previous approach was laden with various templates that created a very cumbersome and time-intensive process; it became too burdensome to sustain itself.

As we began developing our approach, we were very intent to focus the conversation on critical/strategic skills as part of the talent philosophy element of our framework. Once the business strategy and talent philosophy are understood, it is necessary to understand the internal/external supply and demand. This leads to obtaining the appropriate demographic data to gain a clear vision of the complexion and composition of your workforce. An analysis should be conducted of the current workforce through applicable demographics to portray current skill mix by various elements. While conducting this analysis, it is recommended that attention is focused on those critical/strategic skill areas in an attempt to uncover any gaps. Once you have analyzed the data, you can begin to justify recommended solutions and build a case for change. These solutions become key elements of your long-range people plan.

How did you design this approach to address the flaws of the first failed attempt? Many companies struggle to get started with workforce planning or are unable to sustain their initial attempts once they do. I am sure there are many ways to begin, but how did Boeing do it, and what can companies that are struggling learn from your first steps?

The most important first step is to create a burning platform with data. Obviously, a fact-based workforce strategy must be based upon data. Consequently, we began to look at our entire pipeline, from those who were first entering the workforce through the value stream to our most experienced employees. One approach was to align our work with the science, technology, engineering, and math (STEM) pipeline. Based upon our research, we knew that students were not only enrolling in STEM majors in fewer numbers, but many of them were switching to other fields of study before graduating college.

One of our Associate Technical Fellows of Learning Sciences, Dr. Mike Richey, created a STEM pipeline chart (see Figure 2), which was foundational as we sought to provide leaders with valuable insights. Dr. Richey indicated we posit that identifying and understanding the challenges of preparing the STEM workforce and the potential impacts of initiatives aimed at increasing the number and quality of STEM graduates can be improved upon by considering education as a complex, adaptive system

FIGURE 2. WORKFORCE PIPELINE AND STEM SYSTEM SUPPLY–DEMAND CYCLE.

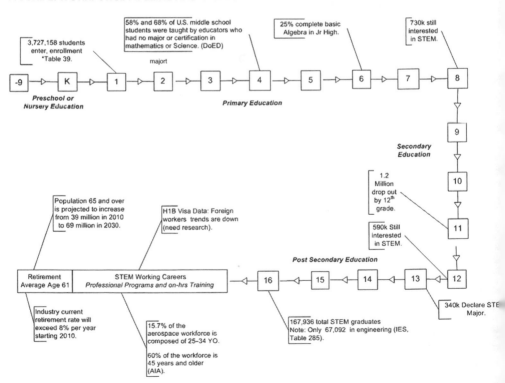

(Lemke & Sabelli, 2008; Stephens & Richey, 2011). In particular, by applying concepts used to examine and model complex systems dynamics to questions of education practice and policy (e.g., emergent phenomena, feedback loops within the system and with its environment, etc.), researchers can gain critical insights on fundamental relationships within the system and, most importantly, observe the ways that the system and its components can adapt over time.

Consequently, this chart provided further evidence of the state of workforce throughout the entire educational pipeline and beyond. Clearly, this chart conveyed facts that became our burning platform. Boeing leaders began using it in our executive center, including our executive courses and in speeches advocating for educational reforms to bolster innovation and competitiveness.

Certainly, our journey has been a grassroots effort from its inception; we began bottom-up rather than top-down. We keep incrementally moving forward with people who want to collaborate with us. We take every opportunity to teach, which leads to greater understanding of our approach. Several people commented, "This makes so much sense; I don't know why we haven't been doing this all along." People relate to the approach because it's simple and is not cumbersome. It's about a dialogue, rather than completing a lot of forms and calculating algorithms. One of our services is to provide consultation for any group that desires to utilize our approach; this has served to be a very valuable aid for many organizations.

Boeing recently delivered the first plane of its new Dreamliner (787) series. It's considered a game changer, a revolutionary carbon-fiber design that will reduce fuel consumption by 20 percent while delivering superior levels of passenger comfort. On the downside, it experienced significant delays and cost overruns. The delivery of such a complex and innovative product must have posed considerable workforce planning challenges. Without being too revealing, what important workforce planning lessons did you learn from the launch of the 787?

Our HR leader in the commercial airplane business shared with us the following insights relative to the 787 program. This leader shared that it is critical to remember that everything on the program was game changing from the business model to the engineering to the production system. The key takeaway is to ensure that purposeful workforce planning is done early in the program development and strategic planning cycle. Workforce planning should be included as part of the initial program planning gates.

So, let's talk future. What is next for workforce planning at Boeing and as a field?

There is a lot of room to demonstrate, with evidence, how Strategic Workforce Planning can bring value to any organization. There is also room to use our capabilities to help build a better supply chain. Consequently, our latest strategic focus area is to collaborate with our internal supplier management colleagues to explore these possibilities. It was very rewarding when one of these leaders referred to us as "a gift" after learning more about our approach. Our involvement in the supply chain helps ensure that we will have the people and products we will need in the future, at all stages of our production.

Through our SWP efforts, the use of data within HR is maturing quickly. As a result, we have recognized a real opportunity to transform from "data informed" talent decisions to "data driven" talent decisions. Consequently, work is under way across the company to begin influencing the culture relative to the importance of this type of transformation. Use of data to drive talent decisions provides further evidence of how SWP brings strategic value back to the enterprise.

Dianna L. Peterson is senior director of Strategic Workforce Planning for The Boeing Company. As strategy leader, she is responsible for determining and understanding how near- and long-term workforce requirements, skills, and knowledge align with Boeing's business objectives. Peterson also provides leadership and operational focus for Boeing's University Relations portfolio, consisting of more than 150 U.S. and international institutions of higher learning.

A 34-year Boeing Human Resources veteran, Peterson has served in a variety of leadership positions supporting many business units, including Boeing Commercial Airplanes, Boeing Capital Corporation, Shared Services Group, and Boeing's Chicago Corporate Office.

She holds a bachelor's degree in business administration with a concentration in human resource management and has participated in the Leadership Program at Duke University's Fuqua School of Business.

Peterson is a member of The Attrition and Retention Consortium and serves on its executive committee and currently is co-chair of The Conference Board's Strategic Workforce Planning Council.

Tina Krieger has been with The Boeing Company for more than 30 years. She began her career with the Space Systems Division as a member of the Logistics staff and has served in the logistics, human resources and engineering organizations.

Currently, Tina is a member of Boeing's Strategic Workforce Planning organization, which helps the company ensure it has access to a skilled, diverse, and sustainable workforce. In this capacity, she is responsible and accountable for the development, deployment, and project management of Boeing's Strategic Workforce Planning framework and approach. Tina also serves as a workforce planning consultant to functions and business units within Boeing.

Krieger holds a bachelor's degree in Organizational Leadership from Biola University. She volunteers in several areas, and currently serves as Vice President of the Board of Directors for the Breast Cancer Care & Research Fund, based in Los Angeles. Tina resides in Orange County, CA, and has two daughters and two grandsons.

The Role of Workforce Planning in Mergers and Acquisitions

Mary Boudreaux Carroll

THE PEOPLE STRATEGY is a critical success factor in a merger and acquisition (M&A), creating an opportunity for workforce planning (WFP) efforts to take the forefront. They can demonstrate their value add to the overall proposition, integration process, and ultimately the outcome of a "new and improved company."[1]

Human resources organization models vary based on the size and nature of an organization, dictating where the role of workforce planning falls within a company. Often, organizations have the workforce planning function embedded within the business itself, or there may be a combination within and outside HR. Coordinated efforts between core HR and financial functions are essential as the role of the workforce planner interacts as a business liaison to implement workforce plans as it relates to the following:

Organization design	Job architecture
Compensation and planning	Training and development
Recruitment/position management	Succession planning
Performance management	Financial planning and forecasting

Workforce planning is not a onetime event; rather, it is an ongoing strategic state of mind required to appropriate and manage talent. HR acts in partnership with business strategy and line management to design a go-forward talent strategy based on the business drivers and current supply and demand. This talent management strategy includes gaps, surplus, training and development needs, performance and succession planning, and so on.

Workforce planners are continually evaluating the workforce, while monitoring the overall health of the organization. Where there is a growth or routine environment, workforce planners often act as strategic consultants—advising but not executing, unless the line leader is ready to implement a particular series of events. Table 1 shows some key areas where workforce planners consult on implementing workforce actions during a steady state.

TABLE 1. WORKFORCE PLANNING METRICS.

Workforce Planning Metrics	
Spans and Layers/Leader Ratios	What is the right depth of layers for our organization? Do we have leaders managing too many employees or too few?
Recruitment Strategies	What is the strategy for percentage of permanent and contingent resources? Metrics for college hires, interns, and diversity hires. Metrics for placement onshore and offshore. Geographic location placement based on long-term planning.
Talent Strategies	Metrics for internal promotions, rotations, rightsizing of job architecture and compensation.
	Attrition and retention strategies for top talent. Managing out low performers. Retirement planning—reskill key resources.

A few examples of attempting to rightsize the workforce at Electronic Data Systems (EDS) occurred prior to the acquisition of EDS by Hewlett Packard (HP) in 2008. Several large-scale workforce planning efforts were set in play to rebalance the job family architecture and compensation structures. This particular workforce adjustment was significantly painful for legacy EDS employees who had received pay increases year over year, resulting in being paid more than market rate for their skill set. This rightsizing was very unpopular with employees, but it was no doubt necessary as overpaid employees will result in loss of revenues.[2]

In 2007, the company had offered in high-costs countries an early retirement package along with options to take voluntary separation incentive packages.[3]

Workforce planners still face challenges and scheduling problems in terms of labor skills by type, complexity, supply dynamics, demand uncertainty as it relates to the sales pipeline, and the competitive marketplace specific to attrition and retention.[4] These challenges still prohibit the ability to drill down or up to the 1,000-foot level, to provide the required detailed workforce planning data for the C-Suite for the skills or capabilities of both very large corporations (more than 100,000 employees) or very small corporations (less than 10,000 employees).[5]

MERGERS AND ACQUISITIONS: ROLE CHANGES

During an acquisition, the roles change and HR moves from a strategic consultant to more of an enforcer as business metrics have been publicly announced and marching orders are now under way. At the same time, you work to blend two workforces into a cohesive high-performing unit. Customers require that you continue to seamlessly deliver integrated services as the "new company." This demands a concerted effort to ensure that the leaders and employees understand the play being called by the business and core sales, general, and administrative (SG&A) functions. During this fragile time, it is essential that the HR business partner, workforce planner, and other HR core functions operate in alignment and that all understand the rollout of significant events to the business.

MERGER AND ACQUISITION FACTS

A disturbing number of M&As are not successful. In fact, some estimate that 70 percent of M&As fail. One of the top reasons for failure points to the complexity of workforce issues. Why? Extra care is no doubt required in order to build a trusting environment between employees and leaders; the effort to adopt the right approach to building this new employee culture is often underestimated.[6] An M&A workforce strategy should assume a normal percentage of attrition backfill while understanding that increased time to fill can occur when required skill sets with expertise exit. Ultimately, these result in additional effort needed to satisfy disgruntled revenue-generated customers. HR business partners and workforce planners understand the complexity of employee emotions during an M&A and the underlying feelings of panic. They can proactively work side by side to mitigate risk by coaching leaders and developing communications to ensure that employee messaging reflects the human factor, reinforcing a combined, engaged workforce.[7]

KPMG reports that 80 percent of large capital transactions fail to meet shareholder expectations and M&A goals, and only 17 percent created shareholder value.[8] Watson Wyatt conducted a survey of more than 1,000 companies, discovering that after M&As, only 46 percent resulted in costs reduction targets and less than 33 percent attained their profit goals. *The M&As did not recognize the benefits 64 percent of the time.*[9] As HR professionals, it is our job to identify key people issues that could turn these numbers around. A repeated reason cited for M&A failure during the post-deal integration phase is culture clash of the two organizations. Culture is a commonly documented issue in M&As; change management programs typically are put in place to address this issue as it still continues to surface as a key cause of failure.[10]

DEALING WITH AN ACQUISITION

One of the first questions after an M&A is announced is always: How many jobs will be cut? The next questions relate to brand, market strategies, real estate, et cetera. A workforce planner's job begins in earnest as the new organization design is unveiled in a practical manner. Once the numbers of layoffs have been announced, questions undoubtedly turn to the new organization structure. The basic interest of individuals is to understand where and how they fit into the new organization. Typically, leaders' communications to employees have involved strategic synergies and cost savings of the acquisition; employees, though, just want to see the organization chart so they know where they fit in their new world.

The M&A storming/norming/forming process is quite different than what is seen in normal team dynamics. Roles begin to transition as a combined leadership team is typically put into place. Position jockeying takes on new meaning during an acquisition, and, ultimately, no one seems 100 percent certain who will end up in charge. Most people are on their best behavior during this period; however, the long hours, stress, and uncertain future take their toll on many, especially within HR.

Immediately, because of the duplication of overhead functions, there is tight scrutiny and examination to identify duplication of efforts, systems, and processes. As a result, strategic plays are called quickly. M&As typically form groups of "special teams" or "clean rooms" to examine the current supply and determine the future workforce requirements.

If you're involved in an acquisition that is combining a workforce of more than 100,000 employees in global locations, working with effective and scalable technology is one of the toughest challenges. Basic issues for workforce planners remain the same; it boils down to *supply*, *demand*, and *timing*. Can we identify our workforce by skill set or capability? Do we have a model or framework to match our resources, both permanent employees and contingent, to our current delivery model? How can we manage our employee information—scale it up and down? How can we encompass multiple geographies with multiple views of the organizational, financial, and business models of tens of thousands of resources? At the same time, how do we design and deploy a robust career management process that retains and develops the skills of this workforce?[11]

FIVE PRACTICAL WFP INSIGHTS

Insight #1: Tools, Metrics, and Data Collection

During an M&A, obstacles include managing the volume of data collected from disparate systems as well as reconciling the data. In the case of HP's acquisition of EDS, the fundamentals in measuring resources were similar yet significantly different. They were similar in that they counted the workforce as regular and contingent, but different in that HP was a manufacturing company that built products and managed a limited level of services. HP's approach to workforce planning counted the workforce "by job level—entry, intermediate, and expert, master."[12]

The next set of dimensions included "business domain—manufacturing, aerospace, finance, etc. . . . and location offshore—Bangalore, Chennai, etc.; location on site—USA, Germany, UK, etc." EDS used a variety of tools to "forecast demand of thousands of skills, but with sparse historical data and hidden structural changes in the data." This presented significant challenges in assimilating the volume of old and new data connection points in a quantifiable and consumable manner.[13]

Insight #2: Changes in WFP Methodology

Merging two HR philosophies and methodologies to adopt a go-forward unified WFP approach may seem easy enough at the surface; however, combining multiple business models, where one size does *not* fit all, can get surprisingly complicated fast. Simple items such as definitions of common metrics may sound like minutia, but progress will be inhibited if common methodologies are not adopted early. More important, understanding the intent of the methodology versus the actual use of the methodology can be more difficult to ascertain during the acquisition.

Bench tolerance is essential to execution of WFP during an M&A, as the bench usually grows as redeployments rise. (*Bench* is defined as the amount of time people spend between billable assignments.) Redeployment business rules and guidelines may differ and create controversy in decision making when large layers of leadership exist. Political maneuvering during an M&A is common; thus, the simplest of rules can become controversial. Much of what is written in business literature focuses on the forecasted plan, and the missing component seems to be the execution of the plan. Defining the necessary business rules required to holistically execute a large, global WFP is a key success factor to actually delivering the anticipated financial targets.

Insight #3: Redeployment Control Factors

Redeployment factors are shown in Figure 1. Note that relocation funds will usually be restricted, so redeployment opportunities may be limited when two factors occur. The first factor is that strategic direction will likely restrict hiring in high-cost locations unless mandated by the client; therefore, minimum opportunity will be actualized for notified employees. The second factor is that predefined control factors are rarely shared during an M&A, so the actual percent of redeployed candidates will be low, and business guidelines could rule out most of these opportunities as it could be managed by extreme exception.

Insight #4: Managing Workforce Reductions

Global Workforce Counsels. Understanding the corporation's geographic strategy is critical to guiding the overall global sourcing strategy. Most corporations tend to stagger these restructuring charges over a period of time, recognizing that

FIGURE 1. REDEPLOYMENT WORKFORCE PATHS.

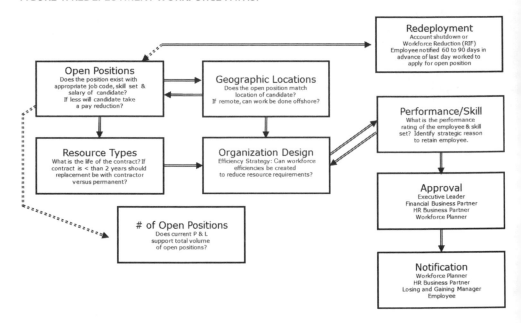

strategic planning in high risk/high costs countries (HR/HCCs) requires plans that must be submitted and approved often years in advance. Engagement with local country counsels is often needed to identify changes in business requirements. In addition, it is also necessary to obtain formal approval if workforce reductions are required in complex European countries such as Germany, Italy, France, and the United Kingdom.

Global implementation requires HR feet on the ground in the country, especially in HR/HCCs. Reliance on trusted people with global WFP expertise, whose experience includes execution of a workforce plan within local laws, is essential to successfully execute a global play. HR must tightly work with finance to plan, forecast, true-up, and reforecast active workforce plans specific to severance packages. It is common for European counsels to accelerate the time line or delay it, depending on the number of layoffs and the dynamics of their countries' economics. Building a contingent plan in the event of delays is recommended especially when execution of the M&A is highly publicized.[14]

Contingency Plans for RIFs. When workforce and financial plans have not been designed to properly execute reductions in force (RIFs) in HR/HCCs, it often results in increased reductions in low risk/low costs countries (LR/LCCs) such as the United States, Canada, Mexico, and Puerto Rico. Poor short-term decisions are often rushed, especially when long-term workforce plans were not actively known and disseminated to key decision makers. Leaders then complain that there was no time to plan. The immediate P&L impact will be negative; however, when managing a workforce plan that spans two to five years, over time the initial investment will break even. Often, HR/HCCs retain highly skilled, expensive resources performing jobs beneath their skill set and competency. The net effect is that instead of returning a profit, these resources could be costing more than the current profit margin on the contract! In a nutshell, it's like being upside down on a mortgage. [Editor's note: *High* and *low* costs are used here in the context of the cost of making workforce adjustments and not necessarily compensation costs. For example, it is usually less expensive to lay off an American than an employee in a European country because of the minimal employee continuity regulations in the United States, regardless of their base compensation levels.]

Although reductions will result in significant severance expenses, these costs typically are built into the overall transition plan and restructuring costs that are expensed during an acquisition. Laser focus on how to extract resources or place additional resources in geographically complex countries should be published from the lowest hiring manager level to the executive running the business. Most M&As occur because one business's profits were too low and expenses were too high. Change management must be embedded in every aspect of the M&A. Failure to disseminate long-term workforce planning guidelines to key decisions makers will prohibit healthy, normal workforce planning on the ground. Workforce planners and financial business partners must work hand in hand to ensure that severance dollars are forecast and allocated correctly.

Understanding the new business model regarding workforce reductions is critical if leaders are required to buy in, or they can get stuck if they have to "deliver a budgetary RIF." RIF selection is extremely challenging, especially when a leader recognizes this is a budget exercise only and the exact type of resources identified for layoffs will be required to source the next deal in the pipeline. Time to up-skill, retool, and reengineer processes will likely go by the wayside. M&A cost-cutting measures tighten expenditures to deliver promised budgetary commitments. Unless strong business justification exists for a revenue-producing unit, RIFs must continue to occur as promised. Remember that a target has been publicly announced and the clock is ticking. Tough calls are often made to meet a higher strategic objective, sacrificing the overall health of a specific function or business unit.

Insight #5: Managing Hiring Decisions

The hiring decision tree shown in Figure 2 is a sample to help hiring leaders walk through a validation workflow to determine sourcing options in a new operating model to obtain optimal margins. The total cost of the workforce must be in the

FIGURE 2. HIRING DECISION TREE.

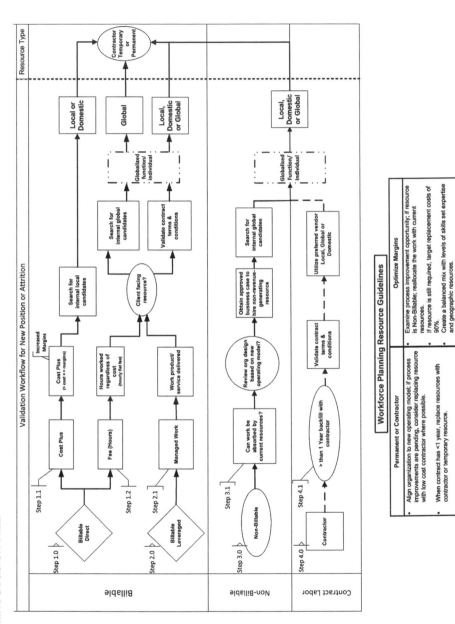

forefront in the key decision makers' thought processes. It is important that all players understand the end-to-end process. The decision to hire a local or domestic resource could be reliant on the contract terms and conditions. For instance, certain clients may require that resources work physically on-site instead of virtually, which could restrict geographic sourcing options to HR/HCCs. A decision tree is a helpful tool to guide leaders through potential sourcing options by identifying whether a local, domestic, or global resource is required as well as whether a contractor, temporary, or permanent resource is the optimum choice.

The benefit of building a strong relationship between HR and finance is limitless. Workforce planners and finance partners rely on one another, and during a financial close, they become each other's "go-to source." Combined, they can build a more dynamic forecast, fitting key pieces of the puzzle by linking the required headcount picture together with open positions, the sales pipeline, attrition, recruiting's extended offers, timing of severance plays, and run-off accounts. The combined effort of the workforce planner and finance business partner enables a more intelligent and likely monthly, quarterly, and/or annual forecast that can be adjusted as the business model changes.

WORKFORCE PLANNING TAKEAWAYS

Supply and demand must be defined consistently and at the same level of detail to enable comparisons. The goals of strategic staffing plans are to fix gaps and surpluses; therefore, it is the role of the workforce planner to work in tandem with the HR business and financial partners to identify and amend action plans accordingly.

What can we do as HR professionals to move the dial forward in creating successful mergers and acquisitions? A key area of change management missed during an acquisition is leadership training. Execution of the actual workforce play often gets bogged down in the actual selection process of reductions and implementation of the workforce plan. Hands-on training would onboard first-line leaders, eliminate confusion and delays, prepare and initiate knowledge transfer, and begin the overall operating model in a more cohesive fashion.

Last, managers should be trained on specifics as they relate to culture and communications, focusing on employee engagement. While HR is juggling many balls, refocusing the manager's attention on employee engagement is essential. Normally, during M&As, key communications are targeted toward the broader employee audience. These communications need the human touch of the employee's immediate management, which provides HR with an opportunity to influence change toward a healthier workforce that is engaged during the challenges of an M&A.

A prime opportunity for a workforce planner is orchestrating an HR integration strategy from the whiteboard to an actual workforce plan to a financial and headcount forecast (actualized), resulting in the new operating model. This challenge depicts a combined strategic effort that requires significant cultural and business change, setting in motion a series of business processes, workforce planning tasks, and talent decisions.

Workforce planning during an M&A provides a unique opportunity to create and renew partnerships within and outside HR that are desirable if you wish to sustain a healthier WFP function for the long term. Monitoring the health of your talent pool can help HR reshape and adapt its workforce toward a new operating model, whether it's designed by an integral business strategy or an M&A.

Notes

1. D. Ulrich, T. Cody, F. LaFasto, and T. Rucci, "Human Resources at Baxter Healthcare Corporation Merger: A Strategic Partner Role," *People and Strategy*, 12 (1989), p. 87. Retrieved from http://search.proquest.com/docview/224606726?accountid=144459.

2. "EDS Pay Cuts Strikes Deep," *Dallas Morning News*, March 3, 2009. Retrieved from http://www.dallasnews.com/archives/2009/03/eds-pay-cuts-strike-deep.html.

3. "EDS Offers Early Retirement to 12,000 Workers," *USA Today*, November 12, 2007. Retrieved from http://www.usatoday.com/money/industries/technology/2007-09-12-eds.html.

4. C. Santos, A. Zhang, M. Gonzalez, and S. Jain, *Workforce Planning and Scheduling for the HP IT Services Business* (Palo Alto, CA: HP Laboratories, 2009).

5. Thomas P. Bechet, *Strategic Staffing*, second edition, (New York: AMACOM, 2008).

6. T. J. Galpin and M. Herndon, *The Complete Guide to Mergers and Acquisitions*, 2nd ed. (San Francisco: Jossey-Bass, 2007).

7. R. P. Steynberg and T. H. Veldsman, "A Comprehensive, Holistic People Integration Process for Mergers and Acquisitions," *SA Journal of Human Resource Management*, 9 (2011), pp. 1–16. Retrieved from http://search.proquest.com/docview/877882922?accountid=144459.

8. J. Kelly, C. Cook, and D. Spitzer, "Mergers and Acquisitions: A Global Research Report," in *Unlocking Shareholder Value: The Keys to Success* (London: KPMG, 1999); R. Schuler and S. Jackson, "HR Issues and Activities in Mergers and Acquisitions," *European Management Journal*, 19 (2001), pp. 239–253.

9. C. A. Boglarsky, "Five Steps to Successful Mergers and Acquisitions," *Human Synergistics International*, printed with permission of *Workspan Magazine* (February 2005).

10. Steynberg and Veldsman, "A Comprehensive, Holistic People Integration Process."

11. Santos et al., *Workforce Planning and Scheduling*.

12. Ibid.

13. Ibid.

14. A. Smith, "Layoffs in Europe: Deal or No Deal?" *HR Magazine*, 54 (2009), p. 71.

Mary Boudreaux Carroll has provided analytic consulting, workforce planning, and HR program management supporting both small and large global mergers and acquisitions. She currently directs Talent Management and Payroll for Anthelio Healthcare. She joined Anthelio as the HR program manager for Organization Change Management to support the PHNS acquisition by the ConJoin Group. Previously, as a workforce planner, Mary supported more than 65,000 employees for HP Enterprise Services for the U.S. Government Sector, Information Technology Outsourcing (ITO), Business Process Outsourcing (BPO), and US Healthcare. As a WFP, her role included orchestrating aggressive restructuring initiatives to optimize the return on human capital investments through location strategy and employee placements.

Mary transitioned into the corporate world after fifteen years of nonprofit work that included marketing, events, and public speaking. She is certified as a Senior Professional in Human Resources (SPHR), holds her associate of business administration degree from American Intercontinental University, and is currently completing her bachelor of business administration with a concentration in HR. Mary and her teenage boy/girl twins enjoy living in the Dallas area and are proud of their Cajun roots. Mary can be reached via email at maryboudreauxcarroll@gmail.com.

Workforce Planning: Does It Hurt Enough to Begin?

David Howerton

IT'S OFTEN NOT OBVIOUS when to begin workforce planning. Sometimes there are just a set of pain points in the organization. The question is: *At what point does the pain cross the line at which you become willing to take action?* And when that time comes, will you be ready with a business plan to address the level of demand for data-driven business insight?

ELECTRONIC DATA SYSTEMS IN THE 1990S

We lived that experience at Electronic Data Systems (EDS) back in the late 1990s. Up to that point in time, EDS was a network of strategic business units (SBUs) acting as independent businesses, each with its own business plan, each assigned a quota to contribute to the enterprise bottom line, and each with its own human resources—owning both the people and the function (though it was not yet called HR). Don't jump to the conclusion this was an inherently bad situation. Since the SBUs owned their own people function, there was very tight alignment to business needs. In reality, this was considered a strength and was a source of pride.

The SBUs prepared and submitted their business plans, which they presented—in depth—to a committee of EDS senior executives. Once the plans of all the SBUs were combined, if the sum of the business targets was not sufficient to meet the commitment of the enterprise—for often "aggregate numbers" had already been shared with the analysts and stockholders—SBU business targets were expanded.

And then, in the late 1990s, as a series of events unfolded, the pains began to increase. With a history of years of continuing growth behind them, the SBUs began to struggle to meet their "optimistic" targets. In the drive to build the business, the SBUs periodically stumbled over each other, at times reaching out to the same potential clients with different proposals and/or prices. A new IT architecture took hold in the market. And with the era of the dot-coms in play, IT competitors were hungry for the skilled people who had been homegrown in the EDS Systems Engineering Development (SED) program.

EDS offerings expanded to be able to stimulate add-on business to existing clients and to reach out to those identified by the sales force as needing just that bit of additional service to close the deal. Meanwhile, on the people side, some leaders began to ask themselves: *Are our systems engineers ready for this? Do we know how to plan and schedule projects encompassing what seem to be endlessly increasing levels of complexity? Do our first-line leaders, especially those new to their roles, have the skills to lead their teams? And do we have enough leaders to continue growing?*

Let's put this into slightly different words to highlight the pain points for a moment. Business targets were becoming more aggressive and more difficult to meet. The portfolio of products and services was changing. Long-standing bread-and-butter IT offerings were in decline. EDS employees were strong in business basics taught in the SED program, but the internal perception was that the program was no longer developing the skill sets needed for future IT business. Competitors were recruiting EDS employees away. Overall growth stretched the leadership pipeline to the point where there wasn't sufficient capacity to support the compounded rate of growth. Rapid increases in complexity of technology and/or contract terms drove SBUs toward dependency upon "heroes" to stand in the breech. And the SBUs increasingly hid these key resources from other SBUs to ensure having the key people they needed for future business success.

The good news is that in addition to the challenges, there were good things happening. To its credit, EDS focused on implementing a Systems Lifecycle (SLC) methodology back in the beginning of the 1990s. Committed to the SLC, EDS strove to ensure that successful development and delivery processes were reused. Processes were continually improved (optimized) so they increased in maturity based on the Capability Maturity Model (CMM) developed by the Software Engineering Institute (SEI). And training and development efforts were channeled into the disciplines that enabled the SLC. The CMM focus wasn't just a "nice to have." There were CMM-based requirements to be able to bid on certain very large IT outsourcing contracts (billion dollar–plus "megadeals"), notably Requests for Proposals (RFPs) from General Motors (GM) and the U.S. government, among others.

THE EVOLUTION OF WORKFORCE PLANNING AT EDS

The single most essential (strategic) driver for the long-term evolution of workforce planning at EDS was its commitment to connect headcounts and resource types to the products and services being offered. We could not have made this commitment without the insights coming from implementation of the CMM and the SLC.

We began to think in terms parallel to preparing a bill of materials required to develop and deliver each of our corporate capabilities. Through the process disciplines of the CMM, we had a clear list of corporate capabilities and we had maturing, underlying processes. The EDS corporate capabilities also connected our workforce planning logic to corporate strategic planning. If the enterprise was considering a decision about the mix of corporate capabilities (add a new capability, discontinue a capability, or act to expand or reduce capacity), we had a logical connection into the decision process! This was fundamental. It made it possible to ensure that our people requirements remained in synch with the business.

A key factor of the underlying reasoning in this structure was the adaptable nature of people. One employee might be a database analyst (DBA) with the required skills for one environment, and yet this employee could readily adapt to an alternate technical environment or updated version of a tool. This was the basis for building reusability of roles and skills into our "skills catalog." A DBA was a DBA wherever that role was required. "Performance tune a database" was a selectable DBA skill wherever the role of DBA was required. Then, looking at the technical environment where the role and skill were to be performed, the tools, methods, and technologies could be selected. So, a *DBA* might *performance tune a database* using *Oracle*. Or, a *DBA* might *performance tune a database* using *DB2*. When the time came to put this into a system, we also wanted to be able to evaluate not only exact matches to requirements, but also "close matches." In our experience, a versatile DBA—one who had worked with multiple databases—could often come up to speed rapidly on an additional database. And in some cases, an experienced and versatile DBA who was, say, an "80 percent match" might outperform a less experienced DBA who was a 100 percent match.

GETTING THE DEMAND SIGNAL FOR WORKFORCE CAPACITY

Getting to the point of having numbers for required workforce capacity required a systemic view of the enterprise. EDS had assembled an enterprise-level process model that suggested the key areas to monitor.

The very beginning point, of course, is enterprise strategy: *What are we in the business of selling?* As mentioned earlier, if there were thoughts being given to changes in the corporate capabilities, or if there were volumetric insights from plans to tap demand in different parts of the globe or to deemphasize or phase out a corporate capability, then those insights were fundamental to planning. If a new corporate capability was being considered, workforce planning needed to examine the similarities of the new capability to other existing capabilities, as a beginning point for estimating any existing capacity that could be tapped. The strategic plan could provide an estimate of the sales volume to be developed over the span of approximately three years from launch of the new capability. Workforce planning would begin development of scenarios to consider alternative approaches to staffing up. The traditional kinds of alternatives included potential merger and acquisition targets with the necessary skilled people, direct hiring, selection of qualified organizations to serve as teaming partners (short-term or long-term), selection of independent contractors, and growing existing employees. The granularity of the skills catalog supported analysis of similar roles, skills, and tools to determine potential internal candidates. And critical here is the understanding that with clarity to the skills delta, the training and development organization could laser-focus on what to teach and how many people needed to be taught. Plus, the incremental value of training could be estimated based on the market value of the corporate capabilities that were sold.

The sales pipeline was the next key data source. Using responses for RFPs, we were able to tap the mature processes for developing and delivering corporate capabilities (which were the building blocks of sales). By understanding the capabilities being included in the response, the project scope and schedule, the initial and target technical environment, the scaling factors unique to each capability, and the task dependencies and associated timing factors, there was clarity as to the people requirements (which skill sets would be needed when). Then, as the probability of a sale was tracked, capacity requirements could be monitored against available supply. When the probability crossed the designated threshold, capacity could be earmarked for specific people resources and when they would be needed.

Sales was an addition to the current book of business. And for an enterprise like EDS, the current book of sold business is a considerable amount of business. It is in this context that revenue is generated—so it is critically important

PROJECT WORK

The nature of the EDS business is project work. Projects, by definition, have a beginning and an end. From a workforce planning perspective, we needed to know the timing for existing projects/contracts so we could anticipate the availability of employees for reassignment. When industry-wide demand for skilled employees is high, the last thing we want to do is shed employees at the end of a contract, only to discover we needed those employees for a project in another part of the enterprise. This required a change in the ability of the workforce management team to be able to "see" the people resources of all organizations. During the "age of heroes" when the business owned its people resources and developed the habit of hiding them, there were issues with knowing if people with the needed skills already existed in the enterprise, and, if so, where they were located. One of the solutions to this was the selection and implementation of an enterprise-wide project management system (a "bolt on" to our Enterprise Resource Management System) in which people were assigned to projects from a single enterprise-wide database.

From the perspective of addressing some of the root causes of the hole in the bottom of the bucket syndrome, we also wanted to ensure that we were offering talented people new and interesting opportunities as one means of retaining them. There was a danger in making an interim assignment while waiting for a contract to begin. At times, the bench strength of the organization (and associated cost) would provoke executive ire, resulting in necessary reductions in force (RIFs). It is difficult to dispute the business need to control the cost. However, if the RIFs were not based on a long-term view of the need for the individuals' skill sets, there was a compounding issue in that the time-to-hire for the skill sets that were lost might actually exceed the amount of time the individuals were to be on the bench. This could result in lost revenue from not having the people onboard, and the added cost of hiring replacements, who were assumed to be equally productive.

A conscious effort also had to be made to provide time between projects for key people to update their skills and to have sufficient "time away" to keep themselves in work-life balance. It is unconscionable to assign a key person from project to project to project, and then indicate she is no longer needed because her skill set has become outdated. Some might counter that the individual should be continually maintaining her own skills. That is admirable but impractical when the nature of the project work or the timing for performance allows no such opportunity. As EDS progressed in process maturity, and the age of heroes passed, this became less of an issue. It is, however, still a matter for managers to consider.

QUANTIFYING WORKFORCE PLANS

We return here to the discussion of factors used to quantify workforce plans. In addition to the sales pipeline data and the current book of business, the enterprise-wide project management system provided critical information concerning when projects were expected to end. However, those ending points were *not* necessarily the end of workforce demand for those clients!

The nature of sales implies there will be efforts made to provide add-on business, thus expanding the scope and altering expected time lines. In addition, for the IT industry, there were numerous cases where the client would put out RFPs for succeeding phases of the work to be done. This might include some expansion of the original scope, or it might lay out a transition in the system lifecycle, such as from development to ongoing production support. While these scenarios might be treated as additional projects to be staffed, they often carried with them a client's expectations that certain key individuals remain with them for the next stage of the work. This requires monitoring and updating of the key individuals' availability flag in the workforce planning tools. It also may be a situation for the sales team to work out with the client, working the relationship to meet the client's desire and at the same time providing an opportunity for the client's current point-of-contact to progress to another developmental assignment.

There also will be unfortunate times when business will be canceled. This may result from many different causes, but two that need to be monitored include bankruptcy of the client and mergers and acquisitions. To the extent these can be foreseen, the employees involved in projects for these clients may be redeployed or reskilled and redeployed. "Timing is everything" in that seasonal fluctuations in demand may impact the ability to retain employees, especially if the cancelled contract is large.

ATTRITION

There is a temptation to look at the high-level picture of workforce demand, as we have up to this point, and assume the supply will be available to meet it. Beyond the issue of finding and hiring some unique and hard-to-fill skill set requirements is the issue of attrition.

EDS was one of the founding members of the Attrition & Retention Consortium (ARC). Through membership in ARC, EDS had benchmark data to use both for comparison of the rate of voluntary attrition, as well as multiple data points for projecting EDS and industry rates of attrition on the overall people inventory. In addition to attrition, though, inventory numbers should consider internal transfers, promotions, and demotions. Clearly, industry norms for attrition do not get down to the point of identifying specific individuals, but they can be used to gain a sense of expected loss rates within larger pools of (key) resources. In recent years, tools associated with the performance management process have carried a flag for assessing the risk of an individual leaving the organization. This can help to bring the understanding of potential loss down to the individual level. It is at this point—when the risk of loss is known at the individual level—that retention plans for key people should be managed. In an increasingly "open book" era of social media, our competitors know by name who our key employees are. The question then becomes: *What shall we do to make sure those key employees know they are valued?* In addition: *What will we do to ensure they are cultivated for their future potential? What specific actions will we undertake to ensure they are retained?*

As this discussion ranges between processes that supply numbers for calculating and balancing workforce supply and demand and details for addressing the individual employees who compose the inventory, you begin to grasp the integrated nature of the HR functions. In attempting to explain this integration one day, a group of us from EDS HR began to draw a picture on a large whiteboard. The picture began with a representation of an individual employee. From that originating point we identified, at a high level, what we recognized as the functions that assigned that employee to an organization, determined his work assignment and associated performance objectives, provided compensation and benefits, developed the employee's skills and abilities, and deployed/redeployed him to projects (work assignment and project assignment not necessarily being synonymous—such is the nature of a matrixed organization), and more. As we worked through creating this illustration, we talked about how the skills catalog enabled all the functions to work together.

This was the basis for the shared, compelling vision that guided our conversations and projects and ultimately guided EDS to integrated workforce management.

David A. Howerton leveraged his experiences as an Illinois State Board of Education Supervisor of Vocational Business, Marketing, and Management programs into the foundation for a thirty-year career as a human resources professional. An early champion of competency-based training, David focused on competencies as key enablers for managing business performance.

During his tenure at EDS, David served as the EDS representative to the Attrition & Retention Consortium, and over six years he progressed through the ARC leadership chairs including terms as Consortium vice chair and chair.

David earned his bachelor's degree in business education from Illinois State University. He lives with his wife and two sons in Plano, Texas.

When Workforce Planning Worlds Collide

Jeff Buchmiller

THE SURPRISING SCOPE AND COMPLEXITY OF WORKFORCE PLANNING

WORKFORCE PLANNING means so many different things to different organizations and professionals, because it spans a broad framework having a large degree of complexity. An organization's workforce planning function is the result of implementing some suite of components according to the needs and style—and stage of process maturity—of the organization (see Figure 1).

An appropriate response to the large degree of complexity is to utilize the "divide and conquer" approach. When the interfaces among components are defined and established, the overall process can be managed, even when the components vary widely in their implementations and have distinct participants who are not well integrated otherwise.

A workforce planning champion therefore needs to act as an architect.

FIGURE 1. COMPONENTS OF THE WORKFORCE PLANNING FRAMEWORK.

Data Analytics	Linkages to Financials	Job Analysis & Org Design	Talent Potential & Development
Futuring & Forecasting	Business Strategy Analysis	Enablement & Engagement	Leadership Talent & Succession
Location Strategy	Workforce Segmentation	Goal Setting & Performance Mgt	Career Mobility

An architect's primary job is to draw solutions on the back of a napkin or on a whiteboard for the stakeholders and participants, in order to achieve a level of coordination among their efforts that would not otherwise occur. Doing so aligns efforts to create something together that none of them could create alone.

When the stakeholders and participants see how their efforts can contribute to the bigger picture, new and more significant solutions are enabled. The synergistic power of the total solution is in harnessing several different competencies and types of information, bringing the multiple points of view to bear.

How the components of the workforce planning framework serve their purposes and interact with each other may be explored in the rich available literature, starting with this book.[1]

What we have experienced in our own organizations and what we have learned from other professionals is that the workforce planning function is typically grounded in a small number of the component areas. The purpose, style, and approach are related to that grounding. It is important for the architect to understand the particular site, the building materials and methods, and the client's requirements in order to fashion solutions that will function properly as well as delight.

THE PEOPLE-ORIENTED WORKFORCE PLANNING MANTRA

The workforce planning mantra at many organizations goes something like this:[2]

Provide the RIGHT skills
At the RIGHT time
At the RIGHT place
For the RIGHT cost

This approach was taken at Electronic Data Systems (EDS) from 1998 to 2008, motivated by the urgent need to coordinate across multiple account teams, which historically had had a large degree of independence. The sheer scale of the organization demanded increased efficiency in cost planning and management, and the majority of its costs were in the workforce.

Ross Perot built EDS in the 1960s through the 1980s as a loose-knit collection of account teams. Each practically owned its own P&L. Each would share client knowledge, technology investments, and other overhead with other accounts in its industry and in its geography, but each would fight fiercely for its key talent, since it was a people business even more than a technology business.

Ross and his team founded the IT services industry and constructed a business model well suited to the resulting market,[3] as evidenced by great corporate success lasting into the mid-1990s. However, it was not an environment in which workforce planning processes were formalized and widespread.

Each account manager created and executed his or her own workforce plans specific to his or her own needs to generate a profit margin, to satisfy the client's needs, and to keep the technical and social momentum strong enough to carry the account into future deal extensions. As the month-by-month account needs evolved, so did the account manager's workforce-related efforts. These focused the account manager's attention on acquiring and retaining key team members with the most talent to be highly productive, to satisfy the client, to master utilization of the technologies, and to lead colleagues.

With the headcount-oriented mantra above, workforce planning efforts focus on capturing projections for the organization's headcounts and total compensation amounts. Use the best available data field for skills, which might be job family, and repeat the spreadsheet for each. Run the same exercise for each location, building out a multidimensional matrix. The smaller-count locations and skills are consolidated until the size of the data set is comfortable for users.

Attrition trends can be used to produce the net supply component, and open positions can be added as "to be hired" employees.

Then a demand side is often developed, where the revenue growth rate forecast is used to scale up the current month's numbers. Do the subtractions to see how many additional employees "need to be hired" and how many are "not needed" by location and skill. (Psst! Don't forget to compound the attrition, as some of those new hires will leave, too.)

This approach is usually taken when workforce planning is championed by HR, and it is a great way to get started when the employees and contingent workers are integral to the business model, so that business managers already are thinking through the ways that business strategy needs to be implemented in terms of the workforce. For EDS, keeping up with offshoring trends while continuing to deliver on commitments to clients was a key driving force (Figure 2).

FIGURE 2. COMPONENTS IN WHICH THE EDS APPROACH WAS GROUNDED.

Data Analytics	Linkages to Financials	Job Analysis & Org Design	Talent Potential & Development
Futuring & Forecasting	Business Strategy Analysis	Enablement & Engagement	Leadership Talent & Succession
Location Strategy	Workforce Segmentation	Goal Setting & Performance Mgt	Career Mobility

A DISCIPLINE OF WORKFORCE PLANNING DRIVEN BY FINANCE

EDS struggled mightily through the 2000s and eventually succumbed to acquisition by HP, to tens of thousands of layoffs, and to integration into the HP services business unit.

Over the course of the two years of integration, we workforce professionals from EDS got pulled closer and closer toward a new understanding of what may be the critical point of failure for the formerly mighty organization—workforce planning—ironically, since we had made great strides in that very area.

Looking back, we could see that the critical point of failure seemed to align nearly perfectly along the axis of the organization's success in its first 35 years. What we failed to do was to transform the practices serving success into their next stage of evolution. This would have involved scaling, translating, and layering them to fit the complex global corporation that EDS had become. There were too many people not understanding their share of the problem or their share of the solution, and there wasn't an architect present with vision and enough influence to arrange it in time.

Prior to the EDS acquisition, HP had developed a robust, respected workforce planning discipline oriented on planning and managing the allowable cost of labor. Each business unit was allowed a TCOW (total cost of workforce) proportionate to its revenues.[4]

HP applied its workforce planning discipline to EDS in 2008 through 2010, realizing the synergies of the acquisition. We lived through that set of gut-wrenching experiences, seeing the many ways we didn't understand workforce planning after all, and learning many new purposes for and forms of it.

The financials approach to workforce planning is a great way to get "in the flow" of the business. Opportunities to generate and sustain profit margins that involve the workforce—improvements and expansions, too, not just reductions—become clear and actionable, as suggested in Figure 3.

FIGURE 3. COMPONENTS IN WHICH THE HP APPROACH WAS GROUNDED.

Data Analytics	Linkages to Financials	Job Analysis & Org Design	Talent Potential & Development
Futuring & Forecasting	Business Strategy Analysis	Enablement & Engagement	Leadership Talent & Succession
Location Strategy	Workforce Segmentation	Goal Setting & Performance Mgt	Career Mobility

WHERE SMALL ORGANIZATIONS OFTEN START WITH WORKFORCE PLANNING

Small organizations lacking the need to implement robust workforce planning functions usually begin the workforce planning journey by extending their existing talent management practices in ways that are more strategic (Figure 4). Often, imminent growth or other change is the catalyst for these efforts. This is a response geared to mitigate these emerging risks to the business.

FIGURE 4. TYPICAL INITIAL COMPONENTS IMPLEMENTED BY A SMALL ORGANIZATION.

Data Analytics	Linkages to Financials	Job Analysis & Org Design	Talent Potential & Development
Futuring & Forecasting	Business Strategy Analysis	Enablement & Engagement	Leadership Talent & Succession
Location Strategy	Workforce Segmentation	Goal Setting & Performance Mgt	Career Mobility

The workforce planning effort at a small organization is sometimes conducted by one person as part of his or her job, at least initially. It is especially important for such a person to act as an architect, guiding others toward the big-picture understanding of the value workforce planning provides, because there is no existing process to support the development of these value-adding organizational capabilities.

THE ANALYTICAL APPROACH TO WORKFORCE PLANNING

It is becoming more and more common, in this era of "big data" and "competing on the basis of analytics," for organizations to adopt a highly analytical approach to workforce planning. Figure 5 illustrates this. The stated goal is often to make data-based or evidence-based decisions regarding the workforce.

Organizations that are already strong in workforce data and analytics will

FIGURE 5. EMPHASIZED COMPONENTS WITH THE ANALYTICAL APPROACH.

Data Analytics	Linkages to Financials	Job Analysis & Org Design	Talent Potential & Development
Futuring & Forecasting	Business Strategy Analysis	Enablement & Engagement	Leadership Talent & Succession
Location Strategy	Workforce Segmentation	Goal Setting & Performance Mgt	Career Mobility

often set off down this path because it is usually easier to expand on existing capabilities than to start fresh on others. What's important is to do the components you choose to do well, at each stage, and keep moving forward at the pace the business needs you to.

The focus in this approach is around the impact workers have on financials, given what they currently do, and around the flows of workers through the organization, into it, and out of it with the resulting changes in impact. Often, these efforts rally around the notion of engagement and its value to the organization.

STATE OF THE ART IN WORKFORCE PLANNING

The most robust implementation of the workforce planning framework we have seen so far is IBM's Workforce Management Initiative.[5]

As the largest, most mature, and most global IT services business, IBM is perhaps uniquely situated to lead in workforce planning. There is tremendous value in it for the company, and the sheer scale of its client base means significant benefits are passed along to global economies in the form of improved services and lower costs. IBM's Smarter Planet brand capitalizes on this tremendous impact (see Figure 6).

The investment required for IBM to achieve this level of workforce planning robustness has been $230 million in its first five years,[6] with additional significant amounts since. Clearly, this level of investment is not appropriate for many organizations, even though IBM has experienced several times that amount in benefits from it.

IBM is approaching total integration of all workforce planning components. An organization that develops such a large capability advantage will eventually develop ways to leverage it, and there is every reason to expect IBM to do so with this capability. That will most likely occur in the form of workforce planning information and processing services, which are likely to be integrated into and bundled with other similar business management services and technologies. Watch for the whole next stage in the evolution of workforce planning, and be ready to embrace it for its speed, high quality, and low cost.

FIGURE 6. COMPONENTS INCLUDED IN IBM'S ROBUST APPROACH.

Data Analytics	Linkages to Financials	Job Analysis & Org Design	Talent Potential & Development
Futuring & Forecasting	Business Strategy Analysis	Enablement & Engagement	Leadership Talent & Succession
Location Strategy	Workforce Segmentation	Goal Setting & Performance Mgt	Career Mobility

CHECKPOINT: WHAT'S YOUR WORKFORCE PLANNING ARCHITECTURE?

The next step for workforce planning champions to do for our organizations—including when we are already partway through the journey—is to reconsider which of the many alternative approaches to the various framework components serve the particular needs we have, without including unnecessary scope that complicates the effort, bogs it down, and increases the risk of failure.

The goal should not be to implement the entire workforce planning framework at once, building an academically complete program. We are learning that it normally takes several years to make the journey, even with the best people involved, sufficient budgets, and a great context for change.

An old saying goes, "What got you this far is often different from what it will take to get you to the next level." Don't let previous success lull you into a false sense of confidence that you already know what needs to be done to take your workforce planning function forward.

There are several proven management techniques from the disciplines of talent management, financial analysis, operations research, and marketing that are useful to apply to the workforce.[7] The architect's objectives are to balance the possibilities with the realities; to balance the academics with the economics; and to select among multiple approaches, materials, and tools according to the specifics of the current situation in order to coordinate the various efforts toward a shared vision.

Completing the vision involves selecting which teams and individuals will be involved at which stages for each component, selecting the tools and technologies to utilize, and designing the coordination processes to ensure that the needed outcomes are achieved. It is wise to start each stage of evolution of each component with a small footprint, then to scale it up after any issues are resolved and as it is proven to work.

Having a well-thought-out, evolving architecture enables each opportunity to improve to be built into the total solution. Winning organizations outperform others by an order of magnitude, not just by 5 percent or 10 percent incrementally. It is by analyzing the situation and the possibilities in this way, and by choosing the most valuable opportunities for improvement, that your organization can stick to its success formula while figuring out how to scale up at each stage.[8]

When you are faced with the challenge of reconciling and integrating two workforce planning functions—because of a merger or acquisition or an internal clash among competing approaches, or at a new point of integration between teams or organizations—realize that it is an opportunity to evolve to a higher-value model by combining the best of both. It does not have to be that one side or the other wins, because it is very likely both sides have great reasons to be doing what they are doing.

REDISCOVERING THE WORKFORCE PLANNING MANTRA

A workforce planning mantra that results from having our own sights raised to the bigger picture would be:

Get the RIGHT minds at the table

Asking the RIGHT questions

To trigger the RIGHT conversations

That guide the RIGHT workforce actions

Success with workforce planning is achieved when business leaders are able to say:

1. There are sufficient leaders and other workers with the right skills in my organization to achieve our goals, and we have a plan in place to ensure that this remains true over the next few years.
2. The costs of labor for my organization are within planned limits that make sense for our particular business strategies, revenues, and goals.
3. I understand the opportunities to stay ahead of competitors and to get ahead of market trends through our talent, and we are prepared to act on them.

However, success is temporary. As soon as the business model, environment, or workforce changes, it is possible that additional efforts are required to achieve the next increment of success. We're never done analyzing and planning around financials, so why would we expect anything different when analyzing and planning around the workforce?

When we implement a multifaceted solution that coordinates and guides multiple disparate components in a way that adds value, then we can say that our workforce planning function has matured.

And when cross-organizational standards are developed similar to those in accounting, finance, operations research, and marketing, then we can say the whole discipline of workforce planning has matured.

Maybe *then*, with compatible and coordinated workforce planning solutions, mergers, acquisitions, and other organizational transformations might not be so painful. Collisions of different workforce planning worlds might instead be opportunities to quickly piece together a healthier and more complete solution.

Notes

1. Thomas P. Bechet, *Strategic Staffing: A Comprehensive System for Effective Workforce Planning*, 2nd ed. (New York: AMACOM, 2008); J. Boudreau and H. Friedman, "Worldwide

Workforce Planning: Facing the Challenge from Definition to Deployment," Human Capital Institute webinar. Retrieved March 2, 2012, from http://bit.ly/HCIwebcasts; M. Collins and P. Howes, "Building a Data-Driven Framework for Workforce Planning," *IHRIM.link* (August 2009), pp. 5–7; J. Jamrog et al., "Strategic Workforce Planning Knowledge Center," Institute for Corporate Productivity (i4cp) website. Retrieved March 2, 2012, from http://www.i4cp.com/strategy/strategic-workforce -planning; Strategic Workforce Planning Human Capital Topic, The Conference Board website. Retrieved March 2, 2012, from http://www.conference-board.org/ topics/subtopics.cfm?subtopicid=150; U.S. Department of Health & Human Services, Office of Human Resources, *Building Successful Organizations: Workforce Planning in HHS* (November 1999). Retrieved March 2, 2012, from http://www.hhs.gov/ ohr/workforce/wfpguide.html; U.S. Department of the Interior, Office of Personnel Policy, *Workforce Planning Instruction Manual* (August 2001). Retrieved March 2, 2012, from http://www.sciencebuddies.org/science-fair-projects/project_apa_format_ examples.shtml; Workforce Planning Workgroup, Human Capital Institute website. Retrieved March 2, 2012, from http://www.hci.org/node/146723.

2. Bechet, *Strategic Staffing*; John W. Boudreau, *Retooling HR: Using Proven Business Tools to Make Better Decisions About Talent* (Boston: Harvard Business Press, 2010); John W. Boudreau, "IBM's Global Talent Management Strategy," SHRM Academic Initiatives. Retrieved March 2, 2012, from http://www.shrm.org/Education/hreducation/ Documents/Boudreau_IBM%20Case%20Study%20with%20Teaching%20Notes_ FINAL.pdf; Boudreau and Friedman, "Worldwide Workforce Planning."

3. Jim Collins and Morten T. Hansen, *Great by Choice* (New York: HarperCollins, 2011).

4. Collins and Howes, "Building a Data-Driven Framework."

5. S. Couch, "HP Workforce Planning," *Strategic e-HR Conference* (February 2008). Jason Averbook's Knowledge Infuser blog. Knowledge Infusion. Retrieved March 2, 2012, from http://www.knowledgeinfusion.com/ondemand/blogs/infuser/2008/02/06/ strategic-ehr-conference-hp-workforce-planning-session/; "Hewlett-Packard's Profitability Driven Workforce Optimization Model," *Corporate Executive Board* (2008); "IBM Tunes Workforce Planning to Supply Chain Precepts," *Manufacturing Business Technology* (2007).

6. Couch, "HP Workforce Planning"; "Hewlett-Packard's Profitability Driven Workforce Optimization Model"; P. Leavitt, L. Trees, and R. Williams, "Getting Started with Strategic Workforce Planning: Developing the Tools and Techniques," Recruiting Trends website (2012). Retrieved March 2, 2012, from http://www.recruitingtrends .com/getting-started-with-strategic-work-force-planning-developing-the-tools-and -techniques; C. Santos, A. Zhang, M. Gonzalez, and S. Jain, *Workforce Planning and Scheduling for the HP IT Services Business* (Palo Alto, CA: HP Laboratories, 2009); Deborah Waddill and Michael Marquardt, "HP and the HR Optimization Model: Case Study," in *The E-HR Advantage: The Complete Handbook for Technology-Enabled Human Resources* (Boston: Nicholas Brealey Publishing, 2011); S. Williams, "Integrating Workforce Planning with the Annual Budgeting Cycle," Infohrm Workforce Planning Summit (May 2009). Retrieved from http://www.prweb.com/releases/2009/ 03/prweb2230074.htm.

7. Boudreau, "IBM's Global Talent Management Strategy"; "IBM Tunes Workforce Planning to Supply Chain Precepts"; Leavitt et al., "Getting Started with Strategic Workforce Planning"; B. Power, "IBM Focuses HR on Change," *Harvard Business Review* (2012), hosted by Bloomberg BusinessWeek. Retrieved March 2, 2012, from http://www.businessweek.com/management/ibm-focuses-hr-on-change-01102012 .htm; T. Starner, "Passion at the Helm," *Human Resource Executive Online* (2008). Retrieved March 2, 2012, from http://www.hreonline.com/HRE/story.jsp?storyId= 136568343; M. Voelker, "Optimizing the Human Supply Chain," *Intelligent Enterprise* (January 2006). Retrieved March 2, 2012, from http://www.informationweek.com/ news/software/enterprise_apps/175002433.

8. Boudreau, "IBM's Global Talent Management Strategy."

9. Boudreau, *Retooling HR*.

10. Collins and Hansen, *Great by Choice*.

Jeff Buchmiller leads Workforce Analytics at Alliance Data. The businesses of Alliance Data—Retail Services, Epsilon, and LoyaltyOne—offer an unmatched breadth of data driven loyalty and marketing solutions. These are all designed to help grow Alliance's clients' businesses through the application of analytics.

Previously, Jeff worked with EDS for eighteen years, then with HP Enterprise Services for three years through the period of EDS integration. As a data scientist and business intelligence expert, he has played a wide range of R&D, IT services consulting, corporate innovation, data architect, business intelligence, and workforce planning roles.

Jeff graduated from Yale University with a B.S. in applied mathematics and later earned an Executive M.B.A. from Southern Methodist University. His friends accuse him of being a "closet professor" living in the business world.

Workforce Planning in China

Naomi Stanford

This chapter explores the context for addressing workforce planning in China. It looks at the issues through the eyes of seven Chinese national HR directors who reveal five areas of significant challenge to them as they work to support delivery of their business strategies through their workforce. Discussion of these is followed by presentation of seven suggestions implied in their interviews that would enable a more purposeful approach to workforce planning than currently being used.

AVERAGE ANNUAL GROWTH of 10 percent in the past three decades has turned China into the second-largest global economy and top exporter. But predictions were that in 2012, Chinese Premier Wen Jiabao would target an expansion of less than 8 percent, and reports suggested that a cut could indicate that policy makers were prepared to tolerate a slower expansion as they moved the economy's drivers to consumption from exports and investment.[1]

It remains to be seen whether this slight putting on of the brakes and change of direction will make any impact on the fraught situation that has faced, and still faces, HR professionals trying to retain employees, fill talent gaps, find new recruits to fuel growth, match competitors' compensation and benefits packages, struggle with high turnover, and maintain a healthy pipeline.

A quick glance at some facts and figures about China gives the barest impression of the challenges and opportunities that face HR professionals and businesspeople as they grapple with business strategies for growth in a country that many outsiders define as a single, comprehensible "China" but that is, in fact, a country of vivid differences that almost defies definition. As James Fallows, a national correspondent for the *Atlantic*, points out:

> The huge and widening gap between China's haves and have-nots . . . is only one of countless important cleavages within the country—by region, by generation, by level of schooling, by rural versus urban perspective, even by level of rainfall, which determines how many people a given area of land can support.[2]

Nevertheless, some facts and figures serve the purpose of painting an impression of the scale of the country. (U.S. dollars are used throughout below.)

Population:	1.3 billion (2010 census)
Area:	9.6 million kilometers (3.7 million square miles)
Capital:	Beijing (largest city: Shanghai)
Economy:	$10.885 trillion (2010 estimate); compared with the United States: $14.624 trillion
Per capita:	$7,518 (PPP); compared with the United States: $47,123 (PPP)
GDP, Compound Annual Growth Rate, 1980–2010:	10 percent; compared with the United States: 3 percent
Cars per 1,000 capita:	65 (2010 estimates, projected to rise to 180 in 2018); compared with the United States: 800
Amount of consumed crude oil that is imported:	50 percent (42 billion gallons in 2005)

In addition, China has twenty of the world's thirty most polluted cities and is the world's largest CO_2 emitter.[3]

Beyond the facts and figures, an Economist Intelligence Unit report notes that:

In many sectors, China is now an emerged, rather than an emerging, market. It is the world's largest market for cars, air conditioners and LCD-TVs, to name just a few products. No doubt, China will soon be the greatest consumer of a whole host of other goods from medicines to designer handbags.

For many non-Chinese multinational companies (MNCs), China is an important market but not an easy one to enter or work in:

China is making greater demands—especially on foreign companies with proprietary knowhow and cutting-edge technologies. Competition is already brutal. To build a winning business in China, foreign multinationals must now plan even more meticulously—as well as make tangible contributions to the host country's continued economic development.[4]

In this kind of situation, the concept of workforce planning—defined as the process of getting the right people with the right skills in the right jobs at the right time—is almost laughable. There appears no way that HR staff can follow a systematic route to:

➤ Identify future numbers of employees required to deliver new and improved products and services

➤ Analyze the present workforce in relation to these needs

➤ Compare the present workforce and the desired future workforce to highlight shortages, surpluses, and competency gaps

➤ Plan how to address the gaps

➤ Address the gaps

Conversations with seven Chinese national HR directors in February 2012 highlighted some of the reasons why workforce planning is not currently at the top of their agenda. Companies called on represent biotechnology, healthcare, HR consulting, products for the oil and gas industry, insurance, refrigeration and heating technology, and energy. Six of these companies are foreign-owned MNCs, and one is a formal joint venture between a Chinese company and an MNC.

The seven people, interviewed separately, were all asked the same five questions:

1. What are the particular workforce challenges facing western multinational companies operating in China?

2. Are these the same challenges that Chinese companies operating in China and in other countries face?

3. What are companies doing to meet these challenges?

4. What lessons can western multinationals learn from Chinese companies, and vice versa?

5. What are the trends in workforce planning in China?

Analysis of the interviews revealed five themes that individually and collectively answered the questions:

1. The short-term business growth strategy trumps longer-term workforce planning.

2. The perception of "good places to work" is changing.

3. Local leadership is critical.

4. The education system is not delivering the needed skills and competences.

5. Drawing on a broader employment market for talent is hard.

Each of these themes will be explored in more detail in the following sections, and, finally, some suggestions for action will be presented.

THE SHORT-TERM BUSINESS GROWTH STRATEGY TRUMPS LONGER-TERM WORKFORCE PLANNING

As several reports note, business conditions in China are volatile and fast moving. While other economies are stagnating, China's is roaring ahead and is a critical engine for global growth. For most companies, the growth strategy is bullish. The U.S. retailer Walmart, for example, has dozens of stores opening every year. In the final quarter of 2011, the company showed a 16.1 percent increase in sales from the previous year. This is nothing compared to the situation in China, however. The *Financial Times* reports that:

> Retail sales are booming in China, doubling every five years or so. The result is unbridled competition, making it one of the world's toughest markets.
>
> Walmart, Tesco, Carrefour and Metro headline the foreign entrants. Japanese and Korean retailers are also pressing hard. Taiwanese and Hong Kong companies have been among the most successful. Then there are scores of homegrown competitors.
>
> "China is a battlefield. You literally have almost everybody," says Torsten Stocker, head of the Asia consumer goods practice at consulting firm Monitor Group.[5]

Confirming this, the UK retailer Tesco, which is a potential Walmart competitor, is looking to increase market share in the next six to seven years, developing as many as eighty hypermarket-anchored shopping malls, adding up to £5 billion in investment. Additionally, Tesco is entering into a joint venture to develop three shopping malls in two eastern provinces, each built around one of the supermarket chain's hypermarkets.[6] Yet no single retailer is making significantly large-scale inroads into the potentially colossal market. There is plenty of room for more growth.

This incredible drive for growth puts enormous pressure on the HR function. In the words of one interviewee:

> The major challenge is not being able to find people to support an organization's growth strategy. This is the bottleneck. If you can't find people, you can't grow. Some industries that are growing 20 to 30 percent per year are finding it very hard to get talent. This is true especially in those positions that require both people management experience and strong technical background. There's a limited pool of people to draw from and poaching staff is rather common.

Hand in hand with the drive for growth goes the difficulty of retaining staff. It is not hard for employees to move to other companies. Consequently, the experience of another interviewee is common:

> My own company had 28 percent overall turnover in 2010. Even in the management ranks where turnover is around 14 to 15 percent, it is difficult to fill the pipeline. This level of turnover stresses the system—there are huge costs around recruitment, training, and the time taken to become fully productive.

This leads to a tension between the realities of a very tight market and the business strategy for growth, which is, anyway, done in the context of a good number of unknowns in both the global and Chinese economic and political climate. Adding to this tension is the fact that business leaders plan with market and competitor intelligence at hand, but rarely do they plan with the employee turnover numbers in hand. When, as is common, turnover is around 25 percent and this is not factored into the business plan, it becomes, as one person said, "a big struggle" to achieve business targets. So as another interviewee confirmed:

Workforce planning is not something that people here do a lot of. Although there may be a certain amount of workforce planning done as part of developing the annual rolling business strategy, it is focused on the market and I'm not sure of the quality of it. HR people tend not to get involved. It's based on certain assumptions which HR is not involved in developing, so what comes out in terms of workforce planning is not robust. This is not surprising as it is very difficult in these conditions to make accurate long-term headcount projections.

In most companies I know of, the workforce element of the business plan is more of a financial input to the process—the cost of headcount. In any situation where we have to watch revenue, we have to think about controlling headcount. It's very common to do this, but it is a short-term perspective and has some serious consequences. Generally speaking, both headcount restrictions and the lack of available talent can stunt company growth, paradoxically as we're trying to grow, and this has a knock-on effect on employee progression within the company. If the company isn't growing, there are no additional openings for staff, and things become stagnant. But China has a tradition that people will be promoted every two years.

On this topic, another interviewee commented that:

China has been raising the minimum wage in recent years, and living costs have also increased year by year. That brings a retention challenge as people, especially blue-collar workers, will change jobs in order to get higher pay. We have recently experienced higher turnover rate in the blue-collar group than in previous years.

While a third made the point that:

The market is very dynamic. In certain industries, the central government and provincial governments decide to adopt certain different rules to regulate the industry. Business conditions can be unpredictable. It's difficult to forecast how many people there will be in each city each year. In our business—pharma—we don't know how many products may come onstream in each province due to ongoing bidding requirements to lower the cost of medical treatment. It's a challenge to plan in this type of unpredictability. The business plans as best as they can and HR has to be adaptable, acting quickly to react to changes. In ideal circumstances, the number of people available in the marketplace should influence the business strategy. It should be more two-way.

THE PERCEPTION OF "GOOD PLACES TO WORK" IS CHANGING

Perhaps because of the tensions inherent in aiming to grow the business and keep a good handle on workforce costs, foreign multinational companies are beginning to lose out to local Chinese companies in their attraction of potential employees. An interviewee observed that:

> Incentivizing people to either join or stay is an option in getting the needed talent, but it is difficult. What happens is that incentives take the form of career development, and here local companies have the edge. Multinationals are not able to compete in the same way on career development and are beginning to lose their attractiveness as employers. Local firms can give broader responsibilities, with more local autonomy and decision making. They are not subject to overseas decisions that have to be implemented locally.

And another one made the point that:

> Big state-run companies are more attractive to new graduates. They pay very well and have a wide market and significant market share. They offer high job security [and] a good benefits package, and a job with them carries social status. Government restrictions are also something to bear in mind. In some sectors government policies are restrictive to multinational growth, enabling Chinese companies to grow by leaps and bounds, which offers good opportunities for promotion and development.

Finally, there was the trenchant comment that "if people can't speak good English in MNCs, their career is limited. There is no language barrier in a local company for local people's career growth."

These individual observations are confirmed by the Economist Intelligence report mentioned earlier. Its findings—based on a survey of 328 senior executives conducted in June and July 2011, as well as in-depth interviews with executives of major foreign multinationals, business scholars, and market analysts—show that "local talent is increasingly gravitating towards mainland companies."

LOCAL LEADERSHIP IS CRITICAL

Part of the reason why state-run or mainland companies are more attractive to workers is that they are run by people who understand local conditions and culture and have the skills and expertise to work these effectively. With this knowledge, they can act more autonomously, delegate more, and make more decisions than leaders who work for multinational companies. These abilities act to attract entrepreneurial types. In addition, local leaders have a longer-term perspective and are prepared to take time and resources to balance the workforce. As one person commented:

> Chinese companies tend to have the right numbers of people but not the right skill sets. People stay with a company because it is the cultural norm—Chinese companies cannot just let people go. They have a social responsibility towards them. But that leaves the challenge of rebalancing the current workforce and the workforce structures to match the future direction of the organization.

With this in mind, a couple of interviewees made the point that western multinational companies are too short-term in their focus. They send in expatriates to lead the operation on a contract of two to three years, which is not enough to establish viable credibility, reputation, and insight into the culture and characteristics of China. As one pointed out:

> There's significant lack of understanding from multinational leadership about conditions in China. It really is essential to have local representatives to lead their company here. Unfortunately, most HQs assign management to work here. It might help if there were Chinese people in [the] HQ to help guide decisions, but there aren't. Multinationals should have a policy of replacing some or all of their China management team with locals, but it seems that there is not enough trust or understanding of local talent to go down that route. In previous decades, if a foreign company had a business here, it was just for exporting goods, and local markets and cost models were not an issue or concern. But China is now a big market. We need local people who understand the markets to lead here.

This lack of local understanding was a point brought up by another interviewee, who observed that:

> Western companies operating in China should be more flexible in the way they approach working in China and the Chinese workforce. One area where it would help is granting more autonomy in determining organization structure, compensation and benefit items, retention programs, etc.

On the other hand, several interviewees pointed out that there were a number of things that Chinese companies could learn from western ones. Below is a typical comment:

> Western companies have very strong, mature management systems, and this is one of their benefits. Chinese companies need to learn to work with these advanced management processes. The advantage that multinationals have is their mature operating systems. In the HR field, we could learn a lot from the multinationals on the processes and systems they use for things like succession planning, career pathing, and so on.

THE EDUCATION SYSTEM IS NOT DELIVERING THE NEEDED SKILLS AND COMPETENCES

The point about learning—Chinese from multinationals and multinationals about the Chinese people and culture—came up in a slightly different way when interviewees talked about new product and service development. For example, one person said:

> Being a manufacturing company presents many labor challenges. Several groups of the workforce are working on new products and services that will require new skills to implement: skills that we currently don't have. We need more technically skilled people and more professional managers with the depth of expertise to carry out our growth strategy.

Another made the point that although there is a certain amount of white-collar worker competence—for example, for R&D jobs—the current education system is not good enough to produce engineers and leaders.

Good business schools to supply managers and leaders are in short supply in China as a whole right now, although things are changing. A *BusinessWeek* article published in 2006 noted:

> The colossal effort by the central government of China to educate the nation's next generation of managers is unprecedented, and it has been undertaken at a speed that is nothing short of breathtaking. In just 15 years, Chinese B-schools raced through the evolution it took U.S. B-schools more than half a century to accomplish.

However, graduate students noted that in some respects the MBA programs they had attended did not match expectations. Of those surveyed by *BusinessWeek*:

> Nearly a third said their schools were merely "good" or "average" at teaching China-specific business—one of the lowest grades among the half-dozen sub-

ject areas rated. "The culture here is different from Western culture. The corporation is run in different ways," says Zhou Shifeng, who graduated this summer from the Tsinghua/MIT program. "We need to know more about how the best Chinese businessmen run companies."[7]

Asked to recommend good business schools, one respondent came up with a list of five—Peking University, Tsinghua University, Shanghai Jiaotong University, Fudan University, and China Europe International Business School—saying that others were not "outstanding enough."

A number of Chinese universities are entering into partnerships with U.S. universities with the dual goals of improving graduate engineering education in China as well as providing opportunities for Chinese students to get a quality graduate education with the goal of retaining them in China. One example of such a partnership exists between the University of Michigan and Shanghai Jiaotong University. Another is the University of California, Berkeley, which announced at the end of 2011 plans to open a large research and teaching facility in Shanghai as part of a broader plan to bolster its presence in China. The Shanghai center will cater to engineering graduate students and be financed over the next five years largely by the Shanghai government and companies operating there. The program was expected to begin in July 2012.

DRAWING ON A BROADER EMPLOYMENT MARKET FOR TALENT IS HARD

The drive to recruit skills and competences for business growth is hampered not only by the lack of skill level, but also by the vagaries of the employment market to draw on. This point was amplified by an interviewee, who said:

> A few years ago there was a lot of migration to eastern cities where multinationals typically started up. Now growth in local economies has been generated, so migration patterns have changed and there are far fewer migrant workers in eastern cities. To balance this, the companies in these eastern cities have to pay more, particularly to blue-collar workers, and this knocks on to manufacturing costs. Last year, there were blue-collar worker pay increases of 13 percent, and this year 16 percent. That's the same for both multinational and Chinese companies.

An article in the *Economist* underscores the changes in China's internal migration patterns, making the point that:

> The shift in migration patterns may also reflect a rebalancing of China's economy. Domestic demand has made a bigger contribution to China's growth in recent years, driven by heavy investment in infrastructure and property. To

serve this expanding internal market, firms do not need to nestle close to a port. The result is a fast-narrowing wage gap between the coast and the interior. In 2004 coastal wages for migrant laborers were 15 percent higher than inland, according to a survey by the National Bureau of Statistics. Now, many workers in Sichuan say that taking into account transport costs and higher living expenses on the coast, less well-paid jobs closer to home are beginning to look much more competitive.[8]

OPPORTUNITIES FOR ACTION

Reviewing her interview notes for this piece, one person commented, "It comes across as a bit negative. I hope the final piece doesn't sound depressing and hopeless. The fact is we have all the good problems." Given the "battlefield" talent and business growth situation outlined above that HR practitioners are working on, perhaps the situation could be construed as hopeless. As she points out, though, there are "the good problems" that could be turned into opportunities for innovative approaches to workforce planning that contributed to addressing the talent shortage. Seven such opportunities are implied in what interviewees talked about.

1. Integrate the Business and Workforce Planning

A business strategy cannot be executed without the available skills and capability in the workforce. From this perspective, business planners need input on the realities of the talent pool in order to adapt the plans appropriately. Not doing this leads to short-term and possibly damaging pressure on business performance. One interviewee cited the difficulties she faces, partly as a result of a lack of input into the business strategy:

> I have to manage the bottom line by reducing costs due to restricted market growth. Yet simultaneously I have to keep up with competitors in terms of compensation and benefits packages, the culture and environment offered to employees, and the career progression. It doesn't work not to have a voice in the business planning process. I feel as if I am being asked to do the impossible.

For HR directors operating in China, this means pressing for inclusion of their own technical expertise and also for the leadership contribution to the strategy of people who really understand the context and culture of China.

2. Develop a Holistic Attraction and Retention Package

It is not enough to think about competing only on pay. The benefits, including training and development, and retirement benefits that come with the job are both attractors and retainers. A report by Mercer, an HR consulting company, on employees in China noted that:

> As benefits increase in importance and organizations look to improve employee satisfaction, organizations can expect a rise in employee demands for more flexible benefits plans that can address individual needs. In fact, 50 percent to 60 percent of participants [surveyed] expressed their willingness to reduce the value of some benefits received and increase the value of other benefits . . . that are important to them.[9]

This recommendation was also made by one of the interviewees:

> I think that what all companies operating in China need to do is to think holistically about the population they are trying to attract and retain. It isn't just a numbers and skills issue. It's about the whole package of career paths, compensation and benefits, the work environment, the management style, and the benefits packages. The companies with the best retention rates are those that offer supplementary, and flexibly offered, benefits like retirement packages.

3. Collect Accurate Data That Can Be Converted into Financials to Feed into the Business Strategy

Given that so much business planning is done on a financial basis, it makes sense for HR directors to collect accurate data that can be converted into the financial costs/benefits of workforce decisions. It is beyond the scope of this chapter to delve into HR metrics in detail, but two books give very helpful information on how to think about and develop a framework that financial analysts and business strategists will be able to work with. These are *Competing on Analytics* by Thomas Davenport and Jeanne Harris and *Beyond HR: The New Science of Human Capital* by John Boudreau and Peter Ramstad.

4. Track the Cost Model That Specifies the Costs of High Attrition and Continuous Recruitment

Once data is collected, develop a tracking dashboard that can be discussed regularly with business planners and strategists. Hand in hand with this goes providing evidence of the benefits of ongoing investment in development, a comprehensive benefits package, and working to slow down attrition against the risks of not making these investments. It is worth the investment for the HR function to approach its work with the business tools of scorecards, cost/benefit analysis, forecasting, and risk management.

5. Initiate Collaborative Partnerships to Plan Innovative Approaches to Tackle Talent Shortfalls and Then Implement Planned Actions

Mentioned earlier are a couple of examples of partnerships between foreign and Chinese universities to develop management and engineering programs that will grow this much-needed talent. One interviewee made the point, "There are some small successes in working with academia and colleges in that they can help cultivate a supply, but again, that takes time."

These partnerships are a good start and could be developed. Research in innovation suggests that at least four different sectors must be linked to get to innovation: national and local government, business, not-for-profit organizations, and academia. Where this happens, "decisions made at every level—investment funds, corporate strategy and HR teams, regional planning boards, philanthropic bodies, academic faculty, and many more—are naturally aligned."[10]

A willingness to intentionally develop communities of economic coordination where multiple parties join forces to "coordinate innovation across complementary contributions arising within multiple markets and hierarchies" would be a powerful way to accelerate addressing talent shortages for the benefit of the whole ecosystem and not simply within a single organization.[11]

6. Consider Virtual and Flexible Working in Order to Widen the Pool to Draw On

One way of expanding the talent market is to appoint remote and virtual workers. This may be a cultural leap and require investment in both employee and management development. As one interviewee reported:

> There is no telecommuting per se. In fact, the work-life balance schemes common in the U.S. don't exist in China. We have people in 200-plus cities. There are cities where we have set up offices, but a lot of people in the second- or third-tier cities work from home. It's difficult for them to have a sense of belonging to the organization—the community aspects. Managing these remote workers is hard; the employee engagement is weak. Our managers tend to stay in touch with them through regular visits, cell phone calls, and text messages.

But given the ubiquity of mobile technology, the rapid development of mobile capability, and the accelerating skills of people in using it, it would be foolish to ignore the possibilities that alternate work forms could bring to help plan for and solve talent shortfalls.

7. Do the Planning

In the heat of battle, it's very easy to get stuck in being reactive. Making time for research, reflection, and planning might seem like a poor investment when someone is in firefighting mode. But the investment in that time is well worth it. It is useful to bear in mind a quote from U.S. President Dwight Eisenhower: "In preparing for battle I have always found that plans are useless, but planning is indispensable."

His thoughts on planning were endorsed by British Prime Minister Winston Churchill in World War II:

> The Commanders who are engaged report that everything is proceeding according to plan. And what a plan! This vast operation is undoubtedly the most complicated and difficult that has ever occurred. It involves tides, winds, waves, visibility, both from the air and the sea standpoint, and the combined employment of land, air and sea forces in the highest degree of intimacy and in contact with conditions which could not and cannot be fully foreseen.[12]

Perhaps what faces Chinese HR directors is not exactly on the scale of World War II, but there is some resonance in reworking Churchill's statement. It is true to say that Chinese HR practitioners are involved in a "vast operation [that] is undoubtedly [one of] the most complicated and difficult that has ever occurred [in recent HR circles]." To get the right people in the right place at the right time requires planning and foresight, which will allow for better judgments in meeting "conditions which could not and cannot be fully foreseen."

References

1. "Wen Seen Paring China's 8% Growth Target on Rise in Inequality: Economy," Bloomberg News, February 22, 2012.

2. James Fallows, *Postcards from Tomorrow Square* (New York: Vintage Books, 2009).

3. Wikipedia; World Bank; General Motors.

4. *Multinational Companies and China: What Future?* (London: Economist Intelligence Unit, 2011).

5. S. Rabinovitch, "China Growth Paradox Baffles Walmart" (2012). Retrieved from http://www.ft.com/intl/cms/s/0/7f5033ca-570c-11e1-be5e-00144feabdc0.html #axzz1nh8DBCCc.

6. R. Jacobs, "Tesco Pushes Further into China" (2011). Retrieved from http://www.ft .com/intl/cms/s/0/5bf484f2-430e-11e0-aef2-00144feabdc0.html#axzz1nh8DBCCc.

7. "China's B-School Boom," *Bloomberg Business Week* (2006). Retrieved from http:// www.businessweek.com/magazine/content/06_02/b3966074.htm.

8. "Welcome Home," *Economist* (2012). Retrieved from http://www.economist.com/ node/21548273.

9. *Inside Employees' Minds: Navigate the New Rules of Engagement—China Survey* (Mercer LLC, September 2011).

10. E. J. Wilson, "How to Make a Region Innovative," *Strategy+Business* (Spring 2012), pp. 20–24.

11. J. F. Moore, "Business Ecosystems and the View from the Firm," *AntiTrust Bulletin* (Fall 2005).

12. *And What a Plan—Churchill's Speech on D-Day (June 6, 1944)*. Retrieved from http://www .parliament.uk/business/publications/parliamentary-archives/archives-highlights/ archives-d-day/.

Naomi Stanford is an expert in business strategy and organization design. Before joining NBBJ as organization design lead, she worked with corporate and government clients, including the General Services Administration, Shell, Gap, the American Red Cross, the Commonwealth of Virginia, and Philip Morris International. Her skills and experience were honed in the U.K. private sector, where she held corporate roles in multinational companies. Naomi has written several books: *The Economist Guide to Organization Design*; *Organization Design: The Collaborative Approach*; and *Corporate Culture: Getting It Right*. Her new book, *Organizational Health*, will come out in December 2012. In addition, she supervises doctoral students in organization theory and speaks, writes, and teaches on many aspects of organization design. Over the last several years, she has worked with the HR Excellence Center in Shanghai, China, delivering workshops and seminars. Her blog, www.naomistanford.com, showcases her interests.

Workforce Strategies for High-Growth Markets

James David Eyring and Alison Romney Eyring

SINCE THE GLOBAL FINANCIAL CRISIS gripped the world in 2008, the growth of corporate revenues from high-growth and emerging markets relative to those in developed markets has shifted markedly. As a larger portion of company revenue comes from these developing markets and this shift is expected to continue, many multinational companies (MNCs) are shifting organization structures and people to the East. This shift in economic centers of gravity has contributed to greater staffing needs and higher demand for leadership capability across Asia.

As western MNCs have increased their presence in Asia, they also have discovered increased competition for talent from Asian MNCs. Over the past decade, the global expansion of Asian MNCs such as Haier, Tata, and Lenovo has improved their attractiveness to university graduates. But this isn't just a trend among younger employees. Increasingly, western MNCs find themselves losing experienced managers to local MNCs that offer managers greater authority and future career opportunities in their home country. Following the global financial crisis, many western MNCs downsized, cut back on hiring, and restructured for greater efficiency, while local companies were hiring and becoming more attractive employers in these countries.

These dynamics of increasing demand and changing preferences of employees have left even the most admired companies struggling to build and maintain leadership and technical bench strength. Conventional wisdom says that lack of talent supply is the culprit. Seldom do we question if the workforce strategies so many western multinationals have deployed are designed to deliver under a range of market conditions.

Over the past twenty years, one thing has not changed: Virtually all the frameworks and tools in use by western multinationals were developed in slower-growing and more highly developed markets. They were created in nations with cultures characterized as individualistic, where people in positions of power or authority are not granted respect because of their position. Too often, HR leaders who see themselves as "global" think that HR or talent practices that work in the United States or the United Kingdom will work in the same way in China, India, or Indonesia. As a Japanese leader said recently in an interview, "They say this is globalization. But it is really Americanization."

This raises two important questions:

1. What is different in high-growth markets?
2. What strategies and tools are best suited to these markets?

In this chapter, we set out to provide preliminary answers to these questions. Our views are shaped by research we have conducted over the past four years on workforce planning and talent management in high-growth markets. They also are shaped by more than twenty years of work with MNC clients throughout Asia-Pacific and Africa. Much of the research cited is based on surveys we have conducted with approximately forty MNCs, including locally owned MNCs, operating in different countries.

A few important notes on the research:

▶   Most of the research data is from Asia. Key countries represented include China, India, Indonesia, the Philippines, and Vietnam.

▶   Much of the research comes from a recent study in which twenty-five MNCs provided information on their workforce strategies and the outcomes they are experiencing at a country level in China, India, and Indonesia.

▶   Multiple HR and line executives in a country completed the survey to help provide a stable estimate of practices for each company.

▶   Workforce practices were correlated with outcomes (e.g., turnover, promote-from-within rates, and ratings of manager readiness). Results indicate which practices are more highly related to good outcome metrics.

CHALLENGES FOR WORKFORCE STRATEGIES IN HIGH-GROWTH MARKETS

Any employee who has visited her company operations in an emerging market knows that these countries have their own unique challenges. It's easy to observe cultural differences, language and communication challenges, and infrastructure issues. It's also easy to observe how rapid growth and change within a company is stretching leader capabilities. Some market dynamics, such as growth rates and competition for talent, are more difficult to observe, but they have profound impact on a company's ability to compete successfully. Successful workforce strategies must address four key challenges in these markets:

1. Rate of revenue growth
2. Limited talent pools
3. Employee expectations
4. Job complexity

Rate of Revenue Growth

In most instances, high revenue growth brings with it employee headcount growth. In emerging markets, growth rates for large companies can hit 20 to 40 percent a year, and newer entrants to a market can easily experience more than 100 percent growth in a year. A small sales group of ten people can grow to sixty very quickly. A company of 1,000 employees can add 300 to 400 additional employees in a year. With offshoring, these numbers can increase dramatically. Having good systems and processes for recruiting and selecting these employees is one of the more obvious challenges of growth.

Unfortunately, workforce strategies often fail to meet the leadership supply demands created in these markets. Many companies have talent management systems that are designed for slower rates of growth (e.g., 5 to 10 percent per year). We've asked many HR leaders throughout Asia and Africa about the size of the key talent pools in which they are investing their development dollars. Most often, they tell us the key talent pool represents 10 to 15 percent of the overall employee population. This is consistent with their corporate guidelines. When we look into their headcount growth and manager turnover (both of which often exceed 20 percent), it becomes evident that demand for new managers far outweighs the supply, and that their key talent pools are not large enough to keep pace with new positions they are adding. Their policy and process are misaligned with their growth needs. This is a core reason why so many companies are fighting a losing battle to build leadership succession in these markets.

Revenue growth also stretches leader skills. In high-growth environments, leaders are frequently outpaced by the growth of their own jobs. Their skills simply can't keep up. Their team size may triple, requiring them to manage through multiple layers. Often, the expectation for continued revenue growth outpaces their ability to identify and exploit new markets. In addition, growth often results in leaders being promoted quickly to fill open positions. This leaves a group of leaders who are stretched in their current roles and cannot move on to larger roles. These leaders may rely on their managers for more coaching—yet their managers also are stretched by the growth and may not have coaching skills they need. These dynamics put further strain on leadership supply.

Of course, growth is not restricted to one company. In high-growth markets, key competitors are also growing. The result in places like China, Vietnam, and Indonesia is a market shortage for many skill sets.

Limited Talent Pools

Talent pool restrictions can occur at many levels in the organization. Even when there is a surplus workforce of entry-level employees, shortages occur. For example, China was expected to graduate approximately 6.8 million university students in 2012.[1] Close to 90 percent of these students will find jobs, but many will go unemployed for months after they graduate. The MyCOS Institute, an educational research group, reports that 600,000 college graduates in China remain unemployed in the six months following graduation. This trend has lasted for three years.[2]

Still, MNCs find themselves suffering from a shortage of qualified entry-level students. This can occur for many reasons:

► Not all graduates have a degree valued by MNCs.

► Graduates often prefer to stay in large cities and do not want to move to Tier II or Tier III cities (i.e., cities with smaller economies and populations than the largest cities such as Beijing, Guangzhou, and Shanghai).

► English-language skill requirements may screen out vast numbers of graduates.

► Students may not have the problem-solving or innovation skills that MNCs would like.

► Companies often recruit from a limited number of universities, underutilizing some schools.

These dynamics can vary by market, but they demonstrate why scarcity can occur in the midst of plenty.

Scarcity among experienced professionals, especially those with specialized backgrounds, is more pronounced. Whereas western MNCs had a competitive edge when recruiting these professionals in the past, this advantage has eroded significantly in many markets. With the headcount reductions that occurred in 2009, many employees began looking for employment with locally run multinationals because of job security. In China and increasingly in India, local companies offer a more appealing employee value proposition. Universum, an employer branding firm, has an ideal employer survey in China that demonstrates this. In 2007, university students polled by Universum identified two Chinese companies in their top ten "Most Attractive Employers" list. In 2011, seven of the companies in the top ten were Chinese. In the survey conducted in India, five of the top ten companies were Indian. Competition to attract and recruit specialized talent is increasing.

The most limited talent pool in high-growth markets is in senior leadership positions. Companies often cite this as their #1 challenge to achieving their growth targets. Lack of mid-level managers is also one of the top five challenges. One cause of this shortage is market growth. The demand for new positions requiring experienced managers always outpaces supply. If internal talent pools are stretched, companies recruit externally out of the same talent pool of a limited number of managers. As with professional positions, local competition for this pool of managers is growing. Increasingly, managers find work for local companies more desirable because they offer more autonomy, provide greater opportunities for advancement without leaving their market, and can contribute to the growth of their home country. For example, in a western MNC, managers frequently report to and manage multiple stakeholders in a matrix structure. Managers in local companies work within simpler structures and have more autonomy. This competition for talent has resulted in pay packages in developing countries that often exceed their counterparts in the United States or Europe; sometimes, the packages even rival expatriate pay packages.

Employee Expectations

With restricted talent pools, employee expectations have increased. Employees with experience with good companies can receive two to three calls a week from recruiters in a high-growth market. Employees in China have told us that if you don't have one or two job offers on the table, something is wrong. These offers can be very compelling, offering salary increases of 200 to 300 percent. This has shaped employee expectations.

For example, employees in India, China, and other high-growth markets expect faster promotion opportunities and title changes and a faster path to large, meaningful jobs. New hires often expect their first promotion in the first year, followed by rapid promotions in the next two years.[3] They often expect to leave the company within three to four years and want to use these promotions to catapult them to their next job with a new company. Although these expectations moderate with tenure, it is not unusual to see mid-level managers in a large MNC move to another company to take over a top functional leadership role. Compared to their counterparts in slower-growth markets, these individuals have less breadth and depth of experience, but they do have experience managing in complex, high-growth markets.

Expectations are also changing around mobility. Many MNCs are experiencing difficulty encouraging leaders to relocate to other markets for experience. However, the causes of this reluctance to move are changing. In the past, managers were driven by a desire to keep their children in good local schools or to keep their family together. Now managers are not as interested in moving outside their home country because they feel this may slow their career growth. "Why would I want an assignment in Germany?" an Indian manager said in an interview. "Germany is irrelevant—India is where the action is." For a growing number of employees within these markets, the opportunities within their country are so great that they don't want to lose out by moving overseas.

Job Complexity

Finally, complexity in emerging and high-growth markets taxes leadership skills in ways that are not typical in developed markets. Leaders have to manage changing regulatory environments, shortages of talent supply, and complex and changing government relations at multiple levels. Often, they must deliver in a market with poor infrastructure and unreliable supply chains or with complex supply chains that span many countries. These leaders also face internal challenges. With high-growth expectations, leaders must build their teams quickly, manage frequent visits from senior management, and manage a highly complex matrix organization where many of their team members report out-of-country. They may have to manage multiple product lines in-country, with limited functional resources to address their own market needs. They may do this without ever having been developed to manage these challenges because their global workforce strategies do not focus on building these skills.

A common metric for examining job complexity is revenue responsibility. The global CEO of an IT company once told us that the job of a sales manager in China or India managing US$100 million in revenue is typically more complex than the job of a more senior manager in the United States managing US$1 billion in revenue. In his organization, the CEO said, support for the manager in the United States was higher, and the product lines and customer segments were simpler. What was higher was the volume of revenue. In this way, revenue was not a "fair" yardstick for complexity of the business. This may not be true for many companies, but all companies still must better understand what complexities their managers in high-growth and emerging markets deal with on a daily basis, and companies must design around these challenges.

These and other challenges all require workforce strategy solutions. Without addressing these challenges, companies operating in high-growth markets will continue to struggle with a scarcity of leadership.

APPROACHES TO WORKFORCE STRATEGY

Given these challenges, what are the best workforce strategies to drive results in these markets? First, let's look at the approaches companies take to workforce strategy and how this might impact the results they obtain.

One model we have adapted and use in our research[4] examines the approach a company takes to its workforce and how this approach impacts its practices and results. Although this model focuses primarily on talent management, we found that these approaches also are reflected in how these companies determine their workforce strategy and in practices beyond talent management. An adaptation of this model is shown in Figure 1.

In this model, the first dimension focuses on whether a company is Inclusive or Exclusive. Exclusive companies focus on relatively small numbers of positions or talent. Inclusive companies focus on larger numbers of positions or talent. The second dimension focuses on whether a company focuses on Positions or People. Position companies focus more of their resources on building capability for positions, while People companies focus on building talent. Broadly speaking, companies can take one of four strategic approaches with this model:

1. *Key Talent.* Company focuses resources on a small group of talent to fuel the leadership pipeline.
2. *Talent Pooling.* Company focuses on large groups of talent to fuel the leadership pipeline.
3. *Position Planning.* Company focuses on planning for key leadership positions (e.g., CEO or marketing positions).
4. *Core Capability.* Company focuses on building core capability across positions and uses capabilities as a competitive advantage.

From our experience, and based on current conventional wisdom, we expected to see most companies taking a predominately Key Talent approach. To our surprise,

FIGURE 1. APPROACH TO WORKFORCE STRATEGY.

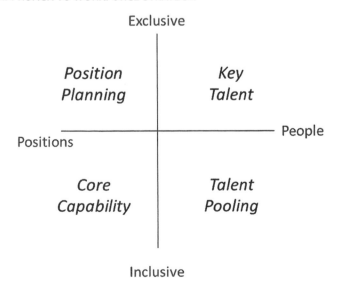

preliminary results from our study of MNCs in China, India, and Indonesia show a remarkably diverse approach. Although few companies took an extremely Exclusive or Inclusive approach, companies were represented in each quadrant (see Figure 2).

We examined a number of outcome metrics for each of these quadrants and found that companies utilizing different strategies performed differently on these metrics. For example, companies with Position strategies (both Inclusive and Exclusive) had lower managerial turnover than companies with People strategies. The companies with the lowest manager turnover used a Core Capability strategy. Companies with this approach had managerial turnover of 8 percent, which was 40 percent lower than the individual industry norms for managerial turnover in those countries. This could be due to the fact that these companies are developing a broader group of employees who can move on to larger jobs rather than focusing resources on a smaller set of leaders. Indeed, turnover for the Key Talent group was highest among the four approaches, with turnover greater than 11 percent. Although the difference in turnover among these two groups is not large, the number of managers impacted in a large organization is meaningful.

As another example, companies utilizing a Key Talent approach were more likely to promote managers within the company than were companies using other strategies. This makes sense. Companies focusing their effort on assessing, choosing, and developing key talent would be more likely to look for opportunities to promote from that key talent pool.

FIGURE 2. REPRESENTATION OF COMPANIES IN CHINA, INDIA, AND INDONESIA IN EACH QUADRANT.

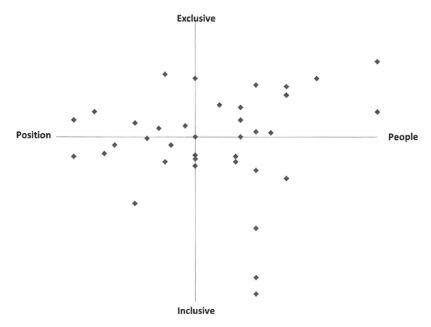

We also looked at how all companies sized their key talent pool. As one might expect, companies with Exclusive key talent pools tended to have a smaller key talent pool relative to the company population of managers. Companies with Inclusive strategies tended to have a larger key talent pool. Results in Table 1 show that the size of the key talent pool matters. Companies with key talent pools in the 20 to 40 percent range promoted more managers within the company (i.e., hired less from the outside). Companies with small (less than 20 percent) or large (more than 40 percent) talent pools had fewer promotions of managers from within the company. This suggests that companies with small key talent pools may not be developing enough people at an accelerated rate to keep up with demand in high-growth markets. Companies whose key talent pools are too large may be diluting their efforts and getting a diminishing return on investment.

TABLE 1. SIZE OF KEY TALENT POOL AND PROMOTE FROM WITHIN RATES.

Size of Key Talent Pool	% Promoted Within
<20%	36%
20%–30%	47%
30%–40%	41%
>40%	37%

Although these are preliminary findings, we can draw some general conclusions:

▶ Companies take many approaches to workforce strategy.
▶ The approach taken impacts important outcomes like turnover and rates of internal promotion.
▶ The size of a key talent pool matters for high-growth markets. Companies that require a global norm are likely to lose competitive advantage in these markets.

OVERCOMING THE CHALLENGES FOR HIGH-GROWTH MARKETS

At a high level, these approaches to strategy help determine how to build a leadership pipeline in high-growth markets. But what specific practices help address challenges for these markets?

To answer this question, we asked line and HR leaders in MNCs to rate the degree to which workforce processes are implemented in their company. Next, we examined the relationship between the strategies used and outcomes attained to identify practices that build a leadership pipeline. We have collected two waves of data covering MNCs operating in China, India, Indonesia, the Philippines, and Vietnam.

Below are some sample practices from our research, surveys, and discussions with companies for each of the four challenges of high-growth markets. These practices seem to differentiate companies that are ready for growth and have built their leadership pipelines from those that still struggle.

Design HR Processes for Revenue Growth

Revenue growth is a blessing. Its curse is a constant lack of managers who are ready for next-level jobs. As mentioned above, some companies are increasing the size of their talent pools to ensure that they are keeping up with demand. But what are they doing about jobs that are outgrowing their leaders?

To address this challenge, some companies hire ahead of the curve on key roles. In other words, they hire a more senior leader for a role than is required by the job evaluation (i.e., the process to evaluate the relative worth and level of a job). For example, with a high-growth expectation, some companies hire at their vice president level for a director-level job, expecting the VP to grow the role and be able to manage a much larger team and portfolio in future.

Locally based companies in high-growth markets do this all the time. They frequently hire without worrying about pay ranges or levels if they think they can get the right person. In contrast, many western multinationals we speak to and work with are restricted by a global compensation structure or job evaluation system that does not give them the flexibility needed to hire a leader who is out of their pay range. Some MNCs have exception processes to get around these issues. However, this slows hiring down and frequently causes the loss of the best candidates.

The best MNCs have changed their processes and have adapted them for emerging markets. For example, one global financial institution adapted its job evaluation system to weight future revenue expectations in determining job size. Instead of looking only at the past three years of revenue, the company also considers the future three years of revenue in determining a job level. By adapting this process, this company is eliminating the need for exceptions and providing better talent that can meet future growth demands. Good business planning and revenue forecasting is important for this to work properly.

Attracting the Right Talent

Limited or restricted talent pools create pressure in recruiting strong university graduates as well as in recruiting experienced managers. A company's employee value proposition (EVP) can help in both of these areas.

Our research indicates that companies with strong EVPs are able to better build capability in high-growth markets. However, a strong global EVP is not enough. The most successful companies had a clearly defined EVP that was: (1) integrated with their local external brand efforts, (2) integrated across HR processes, (3) communicated to employees and managers, and (4) adapted through local market research to be relevant to the local employee market.

As an example, a number of companies have created an EVP relevant to talent in China. They emphasize career opportunities both in and outside China, highlight successful local senior leaders, and widely communicate processes the company uses to grow talent. While these may be important in any country, they are particularly important to MNCs in a high-growth market. Unfortunately, only 16 percent of the companies in our survey managed their EVP to this degree. We found that 23 percent of the respondents had not defined or communicated their EVP. In addition, 61 percent had a corporate-level EVP that was either not communicated or not integrated into their HR processes. This is a clear opportunity for companies operating in high-growth markets.

Successful companies also were much more proactive in recruiting. For experienced hires, these companies were more likely to map talent in the local marketplace and track candidates over the long term. They had their existing managers build networks with these candidates and communicate regularly with them. Again, few companies went to this length. In our survey, 21 percent of the companies did not map local talent at all, and 64 percent only mapped the market for specific jobs (e.g., a senior leader position) when they came open. Companies that maintained a candidate network were better at building capability for the long term.

Similarly, some companies were more likely to use proactive and strategic practices to recruit university graduates. For example, IHG (Intercontinental Hotels Group) has created a public/private partnership to run hospitality academies with almost twenty-five universities in China. IHG executives give lectures at the universities, and the company provides internships and training for students. If the student interns meet IHG's talent requirements, the company also guarantees student employment with its hotels upon graduation. Companies with strategic university partnerships such as this benefit significantly. The partnerships:

▶ Provide a more capable supply of talent for the company

▶ Improve the retention rate as interns are more likely to stay with the company once hired

▶ Improve employer brand among graduates and the universities

▶ Provide a local source of employees who are more likely to stay in the area compared to graduates from a university located in another province

Managing Employee Expectations

Increasing employee expectations contributes to frequent job-hopping. Resumes of job candidates in high-growth markets often show job tenure of one to two years per company. People expect frequent promotions and development.

Unfortunately, many companies are restricted in how they address this because of global policies on compensation. Most companies allow exceptions to their policies on an as-needed basis. However, the best companies have designed and adapted their compensation strategies for local needs. For example, one global pharmaceutical company in our study had broad bands that they used globally. Job titles were strictly adhered to for each broad band, and promotion opportunities were limited due to the breadth of the bands. However, the company's employees still expected frequent promotions, especially in India and China. Title changes were an important sign of that promotion. This was important not only for the employees, but for the employees' families, who see these titles and promotions as signs of success.

To adapt, the company broke the broad bands into zones that were meaningful in the local market. Each zone was benchmarked against salaries and job titles for roles locally. When moving from one zone to another, an employee's job title and remuneration would change. This is similar to having a compensation system with many levels. However, in this case, employees were given merit increases and a title change only when moving between zones. In this way, the employees saw career progression and titles that were consistent with local market practice, while the company maintained its overall broad band philosophy.

In addition to pay structure, companies use management trainee programs and the value proposition behind these programs to address high employee expectations. Many companies, especially in India, hire management trainees, rotate them through a number of positions, and develop them into manager roles early in their careers. One company, Jardine Matheson, is clear in its expectations of trainees. To combat job-hopping, Jardine emphasizes its history of developing leaders internally and the advancement paths that leaders can take within the company. Because Jardine is a large diversified group of business entities focused mainly in Asia, it is able to provide P&L experience early in a manager's career and then progressively move those managers to more complex jobs based on how well they perform. Jardine has combined its manager trainee program and employee value proposition to increase manager retention.

Designing for Complexity

Market complexity results in jobs that are sometimes much more complex than their counterparts in the United States or Europe. Coupled with a competitive marketplace for leadership talent, this means that many job incumbents are stretched in their own roles and typically promoted to the next level when they are barely ready.

To adapt, companies have used a number of strategies. One of the more successful, and practical, is to design jobs with small spans of control to develop leaders into the next level. This allows leaders to have fewer direct reports as they move up to the next-level job. This lowers complexity in one job dimension, allowing leaders to spend more time on the other complexities that they need to manage. As the individual begins to adjust to the new job, spans are expanded.

Although this practice can be used in any market, we have seen more and more MNCs drive toward larger spans globally as they standardize their global structures and drive improved efficiency. Many argue that larger spans are needed to keep leaders focused on "leading" and not "doing." However, companies need to understand the complexities of leading in these markets and then design jobs that allow leaders to be successful. A number of factors should determine job span, not just an ideal cost structure or belief about how to focus leaders.

Another practice is to adapt core management training to close competency gaps in the local labor force. Although many companies have core management training, this training does not always address needs in emerging markets. The best companies design programs to meet these local challenges. Programs often include special functional programs (e.g., marketing programs), government and regulatory affairs training, and mini-MBAs and other courses designed to help managers handle growth in the company. In our research, this one item is highly correlated with having the future leader capability needed to grow. Interestingly, though:

▶ 21 percent of the companies had either limited training or no core curriculum defined.

▶ 56 percent of the companies provided standardized leadership skills training.

▶ Only 26 percent of the companies designed their training to close local competency gaps.

▶ Only 3 percent of the companies regularly adapted the leadership training to build capabilities specific to their strategies.

Clearly, there is an opportunity to better develop leaders in these markets with programs that are relevant to them. Efficiency and standardization should not outweigh the importance of being relevant.

THINK AND ACT GLOBALLY *AND* LOCALLY

One finding that our research has shown consistently is that companies that strictly adhere to global or regional practices fare worse in terms of outcome metrics in high-growth markets.

Many companies are standardizing their talent management practices, high potential programs, employee value proposition, organization structures, compensation plans, and other HR processes. Benefits for moving to global standards include cost efficiencies and ensuring that best practices are implemented to build leadership talent. These are meaningful outcomes. By doing this, however, companies may be undermining their own growth and long-term capability development in emerging markets.

In our most recent round of research, we gathered information on how companies created their workforce strategy. We defined a strategy process as robust when it included a few key areas such as:

▶   Integrating the workforce strategy with business strategy
▶   Forecasting local capability gaps and hiring needs
▶   Ensuring a focus on diversity that was locally meaningful
▶   Understanding and addressing local labor market needs
▶   Planning for three to five years

As Figure 3 shows, companies with more robust strategy processes were more likely to see managers who were ready for growth. Companies with a more robust strategy process also were more likely to be net exporters of talent to other countries. In fact, they exported almost twice the number of employees than they imported. Companies with the lowest scores on their workforce strategy process were net importers of talent.

FIGURE 3. CORRELATION OF ROBUSTNESS OF STRATEGY PROCESS AND MANAGER READINESS.

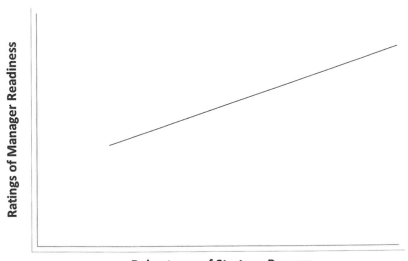

Companies that allowed local design of practices or that allowed practices to be adapted for local use had better leadership pipelines than did companies that strictly mandated global or regional practices. Companies that are driving global standards should consider:

▶ Designing processes and programs that specifically meet the needs for high-growth markets

▶ Implementing a process for local workforce strategy planning

HR leaders and companies must develop locally meaningful workforce strategies or they risk losing competitiveness in high-growth markets.

FINAL TIPS AND QUESTIONS

Even average companies will grow in high-growth markets. The question is: Can they grow even faster and more sustainably with the right workforce strategy in place? We don't yet have the full answer, but we know enough to assert that:

▶ High-growth markets have unique challenges that should be addressed by their workforce strategies.

▶ Different workforce strategies get different results.

▶ Practices for developed markets don't always work in high-growth markets (e.g., size of talent pool).

▶ Companies may be investing in the wrong practices:

- Some practices have more impact than others, but the ROI of practices is rarely examined.

- Many important practices (e.g., core leader training) are not executed at a high enough level in high-growth markets.

▶ Companies with robust, comprehensive local workforce strategies will be more likely to address the challenges in their labor market and improve leadership capability.

How does a company make this shift in thinking to put high-growth markets top-of-mind? Following are a few questions for reflection.

For Global HR Leaders

▶ When did your senior HR leadership team last meet in an emerging market?

▶ How many of your senior HR leaders (especially those leading centers of excellence) have lived in and worked in these markets?

▶ When is the last time you spent significant time understanding labor dynamics in these markets?

▶ Have you implemented a workforce strategy planning process unique to high-growth markets?

▶ Do you encourage adaptation of your global systems to be locally relevant?

For HR Leaders in High-Growth Markets

▶ Are you implementing practices where you have evidence that they work (versus just best practices)?

▶ Are you educating senior leaders and elevating issues that are keeping your country from being successful?

▶ Have you taken time to implement a comprehensive local workforce strategy process?

The economic center of gravity is shifting toward emerging markets. Companies are increasingly relying on growth from these markets, and the percentage of revenue from these markets is increasing. To be successful, companies must adapt their workforce strategies to the unique needs of these countries and ensure that their workforce processes are competitive. Without doing this, workforce strategies that are created globally may actually hamper company growth.

We hope this chapter encourages greater questioning of practices within companies striving to grow in high-growth and emerging markets. While our own research helps point the way toward answers to the questions we posed, it is only preliminary. We have not modeled causal relationships, and the sample of companies at the time of publication is relatively small. We hope that our continued research and that of others in this area will allow us to improve the design and implementation of workforce strategies and talent management practices that work across a broad spectrum of markets.

A FEW NOTES ABOUT THE SURVEY

▶ Items were anchored at four points on the scale with descriptions of what the practice looked like. In this way, companies rated themselves against a standard. The standards ranged progressively from no/low usage toward more strategic and evidence-based use. Example: Companies with university relations practices at the highest level have strategic partnerships in-country (e.g., building curriculum, investing in school, guaranteeing placement). Companies with lower-level practices have relationships and recruit from the schools, but they do not invest further.

▶ Outcomes included both hard metrics and ratings of leader readiness for growth.

▶ Outcomes were correlated with practices to determine which practices were associated with meaningful outcomes. This is correlational research at this point, and causal relations are not fully understood. Only correlations for ratings of leader readiness are shown here.

▶ Multiple respondents (HR and line executives) completed the survey for each company in a country.

References

1. Zhenquo Zhu, "Chinese College Grads to Hit 6.8M in 2012," *Guangming Daily*, translated by *People's Daily Online*, November 23, 2011.

2. Xia Xiao, Jianhua Zhang, and Ju Wu, "'Parent-Gnawers' Live at Home amid Unemployment Rising Living Costs," *Xinhua*, March 30, 2012.

3. C. Schmidt, "The Battle for China's Talent," *Harvard Business Review*, March (2011), pp. 25–27.

4. P. Iles, X. Chuai, and D. Preece, "Talent Management and HRM in Multinational Companies in Beijing: Definitions, Differences and Drivers," *Journal of World Business*, 45 (2010), pp. 179–189.

James Eyring is the chief operating officer of Organisation Solutions in Singapore and leads the global consulting practice. He has more than twenty years of experience in executive development and human resources, specializing in executive coaching and leadership development. James has worked for PepsiCo, Dell, and Motorola and now works with clients such as BHP Billiton, Microsoft, InterContinental Hotels Group, Nokia Siemens Networks, and GSK. Most recently, he has taught at the Helsinki School of Economics and the Singapore Management University and is actively conducting research in the area of leadership and distributed organizations.

James holds an M.A. and Ph.D in industrial/organizational psychology. He has lived and worked in Asia for the past thirteen years. When not working, he enjoys sailing, running, and cooking with his children.

Alison Eyring is the founder and chief executive officer of Organisation Solutions in Singapore. She has twenty-five years of experience in large-scale organization design and change and executive development. Alison works closely with global leaders and their organizations, including Royal/Dutch Shell, BHP Billiton, Chubb Group of Companies, NEC, and Thomson Reuters. She also serves as an adjunct associate professor at the National University of Singapore.

Educated in the United States and Spain, Alison holds a, M.A. and Ph.D in industrial/organizational psychology. She has resided in Singapore since 1999. Alison serves as chair of the board for the Asian Collaborative Organisation Research Network (ACORN). When not working, she trains for triathlons and plays with her children.

Strategic Workforce Planning in the Federal Government: A Work in Progress

Marta Brito Perez

STRATEGIC WORKFORCE PLANNING LINKS TO STRATEGIC PLANNING

AFTER YEARS OF WORKING with organizations in all sectors—public, private, and not-for-profits—and considering why workforce planning was not a more integral part of the business planning cycle, I have come to appreciate the key role business leaders play in determining the value of looking ahead for workforce needs. Without their understanding and commitment, workforce planning is merely a wishful exercise for human resources professionals.

A well-developed strategic plan with a clearly articulated mission and key priorities is the first step in the workforce planning process. Workforce planning should be part of the strategic planning cycle. Those who try to develop a workforce plan without anchoring it in the organization's strategy do so at their peril. In the U.S. federal government, agencies are required to develop strategic plans that lay out direction—where they are and where they are going based on business drivers—and a plan to get there. This is a great place for agencies to begin their workforce planning efforts. A meaningful workforce plan lays out internal and external workforce trends and ways to adapt to those trends to ensure that the agency has the talent to deliver its mission strategy. I will consider the various phases of the workforce planning process, then in the case study on the website, I will dissect one federal agency's recognition of the importance of aligning workforce planning to the development of a robust business strategy.

The importance of workforce planning is not new to the federal government. In 2000, the National Academy of Public Administration (NAPA), which was established by congressional mandate to improve the federal government, defined workforce planning in *Building Successful Organizations: A Guide to Strategic Workforce Planning*. According to NAPA, workforce planning is a systematic process that is integrated, methodical, and ongoing. It includes:

▶ *Identifying the human capital required to meet agency goals*, which consists of determining the number and skills of needed workers and where and when they will be needed

▶ *Developing the strategies to meet these requirements*, which involves identifying actions that must be taken to attract (and retain) the number and types of workers the agency needs

WORKFORCE PLANNING IS PIVOTAL TO THE SUCCESS OF THE FEDERAL GOVERNMENT

In 2006, the Office of Personnel Management (OPM), the government's HR policy-setting organization, predicted in its guidance document, *Career Patterns: A 21st Century Approach to Attracting Talent*, that more than 40 percent of the federal workforce would retire between 2006 and 2015. In the document, OPM urges federal agencies to conduct thoughtful analysis of their workforce and identify interventions to ensure that talent is always readily available. While the 40 percent prediction has likely not materialized because of the economic downturn, the agencies do have workforce planning on their radar screen. Even with the OPM's warnings of an exodus of federal workers, however, workforce planning is not always a natural occurrence in the government. While most agencies recognize its importance, few fully engage the resources required to look ahead to ensure that the necessary skills are readily available for the long term to deliver on the mission.

"The right skills, at the right time, at the right cost" is a phrase often used in the government—yet the analysis necessary to understand the skills required is seldom performed. It is not that agency leaders do not recognize the importance of workforce planning—they do. It is just that the required commitment and resources to implement high-quality planning are considerable. The OPM, the NAPA, the Partnership for Public Service, and other organizations that monitor the government's human capital management practices have often weighed in on the importance of Strategic Workforce Planning (SWP) to the success of federal agencies.

WHAT IS REQUIRED TO DEVELOP A ROBUST WORKFORCE PLAN?

While there are many ways to approach the workforce planning process, there are three fundamental phases that most workforce plan models should include:

1. Planning phase and leadership commitment
   - ▶ A strategic plan that articulates mission and direction for the agency
   - ▶ Leadership prioritizing workforce planning as a mission imperative
   - ▶ Determination of what workforce is needed to achieve future needs
2. Strategic analysis phase
   - ▶ Understanding the internal and external challenges that will impact the agency
     - Workforce segmentation
     - Scenario planning: developing "what-ifs"
     - Supply and demand analysis
     - Environmental assessment and organizational analysis
     - Profile of the future workforce
     - Gap analysis
     - Targeted interventions
3. Accountability for results
   - ▶ Monitoring, evaluating, and revising

Planning Phase and Leadership Commitment

Foundational to the planning phase of a high-quality workforce plan is the commitment of the leaders. Often, leaders provide tacit support to the process and look to HR to carry the weight of the effort. Workforce planning is not about the HR department demonstrating its importance. It is about the leadership, in collaboration with HR, affirming the idea that understanding workforce trends and how internal and external factors impact those trends is mission-critical. Many organizations attempt to assess their talent needs, but few do it well. In the next section, we consider the steps to conduct workforce planning. And in the case study further on in the chapter, we dissect one federal agency's recognition of the importance of aligning workforce planning to the development of a robust business strategy. As the case study shows, the leadership of the National Cancer Institute's Center for Global Health, affirming the importance of the themes of leadership commitment and clear vision, decided to delay the implementation of workforce gap assessment until the agency's strategy had been fully developed and understood by employees and stakeholders.

Equally important in the planning phase is to have a clear vision for what the agency needs to accomplish in order to deliver the mission. During this phase, leaders invest time to consider the mission of the organization and contemplate different paths for delivering on that mission. They should have clarity about what the agency's work is about and how that work will be executed before identifying workforce needs. Once the vision has been understood, leadership and HR determine the scope of the workforce planning effort, identify key personnel to assign to the project, and brainstorm internal and external risks and challenges that will impact the agency in the next three to five years. The time frame for the plan is a function of the business environment in which the agency is operating. The workforce planning effort should consider the new direction for the agency and the current workforce, including possible loss of knowledge as a result of planned and unplanned turnover.

Strategic Analysis Phase

It is important to support the workforce planning effort with sufficient resources. In addition to HR professionals, the planning team should include business leaders who understand all the intricacies of the workforce being analyzed. The analysis of the workforce is a critical element in the planning process. During this phase, the team considers internal and external factors that significantly impact ability to achieve the mission. The team also models solutions and assesses the demand, supply, and necessary interventions to close possible gaps.

In addition to understanding the internal and external trends that influence the organization, the workforce planning process requires a thorough analysis of current and past employee data to provide insight into the workforce needed for the future. Workforce analysis includes reviewing employee recruitment, demographics, promotion, and turnover patterns as well as age and gender profiles of the workforce. Workforce analytics provide further context to workforce planning efforts through a quantitative approach.

Workforce Segmentation. The size and complexity of federal agencies make it imperative to break the workforce into segments along functional lines and relevance to strategic intent. Segmentation provides a technique for prioritizing roles on which to focus.

Scenario Planning. Scenario planning is a useful tool where there are uncertainties about the future needs. Incorporating quantitative and qualitative data about the workforce helps develop a fuller picture of what might be necessary.

Supply Analysis. Supply analysis looks at the agency's existing and projected future workforce. This step involves (1) creating a current workforce profile, (2) reviewing trend data, and (3) projecting future workforce supply. A profile of the incumbent workforce informs the organization about where it is in terms of the right number of people with the right skills. Except for skills assessment, the rest of the data should be available in the agency through employee payroll records, employee files, and various HR databases.

Current workforce data to consider includes:

➤ Permanent and contracted employees
➤ Skills assessment of employees—existing competency assessed against needed work
➤ Workforce diversity (age, gender, and race)
➤ Retirement eligibility statistics
➤ Location for employees

An agency's trend data is very telling of what has occurred in the past. It also helps predict the supply of skills available in the future. The following trend data should be reviewed:

➤ Hiring patterns (time required to fill vacancies, average number of vacancies in year, etc.)
➤ Retirement patterns
➤ Employee turnover statistics

It may be helpful to break down the trend analysis by agency priority areas; otherwise, it is difficult to manage. Information on future workforce supply will emerge from the trend data analysis. This analysis will also help the agency apply assumptions for the future workforce. A robust analysis of trend data combined with information on the current workforce form the foundation for forecasting workforce supply. Equally important is to consider the significance of the envisioned transformation to determine if past workforce trends will still apply.

Demand Analysis. Demand analysis identifies the workforce needed to carry out the mission of the organization. The focus of this step should be on the functions that the organization must perform and not just on the people. One reason this step should be separated from the supply projection is to ensure that changes in functions are considered. These changes might have a significant impact on the size and kind of workforce that will be needed in the future. A restructuring of an agency or part of an agency will have significant implications in the workforce planning process. Again, the magnitude of the change will have a profound impact on the investment necessary to develop a solid workforce plan. (In the case study on the website, I describe the impact restructuring had on workforce demands for the National Cancer Institute.)

Demand analysis provides one of the greatest benefits in workforce planning because it offers the chance for an agency to reexamine its purpose and the direction of its programs in light of changes that are taking place in the external environment. Results include a forecast of the numbers of employees needed in the future (for example, one to five years out) and the skills workers will need. Two ways to determine future functional requirements are through environmental assessment and organizational analysis.

Environmental Assessment and Organizational Analysis. Environmental assessment is the process of examining external trends to obtain a better understanding of what is happening in the environment in which the agency operates. There are several approaches to environmental assessment. The assessment should include trends and issues in the economic, social, technological, legal, and political areas. It is important to track the legislative and appropriations processes to identify factors that may change the agency's mission or program priorities. It is also important to track the changing composition of the workforce and shifting work patterns, including demographics, diversity, outsourcing, and occupations no longer required. An *organizational analysis* should include internal factors such as strategic objectives, business functions, and technology.

Future Workforce Profile. Once the "what" and "how" of future work are determined, the next step is to identify the skills employees need to carry out that work. The future workforce profile shows the number of workers and the set of worker skills needed for the agency's future workforce. The organization's needs are determined by considering the developing trends and issues identified during the environmental assessment. From this review, a desired future state will emerge. The future state for the organization should reflect the best fit for the evolving business strategy, but it should also be achievable.

Gap Analysis. Gap analysis is the process of comparing the workforce supply projection to the workforce demand forecast. The analysis should consider the composition of the workforce, including demographic characteristics, geographic location, size, and employee skill level. The agency will eventually establish workforce strategies based on the results of this analysis. Analysis results will show one of the following:

1. A gap indicates a shortage of needed workers or skills.
2. A surplus suggests that excess in some categories of workers or skills may exist.

Targeted Interventions. Targeted interventions are people management programs and practices that deliver the workforce needed for today and tomorrow. This final step in the workforce analysis phase involves the development of strategies to address future gaps and surpluses. Following are types of interventions designed to close gaps:

► Plan for growth opportunities that take into consideration the long-term development of key talent.

► Develop current employees from existing roles to meet the new needs that have been identified.

► Recruit talent from outside the agency.

► Contract temporary resources.

Strategies include the programs, policies, and practices that enable agencies to recruit, develop, and retain the critical staff needed to achieve program goals. A wide range of strategies exists to attract and/or develop staff with needed skills and to address workers or skills no longer needed in an organization.

Once an agency identifies a workforce gap, it needs to develop and implement effective strategies to close the gap. Such strategies include outreach recruitment, securing contract workers, staff training, and succession planning. Critical gaps should be analyzed with care to ensure that timely action is taken before these gaps become a problem for the organization.

Accountability for Results

Monitoring, Evaluating, and Revising. Ongoing evaluation and adjustments are imperative in workforce planning and are keys to continuous improvement. It is important to identify an individual responsible for the assessment of the workforce information. The review needs to be part of the robust workforce action plan that includes time lines, milestones, and measures of success. Although a workforce plan should look out to five years, it should be reviewed annually. If an agency does not regularly review its workforce planning efforts, it runs the risk of failing to respond to unanticipated changes. Consequently, agencies should establish a process that encourages a regular review of workforce planning efforts in order to:

► Review performance measurement information

► Assess what's working and what's not working

► Adjust the plan and strategies as necessary

► Address new workforce and organizational issues that occur

During the review, departments also introduce and prioritize position changes that have been requested.

The electronic version of this chapter contains additional case study material not available in the print version.

Marta Brito Pérez, senior corporate officer and vice president of Human Resources at Adventist HealthCare, is a senior executive and management consultant specializing in complex reorganizations.

Marta designed and executed significant consolidations and restructuring for AstraZeneca Pharmaceuticals and the U.S. Department of Homeland Security, achieving performance improvements and cost savings in these two distinct environments. She was a presidential appointee while at DHS. Marta also served with the Office of Personnel Management, where she led human capital management reform initiatives impacting more than 2 million federal employees.

She has been honored with the Distinguished Public Service Award from the U.S. Coast Guard and the International Personnel Management Association Award for Excellence. *Hispanic Business Magazine* selected her to its Top 20 Elite Women. She has a passion for not-for-profit initiatives that target public service.

Marta earned a bachelor of arts in criminology from the University of Maryland and served with the International Association of Police Chiefs, designing and delivering crime prevention and public safety programs for domestic and international law enforcement organizations. She holds a master of science in organization development and human resources from The Johns Hopkins University and attended Harvard University's John F. Kennedy School of Government's Senior Executive Program for State and Local officials. She has served on many nonprofit boards and is currently a member of the Congressional Hispanic Caucus Institute Advisory Council.

Marta is a Cuban immigrant. She and her husband, Manuel, have two children, David and Cristina.

Strategic Workforce Planning: Vital Tips for Professionals in the Public Sector

Rachel Bangasser

EVERYWHERE YOU LOOK, you are almost certain to find a sense of urgency that drives both Strategic Workforce Planning (SWP) and change in the public sector, due to issues such as decreased fiscal resources, increased retirement, and altering work responsibilities. The SWP process comes at an important time as the mean age of the workforce continues to rise across the United States. This is particularly concerning in government. In fact, researchers have stated that state government has an older workforce than any other public sector.[1] As the first wave of the baby boomer generation has started retiring, there has been a strain on state government, which is projecting a tidal wave of retirements during the next few years. While trying to maintain and develop institutional knowledge, there is a lack of resources allotted toward talent management or areas such as, but not limited to, organizational research, recruitment, employee training and development, and retainment. Basically, this creates a perfect storm for making SWP an essential practice in current government settings.

The SWP process assists mission-focused organizations in finding long-term direction. This is done by determining the pivotal functions that are geared directly toward achieving an organization's mission while driving toward its vision. Furthermore, SWP is a procedure that assesses the talent supply and demand, focuses on the future, assesses gaps between the current and future workforce, creates a reasonable action plan that closes gaps, and implements and evaluates that plan.[2] Each step offers value to the planning procedure. In essence, SWP is not an easy task. In a governmental setting, SWP needs to occur with limited fiscal resources and in enterprises with multiple union contracts, various legal obligations, and ever-changing environments. Many public organizations offer a variety of services to citizens or to those who serve citizens at the national, state, or local level. The assortment of services offered by a government entity can make strategizing demanding but nonetheless essential.

To assist governmental professionals with SWP, I have provided nine vital tips that I have learned from my own experiences in the public sector while developing, implementing, and consulting in the planning process. I have had a lot of assistance in my learning. Something that I have not provided in my writing is one solid model—an answer to how SWP is done. Although many of the basics of SWP are listed, I have learned that the process changes with each situation. Ultimately, I have learned by trial and error and have taken notes along the way. I am hopeful that these experiences will be helpful to you. These tips are intended to give you a jump toward initial success when doing SWP, regardless of the model you choose or develop to work best for your organization.

SMALL SCOPE FIRST—ENTERPRISE SECOND

If your organization is new to SWP, start in a small department or division. If you are just starting out, your goal in the short term is to learn. Remember that in the long run there is value to SWP at both small- and large-scale levels. Organizations that are more advanced in SWP complete their processes at both levels. The large-scale level provides a strong framework for organizations as they are able to analyze their talent supply and demand, do gap analyses, and make action plans as a whole.

Results have a tendency to be more streamlined on the larger level of the organization because all functions are on the same playing field and are analyzed that way. Realistically, this is very difficult because of lack of knowledge, time, and resources. Because of that, analyses and plans tend to be done at department and division levels. This smaller-scale action can help with hiring different types of positions, since job functions change in different departments even though positions may be the same. For example, an information technology (IT) department will think differently from a communications department. Separate plans will reflect that thinking. Each department may require web-based technology functions but for different reasons and as part of a different strategy. Employees should understand which functions are pivotal throughout an organization. They should also understand the supportive roles behind those pivotal functions.

There are times when this information is applied to a full governmental entity, which typically comes out during a time of crisis. It often starts with information at the department or division level. In fact, identification of "critical employees," is often done during situations such as financial cutbacks, layoffs, or shutdowns, or during some sort of change initiative. Many times, essential functions are based on law or statute, or what is considered to be the safety of the public. During those times, institutions do only what is required for the public versus what is deemed to be in their best interest. It oftentimes has nothing to do with strategy because it may not be an option during times of crisis. For those reasons and for best results, SWP should not be done during time of crisis, but during well-planned opportunities.

START WHEN YOU HAVE EXECUTIVE SUPPORT AND A STRATEGY

There are two things that you need to have before you begin SWP, whether it be in a department, a division, or a whole organization: executive support and a strategy on how you will reach the vision. Whether you are doing this at a departmental or enterprise level, both support and strategy should be worked into your initial discussions, contracting, and planning. Starting with an executive's signature and a clear strategy drives this initiative in the right direction, especially when implementing your action plan. Overall, this will carry the long-term effects of this process much further.

As previously stated, in governmental organizations mission statements are directed toward providing the most exceptional services to citizens, assisting those who serve citizens in the most effective and efficient ways, or a combination of the two. Alongside the mission is a vision for the future, or where the organization is going. The strategy drives that vision and is aligned with the mission. How is the organization going to reach its future? Even if you are working with a department or division or a whole governmental organization, the strategy should align with the mission of that organization.

As part of being supportive, the affected group needs to own and executives need to drive the SWP process. To gather support, inform leaders about the process and potential results before starting. Discuss budget, other resources, and time restraints that may be involved. Provide documents that clearly state where different levels of participation are needed for SWP so questions can be answered. For change to occur, you must be transparent with information and present it to the executives at the right time. Overall, executives need to understand that this process—as well as what you are bringing to your work environment—involves change and may require significant time and resources. You, as a professional, need to understand the depth of your resources, the scope of the project, and the means of the organization's strategy. Your in-depth comprehension and leadership will guide your action plans and implementation processes, as well as assist in gathering the support you need from the right people.

SEGMENT EFFECTIVELY

Segmentation is a primary feature of SWP. It requires you to focus on internal and external supply and demand as well as related global trends that are occurring in the industry. Segmentation is very difficult. In fact, it is the most complicated of the practices involved in SWP and can feel personal. Employees want to work in pivotal functions and struggle when in a position that requires change. It is important to clarify throughout this process that segmentation is not personal. It is based on job functions, not full positions or a specific person.

It is important to remember that SWP in the private and public sector is going to be different in some ways. In the public sector, you need to consider union contracts, a smaller set of resources, specific job classification systems, different employee involvement, and legal obligations that are tied to daily operations. However, many of the concepts that are used in the private sector can be used in the public sector. The philosophy is the same: Change occurs. Government competes for talent in the same industries as the private sector. Government also invests in talent and needs to retain talent.[3] Keeping this investment geared toward what is pivotal is wise.

There are pivotal functions that drive the strategy in governmental organizations, similarly to private organizations. These functions drive the organization forward. Perhaps one way to determine your pivotal functions is by answering this question: In what functions would a change in the quantity or quality in talent compromise an organization's ability to execute their strategy?[4] There is a low percentage of pivotal functions in an organization. Some of these public sector functions are considered essential by, but are not limited to, law or statute when you think about your mission.

After those pivotal functions are determined, you must determine what the core functions are in your organization—those functions that support the pivotal functions. These are most of your organization's functions. Pivotal functions could not be completed without these core functions. Last, you assess functions that are noncore, or those that can be restructured, outsourced, or changed. This is the smallest group of segmented functions. These functions should not be confused with positions. These functions could be a portion of a position.[5] The pivotal functions are critical to driving long-term success of the organization's mission. For example, if the organization's mission is linked to service and protection, such as in a law enforcement organization, it is likely that a law enforcement-oriented function will be linked to the pivotal group. The IT functions may be supportive. However, there may be an IT function that drives a specific investigative program, such as computer fraud. That specific function may be determined as pivotal to that organization.

Pivotal functions require specialized knowledge, skills, abilities, and behaviors (KSABs)[6] as well as competencies that are driven by your talent management system. Assessment of KSABs and competencies will determine the talent that is needed in an organization. An organization's most talented employees are best deployed in applicable, pivotal functions. For example, the mission of a community corrections setting may be to reduce recidivism. Placing the most talented probation officers on caseloads where reduction in recidivism is strategically prioritized and of interest is important. In a financial setting, part of the mission may be to effectively serve those who serve citizens. Depending on the strategy, the best fit for the most talented financial staff may be to manage the largest accounts that serve the highest number of citizens. Essentially, placement of talent is worth considering. Explore your options.

What about the nonpivotal functions, which total the work of most of the employees in an organization? Core and noncore functions do not drive the strategy toward achieving a mission. The focus of supportive, or core, functions is crucial. Pivotal functions cannot operate without strong skill in supportive functions. Separate from that, although difficult in a union-based setting at times, noncore functions should be changed whenever possible so individuals are not spending time on tasks that are not beneficial to the organization. Regardless of your plans with noncore functions, make sure you consider legal and contractual obligations before implementing and announcing potential changes.

FOCUS ON THE FUTURE

In SWP, it is important that the group you are working with has a handle on the current state of affairs. What are the dynamics of this organization? What are the dynamics of the group activities? When the current state is understood, move on to the future and stay in that mind-set. Decisions should be made with the future in mind, or the strategic workforce plan will be outdated by the time the planning process is done.

To assist groups with focusing on the future, there are many futuring techniques that can be practiced. The most important point of futuring is that you choose a multimodal avenue with both qualitative and quantitative approaches. Numerically, solid projection data is helpful for validation and discussion purposes. A qualitative approach that has demonstrated effectiveness, such as scenario planning or what-if strategies, is also important. A combination of the two is most effective; however, it is more important that you provide the opportunity for your team to have innovative dialogue and planning while using evidence in their decisions. Essentially, dialogue is part of a learning and problem-solving environment. Resolutions are created in environments where individuals are allowed to advocate their opinions and ask questions while testing their theories publicly.[7] If you do not have the opportunity to be open in your workplace, it leads to miscommunication, errors, self-sealing processes, and self-fulfilling prophecies. In the case of the SWP process, lack of open dialogue will prevent solid direction, instill an unwillingness to collaborate, and stop a potential change effort before it starts. In my experiences, groups tend to rely on one or the other—either a qualitative planning approach or a numerical projection—to come up with new ideas. Use of both options is best and will result in more creative ideas as long as you include a rich, open dialogue.

PRACTICE A WHOLE SYSTEMS APPROACH

The SWP process is not solely responsible for incorporating talent into an organization or closing skills gaps in a specific area. Looking at SWP as part of a whole system is what Peter Senge describes as systems thinking.[8] There is an interrelationship between SWP and other pieces of talent management, such as strengthening areas involving specific talent, engaging new and current talent, developing and training employees, positioning the right people into the right jobs, promoting the right leaders, and retaining the people that fit into your organization. All of these concepts need to align with each other, as well as the mission, vision, and strategy of the organization. This is an example of a cyclical process that should be validated by evaluation and metrics. Making changes to one piece of the system affects all pieces, especially in the long term. Adapted from the human capital process implemented by Armament Research Development and Engineering Center,[9] Figure 1 demonstrates a whole systems approach to talent management. Figure 1 shows a stronger indication for linking the practices together and evaluating separately, which is important in your continuous change efforts.

For example, you may have an action plan derived from an SWP process that works on the hiring of additional accounting staff with specific skills. In the short term, the plan may indicate only acquiring staff through job fairs, specific job announcements, or other recruiting techniques. In the long term, there needs to be several considerations: engaging and onboarding, making sure that the staff members are in the right positions, and addressing their futures, including retainment. There is a high need for retaining accounting staff in the public sector. Gov-

FIGURE 1. INTEGRATED TALENT MANAGEMENT SYSTEM.

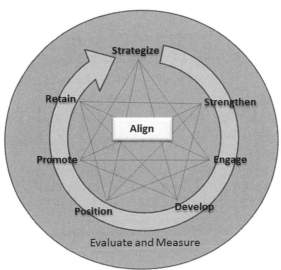

ernmental accounting systems are very specific. The skill is tough to teach and resources are tight. Furthermore, competition between the public and private sectors in hiring accounting staff is high. All of these considerations need to be thought through during the planning process. It will impact your activities, allotted resources, and outcomes.

An example of when SWP, in my experiences, was necessary was when a whole public sector's financial system was updated. The change in the system process positively impacted the way the whole enterprise operated. There was a lot of staff changeover at the time of implementation. Different divisions had to look at how the new technology would change workloads, job functions, and task completion intervals. Staff had to add some tasks and remove others from their lists of job responsibilities. Vacancies needed to be filled differently. It took months of planning and training prior to implementation. Skills that had been needed before were now different. This is a great example of where the SWP process was necessary in filling the gap between current and future workforce needs.

CHOOSE THE ROLES OF PARTICIPANTS CAREFULLY— GO BEYOND HR AND HIGH-LEVEL LEADERS

In many cases, SWP is a responsibility that is left under the umbrella of HR. The responsibility of SWP should be broader than one organizational unit. It is essentially an organization-wide initiative that requires partnership, dialogue, and commitment, while being sponsored by a high-level director or executive. People who are directly involved with the work unit and related functions know the work best. These are people who should be involved in the process. Human resources is typically involved throughout the whole process to assess how these changes may impact the organization through labor relations, staffing changes, or organization development.

In choosing your team, you need a project leader who guides the SWP process; a project sponsor who drives the need and support for the intervention and commitment to the changes; an executive team that develops an initial strategy and shows support throughout the process; a cross-sectional team that completes the planning process; a business intelligence group (research analysts) that assists with data analysis; a team of high-level leaders who give their opinions and support throughout the process; and an implementation team that carries out recommendations of the workforce planning team. You may also benefit from communication specialists, subject matter experts, and project managers who can help with change implementation. Choose your team carefully.[10] People should want to participate and make changes. Based on my experiences, people who have no interest, were forced to participate, or are too busy are not for your team. They should understand your organization and its various job-related functions and be willing to be a part of the change initiative.

Before starting this initiative, team members should understand their roles. Participants will want to have an understanding of what they will be doing and be able to assess how it will impact their own work situations prior to getting started. The purpose of gathering the cross section of people described above is to collect different opinions, broaden ideas, and bring the knowledge of those who work directly with the various functions straight to the planning table. I recall one experience in the planning process that involved little variation in position level. Participants were all managers. The dialogue did not speak to the functions, and it was difficult to steer the team in that direction. They needed a more direct link to skills gaps and areas of talent. To solve that problem, first-line supervisors and a few staff members were added to the planning process, which added deeper perspective.

BE PROACTIVE—REVISIT PLANS AND STRATEGIES

It is important SWP be looked at as a continuous process rather than a project that is over at the time of completion. This proactive approach to SWP enables a strong workforce environment throughout the constant changes in government that extend from adjustment in leadership, elections, variation in funding, workforce decisions, or needs of the clientele. All of this change impacts the whole system within a government entity, including the workforce and its priorities. This can mean that new organizational philosophies emerge, new business ideas develop, job functions change, or a new vision appears. All of this creates the need for a reevaluation of strategy and pivotal functions. This means that ongoing SWP is inevitable. This approach is your best option. The continuous process of SWP ensures that you are ready for change and will make the best hiring decisions for the future.

Although going through the full planning process is ideal, there are shorter ways to plan strategically. It can be done in a short meeting between a manager and HR. Such a meeting may not allow you to gain insights from a cross section of individuals. However, there may be times when holding such a meeting is the best option due to time constraints and lack of resources. For example, there may be an IT manager who has a clear strategy, understands the industry, and knows what she is looking for based on some research that she did, as well as the needs of the organization. She may be versed in applicable data, supply, demand, and trends. If so, holding such a meeting may be best for the department as she works to fill the gaps and reach the strategic goals. This process still requires the development and knowledge of strategy. Sometimes, it is the most realistic process that a person has time to complete.

COMMUNICATION IS KEY

Whatever your SWP process entails, you need to communicate profusely and effectively with the organization. As a professional, you need to assess the level of communication needed at both large and small scales. When leading an SWP intervention, strong communication with the people you are working with is essential so they understand the process and their roles and responsibilities, while the organization may only require information that the process is occurring and updates of how it is going. Prior to implementation of your plans, communication on a larger scale will need to increase from awareness to a clear understanding. The organization needs to understand what will be happening. Regardless, communication will be the key to implementing planning efforts and change that your team is making.

Individuals are more likely to jump on the bandwagon of support if they understand the topic, don't foresee any unnecessary delays, and don't feel hot buttons of emotion being pushed.[11] Communication about what is going well and what is not going well builds a strong sense of trust. Follow up on the things that you say you are going to do. Clear communication demonstrates confidence in your decisions. That confidence also comes through in your work, whether it is in SWP or the implementation of a new model or plans. You will need that support and trust for this entire process.

BE A CHANGE AGENT

Previously in this chapter, it was stated that this process is complex. No matter what your role in an SWP initiative is, your task is difficult when you are making changes in the workforce of a government entity. You may not be the person driving this change effort; however, you may be the person in charge of making the change. This requires strong leadership skills that include guidance of a strong team. Address your immediate struggles, including those with personnel, so the change process will be more effective. This may require you to go down the path of requesting changes in legal obligations, contract agreements, policies and procedures, or general practices. Assess your options, urgencies, and timing. Find a way to make the change and evaluate your efforts. This part is fun, especially when you make a positive, effective difference in how government functions.

In conclusion, there is no single approach to SWP—no cookie-cutter tactic. The path is different for each situation, organization, and industry. You need to assess the situation that is before you and start with an approach that fits with your resources and the group you are working with. By keeping these tips in mind, you will launch a strong foundation in helping your public organization move forward while striving toward attaining your mission.

References

1. G. B. Lewis and Y. J. Cho, "The Aging of the State Government Workforce: Trends and Implications," *American Review of Public Administration*, XX (2010), pp. 1–13.

2. Human Capital Institute, *Strategic Workforce Planning: Participant's Guide* (Washington, D.C.: HCI, 2010).

3. Ibid.

4. John W. Boudreau and Peter M. Ramstad, *Beyond HR: The New Science of Human Capital* (Boston: Harvard Business School Press, 2007).

5. Camden Delta, *XYZ Client: A Guide to Identifying Pivotal Roles* (2010).

6. D. H. Ruse and K. E. Jansen, "Stay in Front of the Talent Curve," *Research Technology Management* (November–December 2008).

7. Chris Argyris, *Flawed Advice and the Management Trap: How Managers Can Know When They're Getting Good Advice and When They're Not* (New York: Oxford University Press, 2000).

8. Peter Senge, *The Fifth Discipline* (New York: Currency Doubleday, 1990).

9. Human Capital Institute, *Human Capital Strategist: Resource Guide* (Washington, D.C.: HCI, 2011).

10. Human Capital Institute, *Strategic Workforce Planning* (Washington, D.C.: HCI, 2010).

11. John P. Kotter and Lorne A. Whitehead, *Buy-In: Saving Your Good Idea from Getting Shot Down* (Boston: Harvard Business School Press, 2010).

Rachel Bangasser is a human resources leader in state government. She continues her employment in government because of her desire to make change that benefits large numbers of people. Drawing on more than twelve years of experience in government and nonprofit organizations, her specialties include Strategic Workforce Planning, human capital analytics, employee engagement, and change management. She has teaching experience in courses related to research methods, stress management, and conflict management. Rachel holds a doctorate in Organization Development from University of St. Thomas in Minneapolis. Questions or comments regarding her work should be directed to rachelbangasser@gmail.com.

Do as I Say, Not as I Do!

Laura Chalkley

WHEN IT COMES TO WORKFORCE and succession planning, especially in local government, how true the words in this chapter's title seem. It's not that we don't want to think about it. The truth is that the busyness of our jobs and daily lives gets in the way of our doing anything but putting out the fires that are popping up all around us. And if truth be told, many think that workforce and succession planning are human resources functions. But are they solely HR? It's true that there is a lack of ownership and/or confusion around who is responsible for workforce and succession planning, and we have come to think the solution is a partnership, a shared responsibility between individual departments and HR.

The all-too-familiar cry in many local governments—*"but I'm doing more with less!"*—certainly doesn't allow for time to think about what may happen in the next five to ten years. And the truth is that many local governments have suffered from significant budget cuts and reductions in staff; however, not too many corresponding services have been cut. But the bottom line is that we do need to think about it, and we do need to do something to prepare for the future.

What further challenges the traditional planning process are the changing demographics of our organizations and the economy. No longer do we hire the person right out of college who comes to work for the government with plans to stay for his entire career until retirement. We hire the very experienced, top-of-the-ladder candidate who has typically retired from a first career, or in rare cases we hire the person with limited experience who plans to stay three to five years and then move on. In addition, the economy has impacted those who are eligible to retire but can't afford to anymore, so in some cases, people are not retiring as early as anticipated. The uncertain economy and rapidly changing technologies also have had an effect on predicting what the work will be five years from now. Will you need building plan reviewers and building inspectors if developers do not have the funding to build?

Peter Cappelli, professor and director of the Center for Human Resources at the Wharton School, spoke at a recent HR People & Strategy (HRPS) conference about "The New Challenge for Talent Management." He said in part that one of the challenges is "generating the supply of talent to match estimated demand when demand is very hard to predict and when the supply of talent won't stay put."

So how can we even plan with all this uncertainty?

There are many models to choose from, and each individual organization has to choose which model best fits its culture and passes the reasonableness test—in other words, what is the organization capable of committing to in order to plan for the workforce of the future? My organization took a dual approach to workforce planning. The first was a focus on internal leadership development at various levels to prepare for the potential retirement of more than one-third of our executive and senior managers within the next five years. The second approach focused on general workforce planning for anticipated retirements in the next five years. We don't have a crystal ball, though we do have some specific retirement dates on the books, but it is still imperative to analyze what our needs will be, decide what skills may be needed for the future workforce, and determine whether we can grow and develop employees to fill the need.

This chapter will mainly focus on the path we took regarding leadership development and will touch on some other models we developed to help individual departments analyze their workforce needs.

LEADERSHIP DEVELOPMENT PROGRAMS

We started the process by collecting data on the retirement eligibility of executive leaders in the next five years as well as the "executive leader readiness" of senior and mid-level managers through a Succession Risk Analysis Tool sponsored by the Corporate Leadership Council. (Note: For our purposes, executives lead departments, senior managers support executives and typically manage divisions, and mid-level managers support senior managers and typically lead individual programs.)

The intention of the tool was to provide information about how strong the future leaders (successors) were; how many of the future leaders were ready to assume a greater leadership role today; whether or not the future leaders wanted to remain employed with the organization; and whether or not the future leaders were receiving valuable developmental experiences. The information gleaned from that survey confirmed all too well what we thought: We could lose approximately one-third of our executives and senior leaders in the short term. The promising news was that there was not significant short-term or long-term risk of maintaining a strong and ready successor pool of candidates for executive level positions.

Then we looked at executive leader readiness among our mid-level managers.

While the executives overwhelmingly agreed that the successors were ready to assume executive leadership positions, when we surveyed the successors, they did not feel they had been provided adequate training or been given the opportunity to be able to deal with developing a department's strategy, supporting organizational objectives, working on projects in which organizational politics make their job harder, and helping turn a struggling business unit around.

To address these needs, the HR department and training and organizational development team designed two new leadership development programs. One focused on mid-level managers, while the other focused on high potential leaders. The two programs were defined as follows:

1. *Mid-level Manager's Program.* This program targeted mid-level managers, seasoned managers, and managers who had completed first-line supervisory programs and wanted to improve their skills and compete for positions of greater challenge and leadership. This program was designed with a strong emphasis on "self as manager." It was a feedback-intensive, cohort-based program lasting five months. The specific components focused on multi-rater feedback and coaching, Myers-Briggs assessment, and an individual development plan; business skills included change management and management versus leadership, developing others, and managers as coaches. It culminated with an experiential learning project: the manager's role in developing employees.

2. *Leader's Challenge Program.* This program targeted high potential mid-level and senior managers and individual contributors to prepare to compete for positions of greater challenge and leadership. The program incorporated action learning for teams to solve real-time county issues, with executive sponsorship. Detailed 360 assessments, Myers-Briggs assessment, and executive coaching were provided for each participant as well as some classroom learning around "self as leader," change management, healthy practices for leaders, leadership presence, and presentation skills.

As you may know, in the public sector, vacancies are filled on a merit-based system, so identifying high potentials needs to be carefully pursued. Our leadership development programs in no way guaranteed or even groomed individuals for *specific* positions. We looked to create a pool of talented and effective leaders within the organization. Our Leader's Challenge Program differed from other leadership development programs in that participants did not have to supervise employees in order to participate. We recognized that there were very strong individual contributors within the organization who had potential for assuming executive leadership positions. Some individuals specifically requested the opportunity to compete for this program and had to have a strong recommendation from their department directors. Others were recommended by senior leaders in their department. We looked for diversity among the pool of applications including ethnicity, job profession, gender, age, and thought process, which we gleaned through an extensive application essay.

While we have seen seven promotions in the past three years from the approximately forty individuals who have completed the Leader's Challenge Program, we have also benefited from graduates who have led high-visibility task forces and teams to solve organization-wide issues. We have been able to "deploy" some graduates to other areas in the organization to allow them to gain an even broader perspective on the challenges facing leaders, providing even further experiential learning.

GENERAL WORKFORCE PLANNING

As I noted at the beginning of this chapter, there is no "one-size-fits-all" approach to workforce planning. We recognized that there was a broader need throughout the organization to look at workforce planning. We also recognized that someone needed to take the lead to begin the discussion and instill this process as a way of thinking throughout the organization. We created a team within HR to work with teams from individual departments if they were willing to devote the time and energy to tackling the issue. The team consisted of an internal organization development consultant, a senior staffing analyst, and a senior classification analyst.

We started the process by getting the teams to focus on a typical gap analysis of future workforce needs. No matter what model you follow, there are some basic components that should be considered. To name a few:

➤ *Forecasting and assessment.* Who is eligible to retire, and what are the future trends for the job? Are there any hard-to-fill or high-risk positions that need a plan?

➤ *Leadership development.* Do we have the internal capacity to groom future leaders?

➤ *Internal opportunities.* Is there a clear career path for employees to follow and take ownership of for their development?

➤ *Recruitment.* Do we have the right mix of internal promotions and new hires?

We provided department leaders with a list of eligible retirees, with clear direction and emphasis on the word *eligible*. We then asked them to do the basic evaluation of potential retirees and identification of staff members who might be able to compete for the position with some skill development.

The following is an example of what we proposed as a *Workforce Planning Process*:

1. Individual departments review retirement date report furnished by HR. Report will be segmented by eligible dates in one- to five-year time frame and six- to ten-year time frame.

2. Review report for "classes" of positions as well as individuals to determine greatest replacement need.

3. List critical skills needed in the next five to ten years, if known.

4. Look at current staff members who may be able to fill positions.

5. Compare critical skills with current staff skill levels.

6. Prepare development plan for internal staff members who could potentially fill those positions.

7. Create a plan for recruiting for positions if there are no internal resources.

We also created a tool that departments could use as a template for analyzing current staff and future workforce needs based on a Workforce Planning Diagnostic Tool developed by the Corporate Leadership Council. Our next step was to ask for volunteers who would be willing to work with our HR team to begin the process. Two departments initially contacted us—a public safety agency and a department of libraries—and we began the work.

Working with the Public Safety Agency

The public safety agency has specific career paths for employees within the organization. Still, it was eye-opening for the leadership of this agency to look at the numbers and to work on a plan for the future of the agency's workforce. The leaders had to look at the gap created by retirements out and promotions up and the change associated with the gap, as well as the need to look at unique skills and knowledge base that would be a struggle to replace if someone in those positions left unexpectedly. We then challenged them to examine the ideal organization and how to get there and to ensure that the desired outcomes and recommendations were aligned with the outcomes of a concurrent job analysis study and potential exam recommendations.

Team review and discussion covered a variety of topics, such as:

▶ Operations, staffing levels, recruitment, retention, staff changes, etc.

▶ Projected retirement and promotional analysis

▶ Feedback solicited from eligible sworn staff regarding projected retirement dates

▶ Projections that were created of upcoming retirements and promotions, reviewed staffing levels for next five years at each rank and determining when and where shortfalls would occur

▶ Specific positions and individuals who were identified who had unique skill sets and knowledge areas that were of concern in terms of knowledge transfer

After reviewing all the data, the team proposed a path to work on that included reviewing the following areas and making adjustments in order to fill the gaps identified in the initial analysis:

1. Recruitment
2. Career development
3. Promotional process
4. Knowledge transfer

There is the recognition that this is just the beginning of the work and that departments will continue to partner with the HR team to provide for the continuity of operations for the workforce of the future within public safety.

Working with Department of Libraries

The second department we worked with took a very different path from either the high potential leadership development route or the all-encompassing view taken by the public safety agency. After more than a year of working on gathering and analyzing data on potential retirements, workforce needs, and industry trends, the conclusion in this department was that there was a huge gap between entry-level positions and mid- to senior-level positions. The department leaders did not feel they had the capacity to fulfill leadership needs in light of the anticipated retirement of senior leaders within the next five to ten years.

The solution to this particular agency's unique need was through the development of an Emerging Leaders Program. The program is designed to identify and define emerging employee talent and develop these people's skills in support of the agency's mission, values, and services. Two additional goals were identified: (1) to increase the diversity of the staff at all levels to reflect the community they serve, and (2) to enhance the retention of highly engaged and talented employees, thus creating a source of successors or future leaders.

With input from HR training and organization development staff, the department leaders developed a nine-month program designed around department-specific knowledge and competencies as well as courses in communication, managing conflict, facilitation, skills, effective meetings, and difficult conversations, all of which were identified as skills needed to move into broader leadership roles. In addition, there are requirements for technology courses (e.g., Outlook Excel, PowerPoint) and participation in luncheon dialogues on topics ranging from "Ethics" to "Making Counting Count." Participants also are assigned a mentor from senior leadership staff in the department.

Anyone can apply for this program, and applicants are selected based on the strength of their application and recommendation from their supervisors. The agency has just implemented its second cohort, so there are no strong metrics yet, but the program is designed to plan for leadership needs in the next five to ten years.

Concluding Thoughts

In closing, I'd like to share a quote from *Effective Succession Planning, Ensuring Leadership Continuity and Building Talent from Within* by William J. Rothwell (New York: Amacom, 2001, p. 16):

> Strategic planning is a process by which organizations choose to survive and compete . . . To implement a strategic plan, organizations require the right people in the right place at the right times . . . Hence, leadership identification and succession is critical to the successful implementation of organizational strategy.

Laura Chalkley is division chief for training, organization development, and staffing in the human resources department of Arlington County, Virginia. She has been with Arlington for twenty-three years. Prior to this position, she was an internal organization development consultant. In June 2004, she was recognized as one of three finalists for the HR Leadership Awards of Greater Washington for enhancing organization efficiency and performance, and she was named "Personnelist of the Year" by the Local Government Personnel Association of Baltimore-Washington Area for outstanding performance in promoting employee growth and development. Laura graduated from Trinity College in Washington, D.C., with a B.A. in business administration, completed the Georgetown University Certificate Program in organization development, and earned the designation of Certified Public Manager through a program sponsored by The George Washington University and the Metropolitan Washington Council of Governments. She is certified as a Senior Professional in Human Resources (SPHR). She can be reached via email at lchalk@arlingtonva.us.

Strategic Workforce Planning: A Rigorous Simulation Optimization Approach

Marco Better, Fred Glover, Dave Sutherland, and Manuel Laguna

INTRODUCTION

CEOS CONSIDER MANAGING TALENT A PRIORITY, as well as a top business challenge for the future—second only to managing business growth.[1] Business leaders recognize that their organization is only as good as its talent, and success depends on having *the right people in the right place at the right time*—a concept we call *readiness*. Achieving high workforce readiness requires the ability to anticipate changing workforce needs, as well as to allocate resources as effectively as possible in meeting those needs. While talent is a top priority, few organizations manage it as strategically as they do their financial and physical assets or their customer requirements.

In most organizations, workforce planning is in its infancy, if it is done at all, and the tools and analytics used to support talent management decisions are not nearly as advanced as they are in other disciplines (e.g., there's no equivalent of a cash flow model or operations plan). Yet the complexity of the task is enormous! The pace of change within economies, industries, and organizations continues to accelerate; labor markets continue to become more competitive and more global; and the workforce continues to become more diverse in terms of its demographics, expectations, and goals.

Advanced workforce planning and talent management tools are needed to enable organizations to determine, among other things:

- The effect of changes in business strategy and customer demand on workforce needs
- Retirement, turnover, and undesired talent loss risks

▶ Cost trade-offs between higher retention and recruitment to close gaps in critical segments of the workforce

▶ The effects on cost and gaps of changing the skill mix of the workforce

▶ The set of retention and recruitment programs that will maximize readiness at minimum cost

The bottom line is: If HR is to have a credible place at the strategic planning table, then human capital decisions must be made based on data and analytics instead of relying solely on anecdotes and assumptions. Experts and thought leaders in the field of Strategic Workforce Planning—among them practitioners, consultants, and academics—are increasingly advocating the use of advanced analytics and decision sciences in their field and in the talent management arena in general.[2]

Simulation and optimization technology can answer this call. Organizations use it to manage risky portfolios of projects and securities, optimize their business processes, and develop new products and services, among other uses. Organizations that are willing to apply this level of rigor to their human capital decisions will create a distinct competitive advantage.

Correctly applied to workforce planning, this technology enables organizations to optimize readiness (right people, right place, right time, and right costs) and representation (diversity) within defined constraints (budget dollars, scarce skills). Whereas traditional approaches limit their scope to projecting future workforce requirements based on static assumptions, the combination of simulation and optimization provides decision-making tools that support the development and implementation of strategies, programs, and policies to meet those requirements.

Think of budget dollars allocated to buckets representing specific practices (policies, programs, initiatives) used to attract and retain valued employees. Then, envision a dial beneath each bucket. You can turn the dial to increase or decrease the resources allocated to each bucket until you find the allocation of resources that is most likely to enable you to achieve specific goals (e.g., readiness, retention, cost), recognizing constraints and considering the demographics of your population.

Other applications include but are not limited to:

▶ Identifying the most effective recruiting channels for the organization

▶ Modeling the cost-effectiveness and risk of using contingent versus regular staff

▶ Supporting the budgeting process by defining and communicating trade-offs between readiness and costs

▶ Modeling the likely impact of compensation strategies

➤ Identifying appropriate bench strength in key areas, given workforce mobility and associated costs

Ultimately, we believe simulation optimization can be applied to any strategic human capital decision-making process. A unique type of simulation modeling, known as "agent-based" simulation, is particularly well suited for this type of application. In this chapter, we describe the components of an agent-based simulation optimization application called OptForce, and how this approach is used to optimize workforce planning decisions.[3] We begin by describing the agent-based simulation model; we then describe the optimization approach; next, we provide a use-case summary of the technology from one of our marquee customers, CH2M Hill; and we conclude with closing remarks about the benefits of our recommended approach.

AGENT-BASED SIMULATION

Agent-based simulation is a modeling technique where key entities (i.e., employees, passengers, etc.) are represented by computerized agents whose behavior is influenced by other agents and their environment. In SWP, agents represent employees whose behavior relates to the likelihood that they will stay in the organization, be promoted or transferred, become good performers, etc., based on environmental stimuli; such stimuli comes from within the organization, in the form of talent programs and practices designed to attract, retain, and promote target employees, or from the external environment, such as the state of the economy, the job market, and the competition for desired talent.

The agent-based model includes accurate forecasting methods for employee retention, not only in the aggregate, but at very granular levels, based on employees' unique characteristics (such as age, gender, marital status) and career attributes (such as tenure, experience, role in the organization, and performance, to name a few).

The forecasting technique must be dynamic and adapt to changes in the employee's attributes, as the employee's age advances, tenure increases, or role changes after a promotion or transfer. The model must also adapt to changes in assumptions about the economy, the job market, and any programs and policies the organization plans to put in place. Thus, the model can be used for scenario planning and "what-if" analysis to assess the sensitivity of the workforce to different sets of assumptions.

In the agent-based model, employees interact with the environment and periodically make decisions about their career in the organization. These decisions are based on their perceptions of the degree to which the organization is meeting their needs, and the likelihood it will in the future. Ultimately, the objective of the model is to determine future workforce needs, how well the current and projected workforce meets those needs, and how to close any resulting gaps.

Simulation in Action

Figure 1 provides a graphical representation of the workforce simulation process. The simulation runs for a number of measurement periods that may be expressed in months, quarters, years, etc. During each period, the following events occur:

1. Each employee makes a decision about whether to stay in or leave the organization. This decision depends on the employee's retention probability, which is obtained from the retention forecasting model.
2. Employees who remain in the organization are assigned to available jobs, contingent upon a match between their attributes and stated job requirements and qualifications.
3. Remaining jobs are filled by employees promoted according to eligibility criteria or probability of mobility/promotion.
4. New employees are recruited from the appropriate sourcing channels to fill any remaining available jobs, as allowed by budget limits.

Consider the process in Figure 1. Circles represent employees and rectangles represent jobs. The top section represents executive-level employees, the center section represents middle management, and the bottom section represents non-managerial-level employees. Finally, circles represent external hires. In this example, the employee decision and job assignment processes occur annually for three years.

FIGURE 1. REPRESENTATION OF THE OPTFORCE SIMULATION PROCESS.

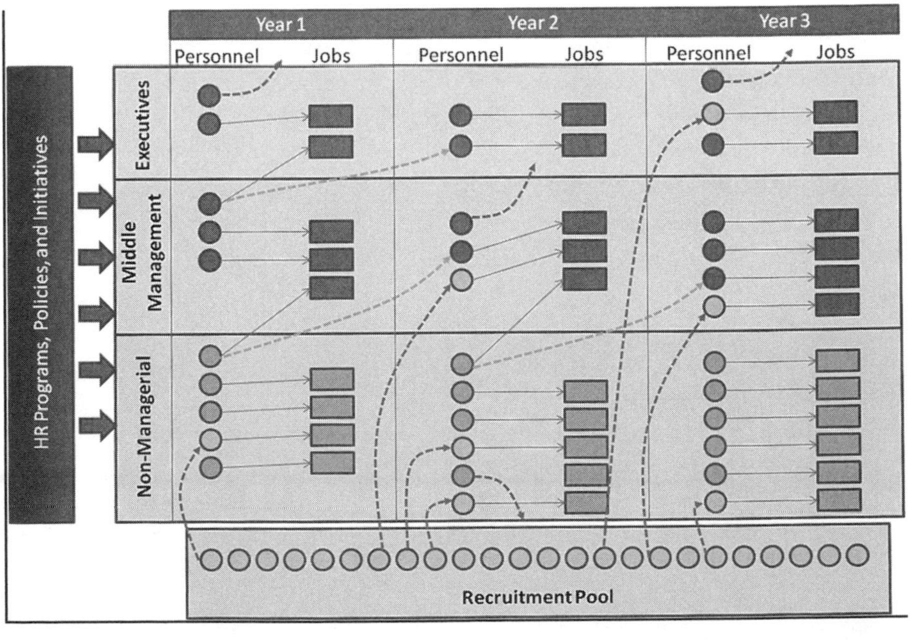

In Figure 1, the initial workforce is composed of two executives, three middle managers, and four non-managerial employees. However, during Year 1, one executive leaves the organization, as depicted by the dashed arrow leading out of the executive section. Remaining employees are assigned to available jobs. In addition, one middle manager is promoted into an executive-level job, and one non-manager is promoted into a middle management job, as depicted by the dashed arrows going from the middle management to the executive section. Finally, a new employee is hired to fill an available non-managerial position.

During Year 2, one middle manager and one non-manager leave; one non-manager is promoted into a middle manager job; and three new employees are hired. During this year, an additional non-managerial job is created, but it remains unfilled due to budget limits.

During Year 3, one executive leaves; there are no promotions; and a new middle management job and a new non-management job are created, requiring three new employees to be hired.

The basic steps in building an agent-based model for SWP are:

1. Defining future workforce requirements (demand planning)
2. Defining key attributes relevant in forecasting employee behavior (retention forecasting)
3. Identifying current and proposed talent policies, programs, and initiatives designed to influence employee retention and mobility (internal supply planning)
4. Determining the impact of each policy, program, and initiative as well as the effect of different economic conditions on retention of employees with different attributes (sensitivity analysis—predictive analytics)
5. Defining current and potential sourcing channels (external supply planning)
6. Defining eligibility and constraints with respect to promotion and mobility within the organization (career development)

These steps are designed to be able to (1) define future workforce requirements based on the organization's strategic plan, (2) determine how the forecasted workforce meets those requirements, and (3) decide how best to close the gap between (1) and (2).

Defining Future Workforce Requirements. Defining future workforce requirements serves as the foundation for effective Strategic Workforce Planning. This estimation of *workforce demand* is used to perform so-called *gap analysis* that identifies the difference between what the organization needs and what it actually has or is projected to have in future periods. Workforce demand planning involves translating business plans into a forecast of specific workforce requirements—number of positions, headcount, skills, timing, location, etc.—and identifying factors that could change the required profile so that contingency plans can be developed.

The most common methods to forecast future workforce needs include aggregation of line manager "guesses," past trends in workforce growth to forecast future growth, and correlation of corporate metrics to historical workforce needs. Such demand metrics may be tied directly to financial projections such as sales, revenue, and gross margin. Alternately, the metrics may relate to operational goals, such as volume, throughput, and cycle time. Metrics may drive the growth in one or more roles in the organization. For example, let's assume that the need for doctors and nurses in a hospital ward is tied to the number of beds. The hospital projects a certain growth rate in the number of beds. The growth rate may be constant over time, or it may vary. Let's imagine that there are two expansions planned, respectively one and two years from now, and that the number of beds grows constantly at a 4 percent annual rate between expansions. Supposing the ward currently has thirty beds, the growth would be as shown in Table 1.

TABLE 1. DEMAND METRIC BASED ON NUMBER OF BEDS.

	Period (Quarters)								
Metric	1	2	3	4	5	6	7	8	9
Number of Beds	30	30	31	34	34	35	35	39	39

Now let's assume that the number of nurses grows at the same rate as the number of beds, but the number of doctors grows at a rate that is 50 percent of the growth in number of beds (i.e., they can attend to two patients at a time). Assuming the ward currently has ten nurses and five doctors, by associating the above metric, we would project the demand for nurses and doctors to be as stated in Table 2.

While historical data might be effective to project future needs for roles that are stable, they cannot be the main driving factor that determines future work-

TABLE 2. RESULTING DEMAND FOR NURSES AND DOCTORS.

	Period (Quarters)								
Role	1	2	3	4	5	6	7	8	9
Nurses	10	10	10	11	11	12	12	13	13
Doctors	5	5	5	5	5	5	5	6	6

force needs in a dynamic environment. For the process to be effective, corporate strategy must be translated into workforce requirements. What is needed is an understanding of the nature of the work required to meet strategic goals. The main source of information is not historical data but the organization's strategic plan. For lack of better methods, focus groups, surveys, and the Delphi technique are often used as tools to accomplish this task. We believe that a more rigorous approach is needed.

We consider both internal and external factors that affect how a particular workforce mix performs against the goals of the organization. Relevant factors include the business environment, market and economic conditions, and technology enhancements. We assume that the exact way in which these factors affect the workforce mix is not known with complete certainty, but it can be estimated and turned into probabilistic models. Specifically, it is possible to model the relationships between a workforce mix and a set of factors to estimate the degree by which corporate goals are satisfied.

Let us consider an example of a claims handling process in an insurance company. For this example, we assume a three-year planning horizon. We also assume that we have five different types of claims, ten tasks necessary to handle those claims, and employees in five different roles and skill levels to perform those tasks. Table 3 shows the expected volume of each claim during the next three years.

TABLE 3. EXPECTED VOLUME OF CLAIMS, BY TYPE.

Period	Claim Type				
	Claim 1	Claim 2	Claim 3	Claim 4	Claim 5
Year 1	20,000	15,500	50,000	37,000	43,000
Year 2	25,000	15,700	55,000	41,000	45,000
Year 3	35,000	25,300	62,000	43,000	52,000

In order to handle each type of claim, several tasks need to be accomplished. Table 4 shows that, for instance, Tasks T01, T03–T07, and T09–T10 are required to process claims of type 1. Each entry in Table 4 indicates the number of minutes of each task that are necessary to process a single instance of the corresponding claim.

Next is the availability and commitment of claims processing personnel to the five types of claims included in the planning model. The example considers five types of roles, and their availability and commitment are given in Table 5.

Personnel in all roles are scheduled to work 200 days per year and eight hours per day. The percentages under each year reflect the commitment of personnel in a role to the five claim types in the model. Variations from 100 percent reflect indi-

TABLE 4. TASKS REQUIRED PER CLAIM TYPE.

Task	Claim Type				
	Claim 1	Claim 2	Claim 3	Claim 4	Claim 5
T01	22	33	18	28	26
T02		44	26	15	
T03	29	17	26	20	
T04	23	34			13
T05	40		16		20
T06	26		18	35	14
T07	42	24	28	8	
T08		10	15		34
T09	16	27		23	19
T10	44	11	13	24	5

rect activities such as overhead not included in the list of tasks. To complete the input data, we need to determine task data consisting of the distribution of a task by role. Each entry in Table 6 indicates the percentage of the task that is performed by a worker in each of role category.

For instance, Task T01 is performed by personnel in Roles 1 and 2 in equal parts. Other tasks require work by other roles, and the assumption in this example is a worker in one role will not perform an activity that requires the skill level of another role.

For each year, the total number of minutes per task is distributed (using the percentages in Table 6) among the different roles. The total number of minutes is

TABLE 5. AVAILABILITY AND COMMITMENT BY ROLE.

Skill level	Days per year	Hours per day	Percentage of Time		
			Year 1	Year 2	Year 3
Role 1	200	8	60%	60%	60%
Role 2	200	8	80%	80%	80%
Role 3	200	8	70%	75%	85%
Role 4	200	8	90%	80%	70%
Role 5	200	8	100%	100%	100%

TABLE 6. PERCENTAGE OF TASK PERFORMED BY EACH ROLE.

Task	Role				
	Role 1	Role 2	Role 3	Role 4	Role 5
T01	50%	50%			
T02			70%	30%	
T03		60%		20%	20%
T04			50%		50%
T05	10%				90%
T06			20%	80%	
T07		25%	25%		50%
T08		70%		30%	
T09	5%	85%	10%		
T10		30%	20%	20%	30%

simply the sum product of the demands and the task requirement per claim. For instance, the total number of minutes of task T01 in Year 1 is given by:

T01 total = 20,000 (Claim 1) * 22 (min) + 15,500 (Claim 2) * 33 (min) + 50,000 (Claim 3) * 18 (min) + 37,000 (Claim 4) * 28 (min) + 43,000 (Claim 5) * 26 (min) = 4,005,500 minutes

The distribution of the total number of minutes among the skill levels involved in performing task T01 is taken from Table 7. In the case of task T01, the calculation is:

Role 1 time = 4,005,500 (min) * 50% = 2,002,750 minutes
Role 2 time = 4,005,500 (min) * 50% = 2,002,750 minutes

The time requirement per role is simply the sum of the times per task required for that role, as shown in Table 7. The total workload for Role 1 in Year 1 is given by:

Role 1 workload = 2,002,750 + 246,000 + 120,325 = 2,369,075 minutes

Workforce requirements are based on both time requirements and talent availability. A summary of the forecasted requirements is given in Table 8 and calculated as follows. A total of 2,369,075 minutes are required of Role 1 in Year 1, as

TABLE 7. WORKLOAD FORECASTS.

Workload
Year 1

Task	Role					
	Role 1	Role 2	Role 3	Role 4	Role 5	Total
T01	2,002,750	2,002,750	0	0	0	4,005,500
T02	0	0	1,775,900	761,100	0	2,537,000
T03	0	1,730,100	0	576,700	576,700	2,883,500
T04	0	0	773,000	0	773,000	1,546,000
T05	246,000	0	0	0	2,214,000	2,460,000
T06	0	0	663,400	2,653,600	0	3,317,000
T07	0	727,000	727,000	0	1,454,000	2,908,000
T08	0	1,656,900	0	710,100	0	2,367,000
T09	120,325	2,045,525	240,650	0	0	2,406,500
T10	0	841,050	560,700	560,700	841,050	2,803,500
Total	2,369,075	9,003,325	4,740,650	5,262,200	5,858,750	

TABLE 8. WORKFORCE REQUIREMENTS.

Skill level	Year 1	Year 2	Year 3
Role 1	41	44	54
Role 2	117	117	135
Role 3	70	63	65
Role 4	60	64	80
Role 5	61	64	77
Total	349	352	411

shown in the Table 7. To find the number of workers needed, the availability of a single Role 1 worker in Year 1 is calculated.

Role 1 availability in Year 1 = 200 (days/year) * 8 (hours/day) * 60 (min/hr) * 60% (availability) = 57,600 minutes /worker

Therefore, the number of workers is :

Role 1 requirements = 2,369,075 (min) / 57,600 (min/worker) = 41.13 workers

Note that the workforce requirements exhibit 0.86 percent growth from Year 1 to 2 and 16.8 percent from Year 2 to 3. This is driven by the projected growth in the demand for claims. However, due to task requirements and labor commitments, both growth patterns are not proportional as the growth in claims demand from Year 1 to Year 2 is 9.7 percent and from Year 2 to Year 3 is 19.6 percent. However, the growth in workforce requirements for those years is 0.86 percent and 16.8 percent, respectively.

A Simulation Optimization Approach to Demand Planning

The demand for products or services is the main source of uncertainty in the example described above; this is particularly true for new products or services. To deal with this uncertainty, a Monte Carlo simulation is used to treat the demand assumptions as random variables instead of point estimates. Each random variable follows some specified probability distribution function. In our example, we assume that the demand for Claim 1 follows a normal distribution with a mean value given by the expected values shown in Table 5. Similar distributions are used to model demand of the remaining claim types with larger standard deviations representing greater uncertainty. Because, typically, demands among products are not independent (for example, during a strong economy, it may be expected that the demand will be relatively high for most or all claims), correlation among demands should be considered in the model.

The uncertainty of key data makes the Monte Carlo simulation an attractive tool to embed in a simulation optimization process as depicted in Figure 2.

FIGURE 2. DEPICTION OF A SIMULATION OPTIMIZATION PROCESS FOR FORECASTING WORKFORCE REQUIREMENTS.

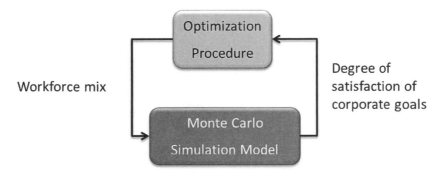

The *workforce mix* in Figure 2 consists of the number of workers required for each period of the planning horizon, at each skill level, and in each location. The optimal mix—that is, the one that satisfies the corporate goals to the highest degree—becomes the workforce demand that will be used in subsequent steps of the company's workforce planning exercise. The optimization procedure can be a general-purpose optimization algorithm based on metaheuristic methods, such as OptQuest,[4] embedded in most commercially available Monte Carlo simulation tools.

For the process to work properly, the degree of satisfaction of corporate goals must include some trade-off component, such as return on investment. In other words, the process should take into consideration the cost of the workforce. For instance, the optimization model may be configured to maximize the degree of satisfaction of corporate goals at minimum cost.

Defining the Key Attributes Relevant in Forecasting Employee Behavior. The second step in defining the model is to identify key employee attributes to consider. *Attributes* describe the characteristics of an employee, such as age, gender, ethnicity, work experience, education, and performance rating. Attribute *values* are used to classify employees for the purpose of assessing differences in retention behavior and the impact of different HR decisions on different groups of employees. For instance, we may want to track employees by two attributes: *gender* and *age*. Then, within *gender*, we have two values: *male* and *female*; within *age*, we have four values: *veterans, baby boomers, Generation X,* and *Generation Y*.

At the core of the agent-based model resides an accurate predictive analytics module, based on decision tree analysis, which we call *Retention Rate Tree* Analysis. More sophisticated than classification and regression trees, this *Retention Tree* not only partitions historic data into groups with homogenous retention behavior, but also recognizes trends in behavior within partitions. Starting from a *root node*, the tree splits on attributes most relevant in explaining differences in retention behavior. The tree-building algorithm selects the best attribute to split on at each level and branch, as well as the optimal splits of the attribute, based on preselected information gain metrics.

The tree uses historic employee data as well as external macroeconomic data to conduct multifactor analysis in order to accurately predict future employee retention behavior. As a result, the agent-based simulation is not only able to simulate the behavior of individual employees, but is also able to determine the key factors impacting an individual employees' behavior based on his unique set of attributes. An example of a rate tree is depicted in Figure 3.

The *root node* of the tree represents employees of a particular organization over some time span (e.g., 233,146 cases in five years), with an average annual retention rate of 90.85 percent; however, if we split the population into five tenure bands, we see great variability in retention behavior. In fact, we see there is a much

FIGURE 3. RATE TREE DEPICTING RETENTION BY FIVE TENURE BANDS EXPRESSED IN TERMS OF YEARS OF SERVICE (YOS).

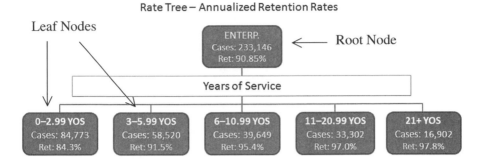

Rate Tree – Annualized Retention Rates

higher than average attrition rate in the 0–3 years-of-service band, while all other tenure bands have above-average retention rates. Managers can target this particular concern with the implementation of a better onboarding program to stem the high attrition of new employees. Deeper examination of the tree could result in better insights into retention behavior.

In Figure 4, the tree from Figure 3 has been expanded to include the organizational division as well as the job level, summarized in terms of bottom, middle,

FIGURE 4. RATE TREE DEPICTING RETENTION BEHAVIOR BY DIVISION, TENURE BANDS, AND JOB LEVEL.

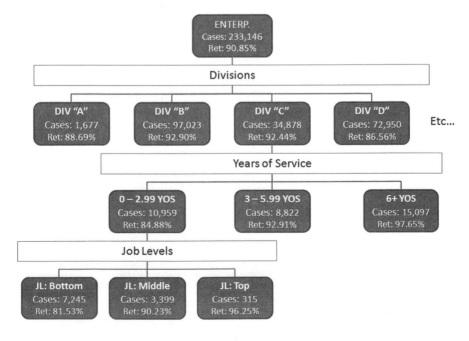

and top. (The figure depicts only part of the complete tree in order to make our point here.) Drilling down into Division "C" of the enterprise, we see that it is not every type of new employee that exhibits low retention, but only those at lower-level jobs, so a less costly onboarding program than previously considered may be sufficient, targeting only this subpopulation.

This feature, more rigorous in nature than other workforce planning solutions, enables decision makers and workforce planners to identify clearly actionable decisions and investments and evaluate their impact on the shape of their workforce of the future.

The retention rates at any node of the tree are used as retention probabilities in the agent-based model, to simulate the probability that an employee with the set of attributes implied by their tree node will stay in the organization from one period to the next.

Identifying Current and Potential Talent Practices. The third step in the planning process is to develop a comprehensive inventory of practices (i.e., formal or informal programs and policies) currently in place that impact attraction, movement, and retention, as well as any proposed modifications to current practices and any practices being considered for future implementation. In order to track costs effectively, costs per employee, as well as any program management costs, should be accounted for.

Determining the Impact of Each Practice on Employees with Different Attributes. The impact of each practice on an employee's behavior is determined based on relevant employee attributes. In the absence of solid historical data and/or external benchmark data, we assume the organization can obtain anecdotal data and informed judgment as to the expected impact of different practices on employees with specific attributes. Like the development of the workforce profile, this is an area where it may be wisest to start simple and build sophistication over time.

As an example, if the organization were to implement a policy that allows for flex-time, we would predict a highly positive impact on the retention rate of female Generation Y employees, whereas we would expect little or no effect on the retention of male baby boomers. Ultimately, the set of attributes chosen to describe the employee population should be selected according to the following criterion: *Does the impact of any of the current or potential practices vary significantly by this attribute?* If the answer is *yes*, then the attribute should be included in the model.

Defining Current and Potential Sourcing Channels. In addition to considering the impact of talent practices, it is also necessary to consider the effectiveness of alternate sourcing channels in bringing employees into the organization. For each current and potential sourcing channel, the following parameters are defined:

➤ A current distribution of the population with the channel, as defined by key employee attributes

➤ A cost-per-hire for the channel

➤ An effectiveness factor for that channel

➤ A maximum number of new hires that can be obtained from that channel

These data can be obtained from the company's recruitment history complemented by external, publicly available data for common channels (e.g., Bureau of Labor Statistics databases, university graduation rates, online job sites), but parameters related to effectiveness and cost will vary by organization.

The probability distribution of the population in a channel represents the likelihood that a new hire will have certain attributes. For example, according to the National Center for Education Statistics[6] of the Department of Education, the distribution of the population of graduating seniors in all public colleges and universities in the United States, is shown in Table 9.

TABLE 9. DEMOGRAPHICS OF GRADUATING SENIORS AT U.S. COLLEGES AND UNIVERSITIES.

	White	Minority*	Asian American
Female	36%	16%	3%
Male	29%	13%	3%

*Note: We define *minority*, for this illustration only, as African American and Hispanic graduating seniors.

These data are entered into a sourcing channel labeled, for instance, "General Colleges and Universities," so that during a simulation, when a new hire is drawn from this population, the likelihood of hiring a minority female, for example, would be about 16 percent.

The cost-per-hire figure for the channel is expected cost to the organization to hire a new employee through that particular channel. It includes setup costs (e.g., travel costs, setting up a booth at a job fair), advertising costs, recruiting costs (e.g., recruiters' time, managers' time in interviews), agency fees, employee referral fees, relocation expenses, and signing bonuses. If the organization cannot calculate cost-per-hire for each channel but has a good estimate of average cost-per-hire by job level, then each channel's cost-per-hire figure can be computed by multiplying the cost-per-hire times the effectiveness factor.

The effectiveness factor represents the effectiveness of the channel in yielding qualified candidates. It is multidimensional and can consider such factors as percent of jobs filled, offers as a percent of interviews, first-year retention rates, and offer acceptance rates. Effectiveness can be measured in many ways, but it is important that the calculation be consistent across all channels.

Finally, the organization estimates the maximum number of new hires it expects to get from each channel, for each role. Ideally, this information will be based on authoritative data sources, such as the Bureau of Labor Statistics, or from verified data consolidation vendors[7] and adjusted to reflect expected future state. In many cases, however, they are based on the best judgment of in-house recruiting experts.

The data in the recruitment channels is used to simulate new hires.

Defining Assumptions with Respect to Promotion and Movement Within the Organization. The last step in setting up the model relates to the mobility of employees within the organization, in terms of promotions, job and location changes, etc. One of the attributes associated with each employee is job level, which may be defined generically for the entire organization or as defined career paths within job families. Mobility is modeled based on eligibility rules or historic rates to predict the likelihood that employees with particular attributes will move within the organization during the measurement time frame.

Table 10 shows an example of a mobility probability table for a services company. In this example, employees are described by tenure, job level, and performance rating, and an advancement probability is computed for each employee according to their attributes. The probability represents the likelihood that an employee with the attributes shown in the first three columns will change jobs or locations during the upcoming period. These data will be used to simulate advancement of employees through the organization.

Once the model has been populated with these data, different scenarios can be tested to predict the outcome of various talent management decisions. These decisions relate to:

1. *Changes in talent practices.* Assuming a limited budget, the organization must prioritize the talent practices it will implement, maintain, change, or discontinue and the level of funding for each. A key application of the model is to determine the budget allocation that results in the highest possible level of readiness while meeting defined representation goals.

2. *Allocation of recruitment budget.* The model considers how budget dollars are allocated across sourcing channels in simulating movement into the organization. A key application of the model is to determine the budget allocations that will most likely enable the organization to achieve readiness, cost, and representation goals.

TABLE 10. PROMOTION/ADVANCEMENT RATES.

Tenure	Job level	Performance rating	Probability (%)
< 5	Non-Managerial	Above	10
< 5	Middle Management	Above	20
6–15	Non-Managerial	Average	10
6–15	Non-Managerial	Above	25
6–15	Middle Management	Average	20
6–15	Middle Management	Above	30
> 15	Non-Managerial	Average	10
> 15	Non-Managerial	Above	25
> 15	Middle Management	Average	20
> 15	Middle Management	Above	50

3. *Economic/business outlook and other environmental parameters.* Economic fore-casts, projected unemployment rates, the financial strength of the organization, and demand and supply gaps for certain skills affect employee retention decisions. How these factors are defined is unique to each organization, depending on the relevance to their workforce.

OPTIMIZING AGENT-BASED SIMULATIONS

Modeling all possible combinations of practices, recruitment budget allocations, and environmental parameters is virtually impossible, even for a small number of options.[8] Therefore, a procedure is needed that allows the user to focus on the set of scenarios that produce the best possible results. That is the essence of the optimization component of the technology. The optimization engine uses the most advanced global search algorithms to efficiently find the best solutions to simulation problems. This enables the user to focus on evaluating a limited number of potential solutions that the optimization has selected to yield the best results.

Figure 5 shows the results of an optimization of an SWP case for an engineering services firm. The performance curve represents the readiness level, and each dot on the performance curve represents an improving solution in terms of readiness. The goals for this optimization were expressed as follows.

The company wants to maximize *readiness* on a three-year planning horizon, while making sure that nonwhite and female employees would represent at least 30 percent of the resulting workforce. In addition, the company imposes a $4 million annual recruitment budget, a $10 million annual program management

FIGURE 5. OPTIMIZATION RUN SHOWING 100 ITERATIONS.

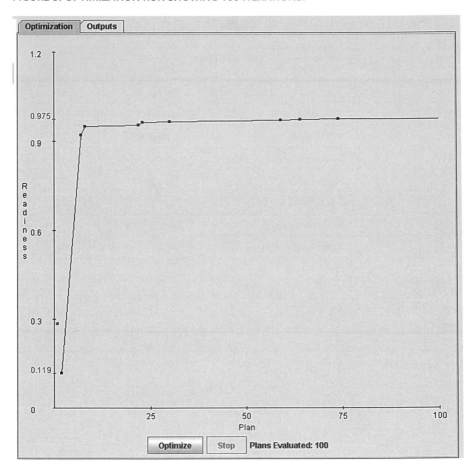

budget, a $100 million annual compensation budget, with the total annual HR budget not to exceed $105 million.

In this example, readiness represents the extent to which workforce demand can be filled by the available workforce at the end of Year 3. In order for demand to be filled, the model matches employees to jobs based on job requirements and employee qualifications. Readiness, r, is measured on a 0 to 1 scale, and is calculated as follows:

$$r = \frac{\Sigma_i\,(p_i | p_i \in E|)}{\Sigma_i\,p_i},$$

where p_i represents job i in the workforce demand scenario, and E represents the set of jobs whose requirements can be matched with a current employee; thus, the numerator denotes the sum of all jobs in the demand scenario that can be filled, and the denominator represents all available jobs.

The best solution found is shown in Tables 11 and 12. From these, we conclude that if the company implements the programs marked "YES" in Table 12, and allocates the $4 million annual recruitment budget as depicted in Table 13,

TABLE 11. SELECTED HR PROGRAMS IN THE BEST SOLUTION.

Program	Program Option	Selected?
Education	No tuition reimbursement	
	50% tuition reimbursement	YES
Flex-Time	No flexibility	YES
	Flexible start time	
	Telecommuting	
Healthcare Plan	HMO	YES
	À la carte	
Retirement Plan	401 K	
	401 K with matching	YES
Incentive Pay	No incentive pay	
	Profit sharing	
	Annual Bonus	YES
Compensation	At-market rates	YES
	Below-market rates	
	Hybrid rates	
Recognition/Awards	None	
	Monthly awards	YES
Ombudsman Program	None	YES
	Full-time ombudsman	
Training Program	New employee orientation	YES
	Annual training program	
Mentoring Program	None	
	Assigned mentors	YES
Diversity/Inclusion	Diversity policy	
	Quarterly diversity training	YES

TABLE 12. RECRUITMENT BUDGET ALLOCATION ACCORDING TO THE BEST SOLUTION.

Recruitment Channel	Budget Allocation
General Universities	10%
Social eNetworks	5%
Ethnic-Serving Colleges	75%
University Job Fairs	0
Online Job Sites	0
Company Website	0
Recruitment Agencies	0
Ethnic-Serving Agencies	0
Network Contacts/Referrals	5%
Publication Ads	5%

then it should expect to achieve a readiness level of 96.3 percent at the end of three years. The total investment in personnel costs and expenses is $94.01 million, of which $3.27 million is spent in sourcing new hires and $90.74 million in compensation, benefits, and other retention programs.

Further inspection of this solution would show that women are expected to grow from 24.7 percent of the workforce to 39.8 percent; minorities from 25.5 percent to 43.5 percent; the age composition of the workforce varies from 35.6 percent to 40.2 percent in Generation Y, 23.8 percent to 42.6 percent in Generation X, and baby boomers from 40.6 percent to 25.2 percent. Average annual turnover is 6.7 percent, and new hires represent 19.4 percent of the workforce. It is also possible to drill down within each job level to analyze similar trends.

Workforce planners can define an optimization objective—i.e., what goal the model will optimize (typically related to readiness, cost, diversity representation, etc.)—and other key measures of success. They can also define parameters that govern the simulation, including length of the planning horizon, programs to optimize, changes in business strategy, and environmental factors (e.g., economic outlook, talent availability), as well as constraints (e.g., budget limitations).

In Figures 6 through 8 we compare solutions obtained from optimization to those obtained from traditional "what-if" analysis. Scenario 1, denoted as *Base*, corresponds to conducting "business as usual"; in other words, no new talent practices are added or modified, and investment in current recruitment channels remains the same. In the second scenario, denoted *What-if*, the user has made decisions to add or modify an HR practice or to reallocate recruitment investments. The third scenario, denoted *Optimized*, refers to the best solution found by OptiQuest.

FIGURE 6. READINESS RESULTS UNDER THREE DIFFERENT WORKFORCE PLANNING SCENARIOS.

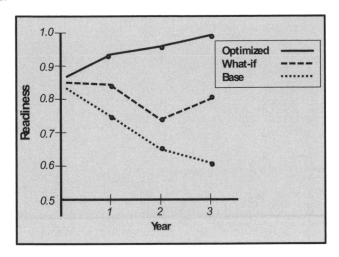

As you can see from Figure 6, although the starting readiness level is about 85 percent, both the *Base* and the *What-if* scenarios perform poorly in terms of readiness (reaching levels of 60 percent and 83 percent at the end of Year 3, respectively), while the *Optimized* results in a readiness level of 97 percent at the end of Year 3.

FIGURE 7. TREND CHART OF NEW HIRES UNDER THREE DIFFERENT WORKFORCE PLANNING SCENARIOS.

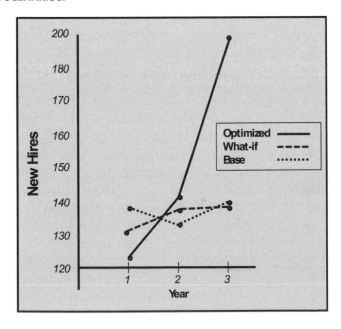

FIGURE 8. TREND IN FEMALE EMPLOYEES UNDER THREE DIFFERENT WORKFORCE PLANNING SCENARIOS.

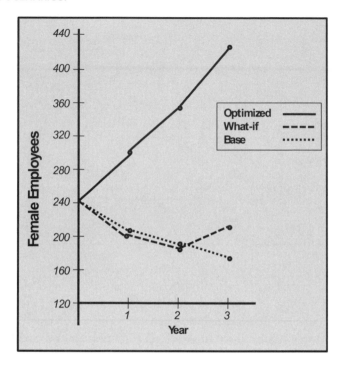

In Figure 7, we show the trend in external hires. In *Optimized*, we observe a small upward adjustment from 131 new hires in Year 1 to 137 new hires in Year 2, in order to account for initial turnover. The trend then becomes stable at 137 new hires in Year 3. Since turnover is much higher in the *Base* and *What-if* scenarios, the necessary adjustments are larger, and the number of new hires each year is highly volatile.

The analysis of new hires is not complete unless we also analyze the composition of turnover. By choosing the correct set of talent programs and practices, the *Optimized* scenario improves retention of the *right kind* of employees, described by a certain type of attribute. Say, for example, that the organization wants to encourage female employees to stay; then the organization would be interested in investing in programs designed to increase the retention of female employees—for instance, a comprehensive healthcare program. Such a program would also likely increase the retention of other types of employees, but its expected impact on female employees would be higher.

In Figure 8, we chart the trend in female employees for three years. In the *Base* scenario, we see the number of female employees decreases steadily if the organization continues with its current talent programs. In the *What-if* scenario, we have specifically chosen certain programs designed to reduce turnover of female employees; however, it takes two years for the downward trend to be reversed, because the hurdle that has to be overcome through hiring is large. Given budget restrictions, the programs chosen under the *What-if* scenario do not produce the biggest impact per dollar invested. On the other hand, the *Optimized* scenario shows an immediate upward trend in the number of female employees. Here, the investment in talent programs is chosen to produce the greatest impact in terms of the female retention goal. This is analogous to the financial arena, where an investor seeks a portfolio of securities that results in the highest return for a given cost.

We now illustrate the benefits of this type of analysis with a real-world application at CH2M HILL, a global engineering services firm with a total workforce of about 30,000 employees, which is using this technology to align its talent strategy with its business goals.

CASE STUDY: Next Generation Strategic Workforce Planning at CH2M HILL

How David Sutherland, head of the Workforce Insight team, is using advanced simulation optimization techniques to mitigate risk and align strategic workforce plans with the company's strategic and financial goals

According to the Bureau of Labor Statistics, there are approximately 75 million baby boomers in the United States but only 45 million Generation Xers coming up behind them, and nearly all of the boomers are expected to be retired by the early 2020s.[9] As this "silver tsunami" (a term referring to the escalating retirement rate of the aging boomer population) approaches, many companies are coming to terms with the risks associated with the impending talent shortage and are looking for effective ways to understand and mitigate those risks. It is no great secret that the engineering industry is particularly susceptible to the aging workforce trend, with many companies having an average age workforce in the upper 40s to low 50s. A recent study by the Corporate Executive Board and Kelly Engineering Resources claim that even if the industry could prevent its eligible engineers from retiring for ten years and hire all new college graduates with engineering degrees during that time frame, the industry is still projected to have as many as 6,000 unfilled jobs annually.[10]

CH2M HILL is a global leader in engineering consulting, design and build, operations, and program management for government, civil, industrial, and energy clients. The firm's work is focused in the areas of water, transportation, environment, energy, facilities, and resources. With $6.3 billion in revenue and 30,000 employees, CH2M HILL is an industry-leading firm in program management, construction management, and design, as ranked by *Engineering News-Record*, and has been named a leader in sustainable engineering by Verdantix.[11] The firm has five times been named one of Fortune's "100 Best Companies to Work For."

In addition to grappling with the aging workforce trend (the company projects three times the number of retirements over the next five years than it experienced in the previous five years), it also faces an increasingly competitive recruiting environment as needed skills and experience become increasingly scarce. The company also has aggressive growth aspirations that are challenging to plan and manage given the project-based nature of its business, which inherently comes with a high degree of uncertainty. CH2M HILL's product is its people and the knowledge, skills, experience, and professionalism they draw upon to fulfill their mission to help their clients build a better and more sustainable world.

To address these workforce-related challenges and risks, the company recognized the need to hire a seasoned SWP practitioner and thought leader in this space. Dave Sutherland was hired in the latter half of 2008 and currently leads the Workforce Insight team, which supports CH2M HILL globally and has the structure and scope of services shown in Figure 9.

FIGURE 9. WORKFORCE INSIGHT STRUCTURE AT CH2M HILL.

Since this was new to CH2M HILL's culture, Dave devised a five-year vision for implementing a highly effective SWP and analytics function to ground everyone's expectations and clarify what it would be and, perhaps more importantly, what it would not be. As Workforce Insight is entering its fourth year, the team has made significant progress. The mission of the Workforce Insight team is to:

1. Enable credible one- to five-plus-year strategic workforce plans for the enterprise and business groups that mitigate risk and align with the company's strategic and financial goals.
2. Provide relevant, actionable, predictive workforce analytics that drive fact-based decisions by business leaders and optimize a sustainable workforce.
3. Support enterprise-wide employee lifecycle surveys and analyze the results.

4. Deliver reliable workforce data and reports to clients in compliance with global data privacy standards via scalable tools and solutions.

5. Provide consultative expertise to HR and other partners to inform the creation or improvement of targeted engagement and retention programs/initiatives.

During these past few years, the Workforce Insight team has successfully implemented several components (processes, tools, solutions) that are essential to building a sophisticated and advanced SWP and analytics capability. However, the challenge of enabling credible strategic workforce plans that link to the company's financial and business goals still remained. The high degree of uncertainty and volatility that comes with a project-based business coupled with a complex workforce presents a unique challenge to creating accurate workforce demand and supply forecasts. CH2M HILL needed a solution that was not solely dependent upon knowing the number and type of projects and programs the company would be engaged in, since that variable becomes highly uncertain as you look further out into the future. What follows is Dave's testimonial to his approach to find a solution.

Not too long after I joined CH2M HILL, we had the chance to connect with another Colorado-based company, OptTek Systems Inc. OptTek had recently received a grant from the National Science Foundation to explore the application of advanced simulation and optimization techniques to better predict workforce diversity outcomes. While OptTek had approached CH2M HILL to explore the possibility of using the company's data for that purpose, it quickly became apparent that, if further configured, this leading-edge technology—embedded in a software package called OptForce—could have much broader application and could usher in the next generation of Strategic Workforce Planning capability to support the SWP process depicted in Figure 10.

FIGURE 10. THE SWP PROCESS AT CH2M HILL.

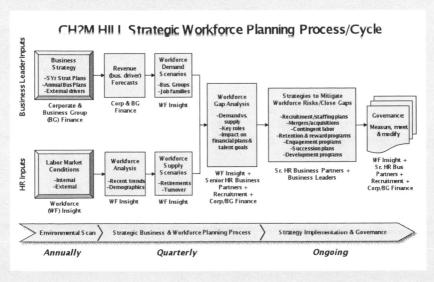

At its core, the software contains sophisticated descriptive, predictive, and pre-scriptive analytics methodologies for demand planning, scenario-based simulation modeling, retention analysis, and selection of investment decisions (in talent pro-grams) to achieve corporate goals.

We are using its demand planning capability to bridge the gap between finan-cial and operational business goals and workforce requirements. Through statistical analytics, we identify our key business metrics that drive workforce needs by different roles and geographical regions. Based on historic financial and operational data and historic headcount data, the demand planning capability also identifies the rate at which growth in a key business metric drives growth in specific roles.

We have also implemented the software's retention analysis methodology that is based on a proprietary algorithm for decision tree analysis. This methodology addresses our voluntary turnover, involuntary turnover, and retirement behavior, all based on key employee attributes as well as other internal or external factors, such as economic climate, unemployment rates, competition for scarce talent in the market, and stock index valuation. The retention tree enables our organization to identify the key factors that explain differences in retention behavior between different types of our employees at the individual role/job/position level and for different demograph-ics, such as age, tenure, and gender. The algorithms can be set to automatically dis-cover the key attributes, or to allow us to select a specific set of attributes of interest, so that we can "see ourselves" better.

Our model combines these analytics in the predictive and prescriptive capabil-ity that allows us to plan our future workforce to support our enterprise as well as busi-ness unit goals. Through simulation-based what-if analyses, we create detailed scenarios with various assumptions to understand potential risks and gaps between demand and supply as well as demographic trends in the workforce, at an individual employee level of granularity. We can easily adjust both internal assumptions, such as staffing multipliers, to model different workforce productivity levels and external assumptions, such as economic performance indicators that affect the turnover rates of our population differently. By comparing ranges of outcomes under different assumptions, we can help business groups understand the uncertainty associated with their business plans, allowing us to work with them to look at various options and solu-tions to help them best mitigate risk. We are also exploring improving the return on investment of our spending on our portfolio of engagement and retention programs.

Through a deeper understanding of what drives engagement and retention in key organizational and demographic segments, we can better tailor implementation strategies to achieve increased levels of engagement and retention than the traditional "one-size-fits-all" approach that assumes everyone values the same things. Based on our cost of turnover calculations, we conservatively estimate that the company could save between $5 million and $10 million (in direct and indirect costs) annually for every one percentage point we reduce our voluntary turnover rate.

A critical success factor for us was to establish a good partnership with our finance counterparts to better understand what metrics drive business performance and how the business and financial planning processes work. For SWP to succeed, it must be integrated with the business and financial planning processes of an organization. This ensure that workforce demand scenarios stay aligned with an organization's financial objectives as conditions change, according to the governance cycle depicted in Figure 11.

FIGURE 11. THE SWP GOVERNANCE CYCLE AT CH2M HILL.

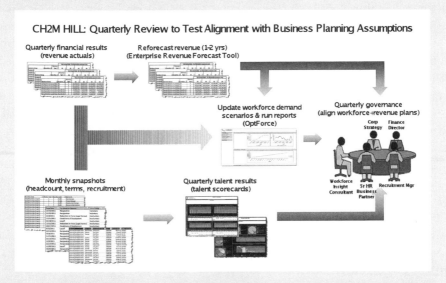

While it will take time to conclusively demonstrate the accuracy and versatility of this technology, early results have been extremely promising. Our initial validation testing using historical data yielded results for one business group that were 95 percent accurate with respect to forecasting workforce three years forward. When testing the much larger population of the company, results improved to more than 98 percent accuracy.

In addition to this level of accuracy, OptForce allows us to analyze workforce demand by pivotal roles and key workforce demographic segments to detect risks and gaps as well as to create actionable staffing plans and mitigation strategies to help the business close those gaps. As we continue to evolve our sophistication with OptForce, we will use the prescriptive analytics from the software's optimization capability to help guide our investment decisions in our portfolio of retention and engagement programs to optimize performance in terms of desired outcomes, such as maximizing workforce readiness, minimizing cost, minimizing risk, maximizing return on investment, and achieving representation and diversity goals.

The race for talent is tightening and will only become more competitive over the next ten years. Lloyd's 2011 Risk Index report ranked talent and skills shortages as the second highest risk to companies' future success. In addition, shortage of talent and skills was one of only two top ten risks that companies felt less prepared to handle today than in 2009, when this risk issue was ranked at twenty-two. Companies that have invested in and committed to creating a robust SWP and analytics function will be far better positioned than their competitors to effectively plan how to address these growing risks.[12]

CONCLUSIONS AND FINAL REMARKS

Agent-based simulation optimization software for Strategic Workforce Planning is based on a bottom-up approach to predicting talent behavior patterns. This technology focuses on accurately predicting individual employee decisions based on demographic and career characteristics, as well as work-related and external stimuli. Individual behaviors are then aggregated into cohorts of interest so that large-scale effects can be analyzed. As the case from CH2M HILL shows, this approach is fundamentally different from traditional top-down or trend-based approaches used by most workforce planning tools in the market, and it produces more statistically reliable results.

In addition to improved accuracy, the agent-based approach enables the evaluation of the impact of alternative investments in talent programs, benefits, and sourcing practices based on the unique set of attributes of your workforce, the work environment, and the state of the economy. The optimization capability takes this process one step further by enabling the planner to identify the best set of retention and sourcing programs that are most likely to achieve the organization's goals within budget.

We believe no other approach to Strategic Workforce Planning can achieve the same level of accuracy at such granularity and with more confidence in the predicted outcomes.

References

1. The Conference Board 2011 Survey of 704 CEOs worldwide.

2. See, for example, Wayne F. Cascio and John Boudreau, *Investing in People: Financial Impact of Human Resource Initiatives* (Upper Saddle River, N.J.: Pearson Education, 2008); Jac Fitz-enz, *The New HR Analytics: Predicting the Economic Value of Your Company's Human Capital Investments* (New York: AMACOM, 2010).

3. See www.OptTek.com for more information and documentation about the OptForce SWP system.

4. See www.OptTek.com for information and documentation about using OptQuest.

5. Compiled from Watson Wyatt webcast "Advanced Workforce Planning: Securing the Future," *Human Capital Institute,* November 20, 2008; "Customizing the Employment Offer," *CLC Solutions* (Washington, D.C.: Corporate Leadership Council, December 2002).

6. See http://nces.ed.gov/.

7. See, for example, EMSI or Workforce Locator.

8. If there were only twenty PPIs and two alternatives for each PPI, there would be about 1 million different combinations to choose from (ignoring any budget constraints).

9. Arlene Dohm, "Gauging the Labor Force Effects of Retiring Baby-Boomers," *BLS Research*, 123 (2000). Retrieved from http://www.bls.gov/opub/mlr/2000/07/art2full.pdf.

10. The Corporate Executive Board, "U.S. Trends in Entry-Level Candidate Availability by Function," (2006).

11. See, for example, http://enr.construction.com/toplists/ProgramManagers/001–050 .asp; www.Verdantix.com.

12. See http://www.lloyds.com/News-and-Insight/Risk-Insight/Lloyds-Risk-Index.

Dr. Marco Better is the Director of Custom Solutions of OptTek Systems, Inc. He obtained his Ph.D. in Operations Research from the Leeds School of Business of the University of Colorado at Boulder. He also holds a B.S. in industrial engineering and an M.B.A. Dr. Better has over fifteen years of professional work experience in the automobile, banking, and telecommunications industries, both in the US and in Latin America. His current interests lie in the application of optimization and data mining technology to solve complex problems in industry.

Dr. Fred Glover is a Chief Technology Officer in charge of algorithmic design and strategic planning initiatives. Dr. Glover is a leading figure in the field of *metaheuristics*, a name he coined in the 1980s – an area that is now the subject of numerous books and international conferences, focusing on the development of models and methods enabling the solution of complex nonlinear and combinatorial problems that lie beyond the ability of classical optimization procedures. He also serves as the MediaOne Chaired Professor in Systems Science at the University of Colorado, Boulder, where he holds the title of Distinguished Professor of the University of Colorado system. He has authored or coauthored more than 350 published articles and 8 books in the fields of mathematical optimization, computer science, and artificial intelligence, with particular emphasis on practical applications in industry and government. Dr. Glover is the recipient of the distinguished von Neumann Theory Prize, an elected member of the National Academy of Engineering, and has received numerous other awards and honorary fellowships, including from the American Association for the Advancement of Science (AAAS), the NATO Division of Scientific Affairs, the Institute of Operations Research and Management Science (INFORMS), the Decision Sciences Institute (DSI), the U.S. Defense Communications Agency (DCA), the Energy Research Institute (ERI), the American Assembly of Collegiate Schools of Business (AACSB), Alpha Iota Delta, and the Miller Institute for Basic Research in Science.

David Sutherland joined CH2M HILL in July, 2008, now with Expedia, where he rose to Director of Workforce Insight, with accountability for global workforce reporting, metrics and analytics, and strategic workforce planning. Headquartered in Englewood, Colorado, CH2M HILL is a global leader in consulting, design, design-build, operations, and program management for government, civil, industrial, and energy clients. The firm's work is concentrated in the areas of water, transportation, environmental, energy, facilities, and resources.

Prior to joining CH2M HILL Dave led Avaya's Workforce Planning function where he had responsibility for delivering metrics on all aspects of the global workforce, creating companywide headcount forecasts and driving the assessment of skill levels for critical positions to ensure hiring, development and retention strategies addressed identified gaps. Prior to Avaya, Dave was a special agent with the FBI and also spent five years with Prudential working in financial analysis, business measurement/process reengineering, and human resources measurement consulting roles.

Dave has conducted numerous speaking engagements over the past ten+ years at a variety of workforce planning and measurement forums including APQC, PwC/Saratoga, The Learning Forum, Human Capital Institute, Inform, SHRM, and The Conference Board. Dave also spoke on a workforce analytics subject-matter expert panel at the 2011 HR Technology conference. He currently serves on the executive committee for The Learning Forum's Workforce Planning Council and was appointed to HCI's Executive Advisory Board to serve on the Workforce Planning Board Committee. He graduated from Boston College with a degree in finance and is a Six Sigma green belt.

Dr. Manuel Laguna is a Senior Research Associate of OptTek Systems, Inc. He is Professor of Operations Management in the Leeds School of Business of the University of Colorado at Boulder. He received masters and doctoral degrees in Operations Research and Industrial Engineering from the University of Texas at Austin. He has done extensive research in the interface between computer science, artificial intelligence, and operations research to develop solution methods for problems in areas such as logistics and supply chain, routing and network design in telecommunications, combinatorial optimization on graphs, and optimization of simulations. His research has appeared in numerous academic-journal articles and books. He is the editor-in-chief of the *Journal of Heuristics* and is on the international advisory board of the *Journal of the Operational Research Society*.

Wisdom on Workforce Planning

Peter Howes

MY JOURNEY IN WORKFORCE PLANNING (WFP) commenced in detail some thirty-five years ago. At that stage, I was a lecturer at the Queensland Institute of Technology (QIT, now the Queensland University of Technology) in Brisbane, Australia. In 1978, I introduced a course on workforce planning as an elective in the human resources management degree at QIT. The course was called Corporate Manpower Planning.

The only text I could find at the time was a small book called *Practical Manpower Planning* by John Branham, published by the Institute of Personnel Management (now the Chartered Institute of Personnel and Development, or CIPD) in London. To run the course, I mainly used various articles. These included articles from the Institute of Manpower Studies in the United Kingdom (now called the Institute for Employment Studies) and articles from the newly formed Human Resource Planning Society in the United States (now called HR People & Strategy).

During 1978–1979, I was on the organizing committee for the first national conference for the Institute of Personnel Management Australia (IPMA, now called the Australian Human Resources Institute AHRI), to be held in Queensland. I was responsible for the content for all of the keynote and stream sessions. I made workforce planning the focus of every session in the entire conference.

During 1981, I completed my sabbatical at BP (then called British Petroleum) in Melbourne. The focus of my sabbatical was to build the WFP systems for BP in Australia. This experience became the catalyst for me to leave an academic career and establish my own consulting firm, called HRM Consulting. (Many years later, we changed our name to Infohrm. In 2010, Infohrm became part of SuccessFactors, an SAP company.) I spent the next thirty years working in the field of workforce planning and workforce analytics. Our primary business in the early years was running public workshops in human resource management, including a three-day workshop called Practical Techniques in Manpower Planning, which I first ran in September 1982.

Over the next three decades, I and others within HRM Consulting/Infohrm ran variations on this workshop more than 500 times across fifteen countries, as well as conducting more than 200 major consulting projects in WFP across ten countries. In 1991 I first partnered with Dr. Jac Fitz-enz to set up the Saratoga benchmarking program in Australia. This commenced my journey of integrating workforce planning and workforce analytics. In 2006 Infohrm first developed web-based workforce planning and analytics software that is used by many companies large and small around the world. This software is now the SuccessFactors Workforce Planning software, which in February 2012 became the basis for SAP's cloud-based Workforce Planning software. The reflections and observations presented here are based on this background.

There are some key principles or personal reflections about WFP that I think are important for any company to consider. These are:

➤ WFP is a risk mitigation process.
➤ It is useful to think of workforce planning as a strategic staffing process.
➤ WFP is a planning process, not a budgeting process.
➤ Focus on the gap and not the actual forecasts.
➤ Developing a methodology or framework for the WFP process is a critical factor in success.
➤ Scenarios are an essential component of the WFP process.
➤ The biggest challenge in WFP is how to institutionalize the process by creating a Centre of Excellence and using effective technology.
➤ Forecast competencies as well as numbers.
➤ Ensure that WFP leads to action.

This chapter focuses on these reflections rather than on the specific techniques of workforce planning.

THE RISK MITIGATION PROCESS

I like to think of workforce planning as being a risk mitigation process, meaning that we undertake WFP only when the risk of not doing it is too great. I believe any organization needs to be very pragmatic in its reason for undertaking workforce planning. We do not undertake WFP because it constitutes "best practice" in our people management practices. If an organization is confident that in the future it will easily be able to find people with the right skills that it needs, and if these recruits could be quickly onboarded and could quickly become fully productive, then there is little need for workforce planning. What the company needs is simply very good staffing practices. If a company can offer good career paths for its workforce, again, there is little need for WFP. In my experience, these two situations rarely take place across all or even most workgroups. Hence, for most organizations, workforce planning is a critical requirement to reduce the risk of not being able to fill critical job roles in the future.

An example of risk mitigation as an outcome of workforce planning can be seen in a case study for National Grid. National Grid is a major utility company with operations in the United Kingdom and the United States. National Grid presented its story at the Infohrm conference in London in December 2009. A couple of years ago, Infohrm completed a workforce planning project within the high-voltage electricity transmission business in the United Kingdom. As part of this project, we forecast that the projected gap between supply and demand for power engineers out till 2020 was likely to be in the order of 350. While this number may not appear large, further research estimated that this was going to be more than the total output of power engineers from all universities in the United Kingdom over this forecast period.

National Grid would also be in competition with other energy companies in the recruitment of these graduates. This finding led the CEO of National Grid to say, "This is one of the biggest challenges we face as a business." Based on these findings from the WFP project, in 2010 National Grid offered fifty scholarships to technical officers to upgrade their qualifications to degree level. This is risk mitigation.

STRATEGIC STAFFING

As previously stated, I like to talk about workforce planning as being the equivalent of strategic staffing. Almost all HR practitioners and line managers have been involved in staffing processes many times in their careers. I like to differentiate between tactical staffing and strategic staffing. A tactical staffing action within a company commences with a vacancy, which then kicks off a two-step process: (1) a recruitment process, and then, when we have more vacancies than positions to fill, (2) a selection process to assess the candidates.

From a WFP perspective, my interest is in the recruitment process. I believe that over the past two-plus decades, we have confused recruitment technology with recruitment methodology. Some twenty-five years ago, we had the automation of the recruitment process with technology systems like Resumix. Then, about ten years ago, we saw the growth of Internet job boards like Monster.com. Over the past few years, we have seen the growth of social collaboration websites like LinkedIn growing their impact on the recruitment process. Within success factors, we have also seen the acquisition of Jobs2Web as part of the next generation of recruitment technology.

I'm fully supportive of the growth and evolution of technology to support the recruitment process. This technology, however, does not change the underlying methodology, which has not really changed for more than fifty years. This ongoing methodology of tactical staffing is, effectively, we advertise and pray. We simply hope that more appropriate candidates apply than we have jobs to fill, whether we have a one-off position like an actuator or geologist or a group of positions, such as taking on 100 graduates as part of a graduate recruitment program. Traditional tactical recruitment is appropriate *if* there are enough candidates in the marketplace who will or are likely to apply for positions within the company as the vacancies occur. In today's business environment, for specific job roles like engineers and most jobs based on a math or science foundation, this is a high-risk approach to recruitment.

With strategic staffing, we make our best forecast of the projected vacancies by job role over a more extended period, typically two to five years into the future. When we know the magnitude of the projected vacancies over multiple years, we can determine new recruitment strategies that cannot be implemented when we are dealing with a short-term vacancy. Some of these strategies include:

▶ *Developing new career paths.* With extended lead times, I believe most companies can build required future job roles internally. This generally means moving people through a different sequence of positions to historical career paths combined with short-term projects and secondments (a temporary transfer within the company). By having the clarity of future requirements as a result of a workforce planning process, most companies can have more confidence about future requirements and consequently make the investment to build new career paths. This will become a more critical staffing strategy to address shortages in critical job roles in companies in the future.

▶ *Developing and articulating the employee value proposition for critical job roles.* In an ideal world, organizations would build out the EVP (employee value proposition) for all job roles, but this is not realistic because of the resources required. I would argue that EVPs should be developed for all critical job roles within a company. I would start with those critical job roles where we forecast that there will be a significant gap between projected demand and projected supply over the next few years. The more we can articulate the EVPs, then the more we are likely to attract external applicants as well as retain individuals currently in these roles within the company.

▶ *Developing the employment brand of your company.* I do not believe it is feasible for any organization to fully develop the employment brand for the company as a preferred employer across the board for all occupational groups in all business units in all geographical locations. Once a company knows the job roles where it expects to have the largest gap between projected supply and demand, and it assesses that these job roles may be difficult to fill from the external labor market, then it makes sense to work on building the employment brand in these job roles first.

How can a company build its employment brand? One option is having specialists in the job roles with the projected shortages or their managers speak at conferences and seminars, provided they are articulate and engaging and will present the company as a great place to work. Another option is to build the company's profile in the print and electronic media around topics associated with the critical job roles. This can include press releases, interviews, and blogging. It is also advisable to build the employment brand at universities for those disciplines where shortages are expected in the next two to ten years. The basic activities would include having key specialists from the company giving guest lectures in various subjects. A more strategic approach would include working with key academics from targeted universities where you want to focus your graduate recruitment. This could include building assignments for selected subjects around your workplace, having a strong summer internship program where academics help select the students you take on, or co-funding research for selective universities. Another option can be funding a research post or postdoctoral fellowship in selective universities where the academic filling the role can be the link with the outstanding students you want to engage with. The workforce planning or strategic staffing is the link to tell us in which disciplines it is most strategic and cost-effective to make this type of investment.

In summary, I think of workforce planning as being the same as strategic staffing. The forecasted gap between projected supply and demand provides the cumulative recruitment scope for the multiple years of the forecast period. This allows us to be more creative in our recruitment strategies than we can be with tactical staffing.

WORKFORCE PLANNING IS A PLANNING PROCESS, NOT A BUDGETING PROCESS

While this might sound obvious, it's amazing how often individuals confuse WFP as a budgeting process rather than a planning process. One of the key differentiators between WFP and budgeting is the time frame for the forecasts. Most budgets are out for a maximum of twelve months, whereas a workforce plan has a forecast period of between two and ten years. Forecasting the workforce requirements for six to twenty-four months is a very important task, but it's not workforce planning. I like to call this shorter time frame planning "resource planning."

In addition to the time frame of the forecast, there are other factors that differentiate resource planning from workforce planning. One factor is the population covered. Resource planning is typically undertaken for the entire workforce, while

WFP is undertaken only for critical job roles. Over the next six to twenty-four months, all organizations need to know the total labor cost to run their business, broken down by job family and occupational group as well as by organization unit, location, and grade. These are normal workforce reporting and segmentation activities required to run any organization. Under workforce planning, we are primarily focusing on the critical job roles that we are at risk of not being able to fill. If we attempt to undertake workforce planning for every job role, then I predict the process will collapse as the resources required to complete it are too great for the return achieved.

To stress the planning orientation of workforce planning, I like to use the metaphor of a road sign. Imagine driving along a country road at 60 miles per hour, going around a curve, and seeing a T intersection road sign. Under the T intersection sign is another sign saying "300 yards." The question I start with is: *What is the purpose of this road sign?* The answer is that there are multiple purposes. One purpose, but not the primary purpose, is to let us know that in approximately six seconds' time we will need to make a ninety-degree turn to either the left or right. The primary purpose of the road sign is to tell us what we need to do immediately—take our foot off the accelerator—and what we need to do progressively over the next six seconds—put our foot on the brake, move our indicators to say whether we are turning left or right, place our foot on the brake again, and then begin turning the steering wheel either left or right depending on which way we want to turn.

Similarly, the primary purpose of a workforce plan is not to tell us the cumulative workforce requirements we will have in, say, five years—or more correctly, the cumulative workforce gap we will have in five years. The primary purpose, and hence the real benefit of a workforce plan, is to advise what type of HR or people management actions or interventions we need to start initiating now and progressively over the forecast period (say, five years). Like the road sign, the purpose of a workforce plan is to help us initiate actions now and progressively over the forecast period so we can address our future staffing gaps for our critical job roles. If we could instantly fill jobs, then this would be like we could instantly stop a car. Since physics doesn't allow us to instantly stop a car, we need road signs. And because we can't be confident of filling all of our critical job roles instantly as they become vacant, we need a workforce plan.

When we hear people make statements like . . .

➤   We can't undertake workforce planning because we are in industry that is changing too rapidly.

➤   Because of mergers and acquisitions/industry consolidation/changing legislative environment/etc., we cannot undertake workforce planning.

➤   We need to consolidate our business planning before we can undertake workforce planning.

... then we know these individuals don't really understand the basic premise that workforce planning is based on. If you have more clarity and certainty about the future, then WFP adds less value. The more uncertain the future is for an organization, then the more value WFP will add.

MIND THE GAP

Anyone who has traveled on the London tube system will be very familiar with the phrase "mind the gap," which is painted everywhere. This phrase is also very applicable in workforce planning. I like to think that the core of a workforce plan is the gap between the demand forecast and the supply forecast. It is the magnitude of the gap that we are concerned with and not the actual demand and supply forecasts.

Let's assume we are a hospital system and we have today 2,500 nurses. Assuming the hospital has a strategy for organic growth over the next five years, let's assume that its demand forecast for nurses in five years is 3,200. When we look at supply forecasts, we are not forecasting how many nurses the hospital will have in five years. What we are forecasting is how many nurses of the current workforce will be with the hospital system in nursing positions in five years. Factors we consider are age distribution and tenure profiles to forecast retirements, historical voluntary turnover rates to project resignations, and internal transfer and promotion rates to assess internal movement. Based on our modeling of these factors, we may assess that 1,400 of the nurses will still be employed in five years. Then, we can see that the gap is 3,200 – 1,400 = 1,800. This shows the cumulative gap over our forecast period of five years. This number 1,800 also represents the strategic staffing of nurses over the five-year period as opposed to traditional staffing that considers existing staffing. It is also possible for this number to be a positive number in terms of projected supply being greater than projected demand. In this case, we are projecting a surplus of staff in the particular job family we are forecasting. As we can see the surplus by year of our forecast, we have the option to proactively take action to prevent the surplus staff. For example, we can stop or minimize external recruitment as well as internal promotions and transfers into the particular role(s). Alternatively, we can also accelerate our existing transfers and promotions out of the particular job role(s) and perhaps create new career paths out of the job role(s). This is all part of what I would call strategic staffing.

There are other gaps we need to consider in WFP. If we use scenarios as part of our forecasting methodology, then we are also interested in the gap between the various scenarios, as this helps us to assess the risk associated with the gap. If we have two scenarios that have significant variations in the demand forecast under each scenario, then we have a significant variation between the two gap forecasts. In this case, we need to develop contingency staffing options for how we will address the gap. This situation also means that we will more vigilantly monitor the underlying scenario options to see which of them comes true. The second type of gap can be associated with forecasting how the competencies making up the job role may change over time. If we anticipate that the competencies required in a job role in the future are different from the competencies required today, then this is also a gap we need to proactively manage as part of the WFP process.

WORKFORCE PLANNING FRAMEWORKS

I believe it's essential for any company undertaking workforce planning to develop a framework to explain the interaction between all of the tasks that make up WFP. When working with companies, I start with two or three generic frameworks that I have developed over time, and then I work with the client to customize one of the frameworks so that it specifically works for the client's structure and processes as a company. In the following sections, I will share three frameworks on workforce planning. The first is the most simple (to highlight the key points), the second shows some of the extra details that need to be incorporated, and the third is more of a process model for workforce planning.

Simplified Workforce Planning Process

The most simplified WFP process is shown in Figure 1. It highlights some key aspects of workforce planning from my perspective. The core activity is the box labeled *Matching Workforce Supply & Demand Forecasting*. I see this as the core as all of the inputs into this activity are undertaken only to improve the quality of matching process. The return for WFP is based on the quality of the matching process. Here are my initial principles for workforce planning:

▶ Demand forecasts must be based on the future business plans for the organization. Demand forecasts must be completed by line managers. The role of HR practitioners is to facilitate the generation of the demand forecasts. Historical staffing numbers and productivity measures are useful inputs into the demand process, but they are not the basis for preparing demand forecasts, as more and more, the past is not a good predictor of where companies will move to in the future.

▶ Demand forecasting incorporates forecasting both numbers and job roles (or competencies). Forecasting numbers is mandatory if the WFP process is to have credability. Forecasting how job roles will change in the future is an important but often neglected aspect of demand forecasting. Most companies have their own term for defining job roles. It might be called competency profiles, skill sets, skill database, etc. The core to this part of workforce planning is to understand how the skills or competencies required to do the job are likely to change over the period of the forecast. In many cases, the change in skills required has a greater impact than the change in the actual numbers required.

FIGURE 1. A SIMPLIFIED WORKFORCE PLANNING PROCESS.

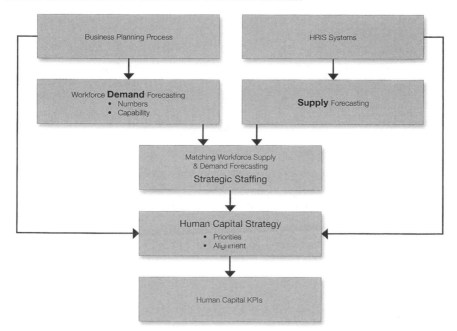

▶ The supply forecasting process has much more potential for automation than demand forecasting. As mentioned earlier, by analyzing retirement patterns, voluntary patterns, and transfer and promotion rates, we can be fairly predictive in assessing the projected supply by critical job role into the future. Fortunately, software is available today to automate this process in a way that cannot practically be done with Excel pivot tables. The data required for modeling the supply forecasting is typically available in the core HRIS/payroll system of any company.

▶ The *Human Capital Strategy* process shown in Figure 1 is a core part of the WFP process. I see WFP as an input to shape the formation of the HR strategic planning process, not an output from this process. Regrettably, too few companies use the output from a workforce planning process as input into the HR strategy formulation process. I see two other inputs into the formulation of the human capital strategy. I believe that the business planning process (which can go under many names, including strategic planning and corporate planning) is the single most important driver in formulating the HR strategy. I also see workforce analytics as an important input into the formulation of the HR strategy. Unfortunately, most companies confuse workforce reporting for workforce analytics but use neither as an input into formulating their HR strategic plan.

▶ An important output from the HR strategic plan is the formulating of the human capital key performance indicators (KPIs) for the company. In most companies today, an HR strategic plan is more a PowerPoint presentation pack than a comprehensive document with action plans and accountabilities for execution of these actions plans. The HR strategic plan is more about building a shared mind-set within the company as to our people management priorities. In this case, the KPIs are the vehicle by which to operationalize the HR strategy. I believe any company can have only five to ten people KPIs out of 1,000-plus possible people measures. For a measure to become a KPI, it needs to meet three criteria. First, the measure must be aligned to strategy. Individuals must be able to articulate how execution on the KPI measure directly supports execution of the HR strategy and how this directly leads to the execution of the business strategy. The second criterion is that we know our results for the KPI and we have set a target, and hence we have a gap. We typically do not have the same target across the entire company as the workforce is heterogeneous not homogenous, and, hence, this needs to be reflected in the targets we set. Benchmarks are a useful input into setting the target but should not in themselves be the target. The third criterion for a measure to become a KPI is that the company needs to invest resources into interventions to achieve its target. In addition to formulating a few people KPIs to ensure execution of our HR and business strategy, I believe companies should monitor their performance on fifty to 200 other measures. I worry about companies living in blissful ignorance when it comes to their workforce, but this is a topic for workforce analytics rather than workforce planning.

More Advanced Workforce Planning Framework

Figure 2 shows a more advanced workforce planning framework. Let me summarize some of the additional elements that this framework shows.

FIGURE 2. A MORE ADVANCED WORKFORCE PLANNING FRAMEWORK.

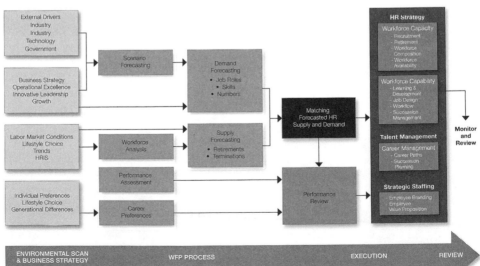

Scenario Forecasting. I would almost consider it mandatory to use scenarios in a workforce planning process, particularly for demand forecasting. It is rare for any company to know what the exact nature of its business will be in five years, and, hence, exactly how many people it will need by job family by location. The more external factors there are that will impact the business, the more scenarios become essential. Typical external factors considered in scenarios include economic growth rates, commodity prices, foreign exchange rates, government policies, market share, commodity pricing, etc. In scenarios, I like to look for factors beyond the organization's control that will impact its business and, hence, the required workforce over the forecast period.

For any company, there is an infinite number of permutations of scenarios for the future. I favor alternate scenarios when managing the trade-off between complexity and return. This gets beyond the simplicity of a single forecast but minimizes the complexity of multiple scenarios. When companies use three scenarios, the scenarios are often labeled as *optimistic, pessimistic,* and *most likely.* When this happens, too many individuals focus only on the most likely scenario. When we have only two scenarios, we are forced to think about the people management strategy implications of the variations between the alternate demand forecasts and, hence, the resultant variations in the projected gap between supply and demand. This helps as then WFP is a true planning process and not a budgeting process. When there are variations between the alternate scenarios, I stress that clients think of the variation as being the maximum *plausible* variation that could realistically be expected over the forecasted period and not the *theoretical possible* extreme that could occur. If I was working with an organization that had identified market share as an important dimension for its scenario, and if the organization's current market share was, say, 35 percent, then it might be plausible for its market share over a five-year period to range from 25 percent to 45 percent. It's unlikely that it could range from 10 percent to 70 percent, even though this is theoretically possible. It is essential that the senior executive team of the company signs off on both the scenario factors to be selected and the boundaries to the plausible range for each factor.

Labor Market Conditions. If we want more accurate supply forecasts, we need to consider the anticipated impact of the external labor market and the economic conditions. External economic conditions and the external labor market do impact voluntary turnover rates. I doubt there are many companies in the world that have experienced an increase in their voluntary turnover rates in the past year. This is not likely to be a result of better HR interventions but simply the result of more employees deciding not to resign in a period of poor economic conditions.

If an organization prepared a supply forecast in 2012 for the next five years out to 2017, I would anticipate that the company underestimated how many employees would resign over the five years if the company took its 2011 turnover rates and used them to extrapolate each year over the next five years. While 2011 rates might be useful for predicating 2013 and 2014 rates of voluntary turnover, I predict that they would underestimate the voluntary turnover rates in 2015–2017. My assumption is that as and when the economies around the world improve, many individuals will be more prepared to leave and join other companies as there will then be more opportunities. I also think that in many organizations, a growing group of employees are staying only because they are not prepared to take the risk of changing jobs in a poor economy. As the economy improves, their risk profile will change, and many will leave to join other companies.

This does not apply to some industries and occupational groups. Mining companies around the world have been experiencing higher turnover because of the increased demand in the labor market for virtually every occupational group they employ. In addition, occupational groups like nurses and cloud computing specialists have high turnover because of the shortages in the labor marker for their skills. In all these cases, we need to assess the external labor market to determine the impact these shortages will have on the current voluntary labor turnover rate within the company.

When we look at retirements, we also need to look at the impact of the external economy, particularly as companies move their workforce from defined benefits to defined contribution pension plans. Historically, companies could accurately predict when the segments of their workforce on defined benefits pension plans would retire, as it was generally a formula of age and tenure that gave the maximum pension payout. With the prevalence of defined contribution plans, which inevitably will lead to a lower annual pension payment, many people will not be able to retire by age 65. In the future, we will see many individuals forced to stay at work till they are over 70 years of age, and if their investment funds are not performing well financially, we can expect segments of the workforce to work till they are 80 when they would have preferred to have retired before they were 65. This is a workforce planning issue very few companies have even started to think about.

HR Strategy, Talent Management, and Strategic Staffing. In discussion of the simplified model, we spoke about how WFP was an input into the HR strategy formulation process. We need to also think about how WFP can impact both strategic staffing and the talent management process. Earlier, I spoke about how workforce planning can be thought of as a strategic staffing function. I would argue that all HR functions need to think about the strategic staffing function as well as the traditional (tactical) staffing function. By understanding the cumulative vacancies we expect in critical job roles over the forecast period, we can have more creative staffing options that are not possible under traditional staffing models, where we know only our current or short-term vacancies. The additional staffing strategies include developing new career paths, articulating the employee value preposition for critical job roles where we are forecasting to have significant vacancies over the next three to ten years, and developing the employment branding for these critical jobs.

The talent management process within any organization should be integrated to the WFP process. A key tenant in talent management is that it takes time to build capability. If we need a specified amount of capability in the future with specific competencies, then we need to understand both the magnitude and the profile of this future capability if we are going to be confident of building it. Workforce planning provides this insight for the talent management process. To use an older term, we can think of workforce planning as being the strategic training needs analysis process of the talent function.

Workforce planning can play a very important role in improving the financial performance of any organization. Having individuals attending job training is one of the most expensive processes available to a company to build the new capability required in its workforce. I believe that most of the new capability required within the workforce in the future can be built in a much more cost-effective manner. It has been my consistent experience that future capability can be acquired within a company if it moves individuals through a different sequence of job roles, building new career paths, complemented by how the company uses project teams and secondments. Organizations can build future capability as a by-product of doing real work with this combination. We need the workforce planning process to tell us the new competency profiles we need and the magnitude we require, as well as telling us the magnitude of gap required over our forecast period for existing capability. Having access to this information gives the talent management function and the senior management team the confidence to build new career paths now to start building future capability as a by-product of getting today's work completed.

When selecting individuals for project teams, organizations need to consider three criteria where today I think they consider only two. The two existing criteria used are *who do we know has the current capabilities to complete the work required in the project team* and *who is available*. While not perfect, most companies work through this process even if they do not have a robust skills inventory. My third criterion, which is rarely used in selecting individuals for project teams, is *who will gain the most from the project in assisting the organization in building its required future capability*. We can utilize this third criterion only if we have a robust workforce planning process within the company. This is a significant payback for our investment in workforce planning.

Performance Management and Workforce Planning. I believe that in all organizations, we need to improve the integration between the workforce planning process and the performance management process. In this case, I'm referring only to the use of the performance management process as a development function, not when it is part of the compensation process. As shown in Figure 2, there is generally a direct link in most organizations between the performance assessment process, the performance review process, and the individual development planning process. The individual and the manager assess the individual's strengths and weakness. This is discussed during the review process and is used to formulate a development plan for the individual. In this process, I'm not concerned with the assessment methodology (360 review, assessment centers, behaviorally anchored rating scales, etc.). I believe there is a fundamental link missing in this traditional methodology. I believe that there should be a direct flow from the WFP process (matching supply and demand forecasts to determine projected gap by critical job role).

I believe the development component of the performance assessment process in organizations needs several inputs. We need an assessment of performance and potential, the individual's assessment about career preferences, and an assessment of projected future opportunities from the WFP process. Without the input about the forecasted future opportunities, I believe the career assessment—in the absence of any workforce planning data—is based on the implicit assumption that future opportunities will be similar to past opportunities. This is a very dangerous assumption and positions the organization to not be preparing for evolving and new job roles. It may also be preparing individuals for jobs that may not exist in the future or may be reduced in number. Workforce planning is essential if we want the performance assessment process and the overall talent management process to have a future orientation rather than a retrospective orientation.

Workforce Planning Process Model

Figure 3 shows a current process model for workforce planning. This model was evolved from previous models within Infohrm during 2007 and 2008. Acknowledgment is given to Amy Hammond and Anastasia Ellerby from Infohrm, who worked on this model.

I feel this model is fairly self-explanatory, but I will make a few comments. Based on my workforce planning consulting experience over the last three decades, I feel it is essential that any organization understand the essential prerequisites before commencing a workforce planning initiative. We need to be able to articulate what business need(s) we are going to address with workforce planning, and we must determine if we have adequate engagement from key business leaders to the project. From a project management perspective, we need to make sure we have scoped the resources required, we have adequate WFP capability, we can access the required data for preparing both our demand and supply forecasts, and we have an adequate methodology for undertaking the WFP projects. The key challenges for most companies are having the workforce planning capability and methodology and having adequate resources.

My standard recommendation to most companies is to undertake a pilot

FIGURE 3. A WORKFORCE PLANNING PROCESS MODEL.

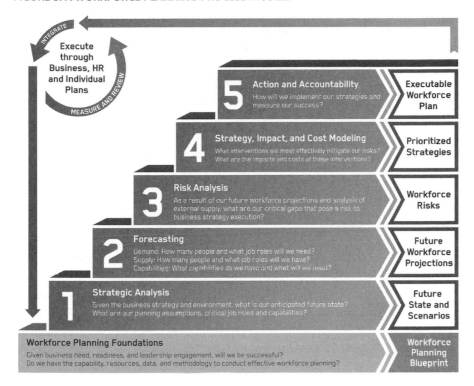

project first. This requires fewer resources, utilizes both internal and external consultants to assist, and has a much shorter time to completion so senior leaders can
see the results quickly. I believe a pilot project can be completed in 100 days. If a
company does not have the workforce planning capability, then it is logical to
team with a consulting organization that has this expertise and to use the pilot
project for skills transfer to the internal team. The major challenge here is to retain
the internal staff involved in the pilot so that these people stay in the WFP function for the next two to three years. I believe it takes people two to three iterations
of doing a workforce plan before they become confident in the area. Retaining
internal skills is one of the biggest challenges most companies face.

Strategic Analysis. Because I believe that the linking of the workforce plan, and
particularly the demand forecasting, to the overall business strategy is so critical,
I like to show this as a separate step in the overall workforce planning process. This
step involves understanding the strategic direction of the company in order to
kick off the workforce planning process. I like to begin with a review of previous
reports and presentations on the future of the company. This might include formal strategic plans or a study of proposed capital expenditure over the next five

years. It could be studies of new products or services to be offered. Generally, there is a lot of prior research that is valuable for workforce planning. We must find and review these documents so we are not reinventing the wheel. The next step is a series of interviews with the company's senior leaders. I start this at a very broad level in terms of what keeps these people up at night. What do they worry most about? This then becomes the basis for preparing the underlying scenario assumptions.

Once the strategic analysis is completed, we are in a position to finalize the selection of critical job roles we are going to undertake in the workforce planning project. It is not possible—or at least it is not sustainable, in my experience—to undertake WFP for the entire organization. The resources required lead to the process being abolished after one or two iterations. I thus do not believe it makes sense to attempt workforce planning for the entire organization. For example, it does not makes sense to undertake three- to ten-year workforce plans for those job roles where it will be relatively straightforward to recruit applications from the external labor market and it doesn't take too long to have them fully productive. It makes more sense to me to allocate the resources available for workforce planning into doing a better job on the fewer critical job roles. Here are some of the type of criteria I would use for selecting the job roles for workforce planning:

▶ Those job roles that we anticipate we will have difficulty in recruiting from the external labor marker (e.g., jobs requiring math and science)

▶ Those job roles that have a long lead time before a person becomes productive

▶ Those job roles where we have large numbers of people in the same job family and where getting more accurate forecasts can have a major impact on staffing

▶ Those job roles that have a disproportionally high level of impact on the overall performance of the business

It may not be possible to undertake a workforce planning pilot on all critical job roles in the first iteration. It is more important that we focus on a few critical job roles that are seen to be a valid representation of roles to demonstrate the value of workforce planning. Then, in the second or third iteration, we can expand the scope to include all of the critical job roles. In some organizations, it may be useful to update the workforce plans every two years rather than on the conventional annual cycle. These companies may want to complete the forecasts for half the critical job roles one year and the other half the next year.

Forecasting. This is what I would consider to be the central component of the workforce planning process. Here are some additional comments I would add to my previous statements.

Demand and supply forecasting are undertaken only for critical job roles and not for every job role in the organization. In undertaking demand forecasts, we can use a combination of quantitative and qualitative demand forecasts. The typical quantitative techniques include regression analysis, time series analysis, decision analysis forecasting, and productivity benchmarking measures. More advanced statistical techniques such as linear programming and other optimization modeling are typically not used. It is important to be conscious of the limitations of quantitative techniques, which are based on the proposition of using the past to extrapolate the future. As the rate of change in society and organizations increases, then quantitative techniques become less appropriate. However, I still believe quantitative techniques have a role in workforce demand forecasting. I like to think of quantitative techniques as helping me to determine the "null hypothesis" future. By this, I mean that quantitative techniques play a valuable role in determining the future workforce required under the current levels of productivity. We then need to assess the levels of productivity change we expect as a result of new technology, revised work practices, outsourcing, or process reengineering. I like to think of quantitative techniques as being inputs in the qualitative process of decision making as to the demand forecast.

In demand forecasting there are a number of qualitative forecasting techniques that we can use: interviews, focus groups, nominal group technique, Delphi technique, and reparatory group. I like to think of the qualitative techniques as being techniques for group decision making. In demand forecasting it's very rare that one individual has all of the information to prepare a demand forecast. Qualitative techniques are about structuring the interactions to facilitate the generation of the most accurate forecasts that can be complied.

In supply forecasting we can be more confident in using historical data as the basis of preparing Supply Forecasting. The basis of supply forecasting is to determine of the current workforce how many will still be here in the future at our forecast points, one, two, five, or ten years in the future. In supply forecasting we are thinking of the current workforce as the cohort and assessing the retention. For supply forecasting we ignore the external recruitment that will occur over the forecast period. This is essential if we are to assess the projected gap by job family/occupational group over the forecast period. There are three factors we take into account when determining the supply forecast: retirements, voluntary termination rates, and the internal transfer and promotion rates.

In determining retirement rates we need to understand the age distribution and the tenure profiles. When individuals are members of "defined benefits" pension funds it's possible to be very accurate in projection retirements as the rules of most of these retirement plans maximize the payout based on a combination of tenure and age. It's not unnatural that individuals would elect to retire when the payout is at the maximum amount. In most companies there has been a movement from defined benefits to defined contribution pension plans. Basically these newer plans are less generous to individuals, and the amount available for pensions depends on the financial performance of the plans the funds have been invested in.

It's likely in the future that as more of the workforce in companies reaching retirement age will be in defined contribution funds, we will not be able to determine retirements based on age and tenure. It's likely that many individuals will not be prepared to take retirement at 60 or 65 years of age as their funds will not support retirements. This will become a major issue for companies over the next twenty years.

The second factor in calculating future supply will be assessing how many individuals will voluntarily leave the company over the forecast period. To assess this we need the following information. We need to assess voluntary turnover by occupational group, organization tenure, organization unit, and by location. Once we have the turnover rates for all of these segments, we can extrapolate the turnover and projected loss. It is very dangerous to try and use total voluntary turnover rates or turnover rates by occupational groups as the basis for determining supply forecasts. While the aggregate numbers may turn out to be correct, they will hide the higher and lower numbers from all of the segments. In supply forecasting we are not trying to just understand the projected total workforce that will still be with us in, say, five years' time. We need to know these forecasts by occupational group/job family, by organization unit (division, branch, etc.), and by location. We need the segmentation to ensure the accuracy of the forecasts. For example, if we knew that the voluntary termination rate for mechanical engineers in the mining division was 10 percent and we had 500 mechanical engineers, then it would be incorrect to say we will lose fifty engineers per year, and hence we will lose 250 over the five years, giving us a net supply of 250. It would be more accurate to say that we will lose 50 + 45 + 40 + 37 + 32 = 204 over the five-year period. While more accurate, this will still overestimate how many will leave. If the total voluntary turnover is 10 percent, then we know that this will vary with tenure, so it might be 15 percent in the first year of tenure and 5 percent in the fourth and fifth year. In this case using the average of 10 percent will overestimate how many mechanical engineers will leave. In our fourth year of forecasting we should look at the turnover of individuals in the fourth year or longer in tenure and ignore the turnover rate in the first three years of tenure or the average over the total tenure profile. In order to complete this level of analysis, we need technology to automate the process.

When we have analyzed the voluntary turnover rates, we need to look at the external labor market. If the current labor market for the occupational groups we are forecasting for are relatively depressed, then we need to assess if we believe the external labor market will grow, shrink, or stay steady. If we think the labor market will grow after, say, three years, then we need to increase the projected voluntary turnover rates in three years' time. If we simply project historical rates, we will underestimate loss rates in the market if projected to grow more rapidly, and we will overestimate loss rates if we forecast labor markets will become less strong.

Risk Analysis. The central phase of the overall workforce planning process is to assess the risk associated with the projected gap between the demand and supply forecasts. The risk is different from simply understanding the magnitude of the gap. There may be large gaps for some job families, but we assess there is an adequate pool of candidates in the marketplace, so our main focus will be to gear up our recruitment activities, both externally and internally. Generally, it's business as usual but with a large volume of work to do. We may have other job families where the gap is not as large numerically but there is a much greater risk because of the lack of supply in the external labor market, typically combined with a long lead time required to build this capability internally. Examples of job families include relationship managers in private banking, geologists and geophysicist in mining and oil and gas, loss adjusters in general insurance. The focus of workforce planning in the past few years has been to think about risk and not just the size of the gap. With job families where we assess significant risk in the size of the gap we often have to develop new career paths rather than relying on traditional career paths. We may need new career paths to not just accelerate the level of capacity that we need in the future, but also to build new capabilities that will be required in the job family in the future. From my experience, most of the risk identified in workforce planning is to build new capability that will be required in the future that has not been required in the past.

Strategy, Impact, and Cost Modeling. Traditionally this step in the workforce planning process involved building HR interventions to address the projected gap for the critical job roles for which forecasts had been prepared. This then becomes a logical extension of the risk assessment previously prepared. In my experience, this is the most straightforward aspect of the workforce planning process, but it consumes the most resources, particularly in the execution stage. This step is where we are able to draw upon our knowledge as to best practice HR interventions to address the strategic staffing gaps we have identified. It is much easier to select or develop HR interventions once we have a good "road sign" as to the future risks in our workforce. The types of strategic staffing interventions that are available to a company are well known. David Ulrich, for example, talks about the "Six Bs": Build, Buy, Borrow, Bounce, Bind, and Boost. There are, however, additional strategic staffing interventions that can be implemented when we have the clarity of workforce planning.

In formulating our strategic staffing interventions, we need to assess the impact of our interventions on addressing the forecasted gap and then use this to determine the level of investment we make into each intervention. This is an interactive process, and it helps us balance the level of investment with the degree of risk we are trying to mitigate.

Action and Accountability. The final step in the workforce planning process is to allocate accountability for the implementation of the proposed strategic staffing interventions. This process is reasonability straightforward and is based on the principles of project management and change management. The role of workforce planning is to identify the projected gaps in critical roles over the forecast period. We then used our HR expertise to design and implement interventions to address these gaps. Like the road sign we start immediately with the initiatives we need to start now because of the lead time to build capability.

SOME FINAL SUGGESTIONS

To conclude this chapter I will briefly highlight some additional suggestions based on my experience over the past thirty-five years working in the field.

When undertaking workforce planning it essential to forecast the numbers required by critical job roles over the forecast period. Without forecasting numbers we will have little credibility with senior executives when we present our findings. In addition to forecasting numbers I believe it's critical to forecast competencies. In my experience, there are more organizational consequences of changes in competencies than there are consequences in change in numbers. In this context I'm using the terms *competencies*, *skills*, and *job roles* interchangeably.

When working with senior managers on the demand forecasts I find many managers and executives reluctant to commit themselves to actual forecasts during demand forecasting interviews and focus groups.

In my experience, most managers are comfortable, with the right information, to prepare demand forecast over two years. Their level of confidence in the forecasts as the figure above shows is high. Most managers felt uncomfortable preparing forecasts beyond two years, and this becomes a tipping point where the level of confidence in the forecasts drops dramatically. In many ways this is not surprising as many more factors that can affect the business and hence the demand forecasts can change over a longer period. Managers are less confident about the impact of the economy, changes in commodity prices, interest rates, economic growth rates, competitor practices, government regulations, and so on. After drawing this simple diagram I then update it where the two-year forecast becomes the current headcount, the third-year forecast becomes the new first-year forecast, and so on. I stress to the managers that we do not prepare, say, a five-year forecast and never come back to it. Clearly we have less confidence in a five-year forecast than a two-year forecast, but over the next year we are not going to implement specific actions that impact us five years out. We want our best effort to get the correct directional forecast five years out but we will have several opportunities to revise the forecasts over the five-year period.

Another suggestion in preparing demand forecasts is to not allow managers to use the same level of rigor in the numbers that they are used to in budgeting. An example: If you have 500 mechanical engineers and you expect the numbers to grow at a steady rate over, say, five years, I would only allow forecasts that are rounded to the nearest 10, with forecasts such as 520 or 570. To have a forecast of, say, 519 takes away from the fact that workforce planning is a planning process and not a budgeting process. If you have 5,000 mechanical engineers, then I would round my forecasts to no less than the nearest 50. Although a small issue, it helps to keep it as a planning and not a budgeting process. Our goal is to understand directionally what the gap is.

My single biggest frustration from consulting in workforce planning for the past 35 years is how often the workforce planning process is not sustained in companies. While it's legitimate to have a one-off project in workforce planning within a company I believe the real benefits come from having a sustainable process. There are two prerequisites for making it sustainable. First we need to create a Center of Excellence in Workforce Planning. I actually prefer it to be a CoE in Workforce Planning and Analytics. This would follow all of the standard processes in creating a CoE. The second prerequisite to making workforce planning a sustainable process over time is to implement workforce planning technology to automate the process. This can be technology developed in-house, such as HP did, or it can be third-party workforce planning and analytics technology. I do not consider Excel pivot tables to be workforce planning technology. Excel is a good prototyping environment but is not sustainable over time as it's far too labor intensive to maintain and is not appropriate technology for modeling supply forecasting, career paths, etc.

My final comment is that we must position workforce planning as a business process, not an HR process. Workforce planning is a process that assesses the risk of business execution from not having the right human capital available. Workforce planning is one of the most powerful vehicles to make HR a critical strategic resource within companies.

Peter Howes has 40 years of experience in HR as a practitioner, academic, and consultant and is now in his third year as Vice President at SuccessFactors. His focus is Workforce Analytics and Workforce Planning. He was formerly CEO of Infohrm, a consulting and technology company specializing in Workforce Planning and Workforce Analytics that he founded in1982.

Peter is a Life Fellow of the Australian Human Resources Institute and a Fellow of the Australian Institute of Management. In 2003 he was awarded the Outstanding Alumni award for the Business Faculty at Queensland University of Technology.

His favorite pastimes are rugby and wine. He is married with two adult children. Peter is based in London and Brisbane.

Pioneering New Business Frontiers: Unaware of What "Shouldn't" Be Done

Dan Hilbert

NEARLY A DECADE LATER, I sit on my back porch overlooking the Texas Hill country and humbly laugh about the events that occurred that resulted in the breakthrough strategic human capital advances my team pioneered at Valero Energy. I lean back a little farther and smile ironically, thinking about how today my company, OrcaEyes, helps businesses measurably deliver breakthrough results in shareholder value, operational performance, and risk mitigation. If I were a different sort of person, I might stand up in front of an audience and pontificate about some divine intervention or moment of inspired brilliance. But if I committed that type of self-deceptive absurdity, I couldn't enjoy the real-life humor of the amazing occurrences. It all happened because I simply didn't know "what I shouldn't do" at the Fortune 15 company Valero Energy.

I'll never forget the first meeting I had with the Executive Plant Management Committee at Valero. I was unaware that HR seldom was able to speak to the committee. At Valero, this committee was arguably the second most powerful group outside of the board of directors. EVPs, SVPs, and GMs (general managers) of refineries are analogous to starship captains in *Star Trek*, exploring dangerous new worlds. A refinery is a very dangerous place. One small mistake results in deaths, and this happens multiple times every year at refineries. One major mistake and a small city is incinerated—literally.

These executives and GMs never completely rest. When on the road, they live by their cell phones, always on guard waiting for a crisis. I played golf with these leaders on a number of occasions. Golf was supposed to be relaxing. I learned by the third hole that these executives never completely relax—not even close. When the cell phone rang or they received a text, a frown immediately engulfed their faces.

When I look back to that first Executive Plant Management Committee presentation, inevitably, the first memories that arise are how lucky I was not knowing what I shouldn't know and shouldn't do.

Before me, the head of organizational development presented. Her excitement and accompanying anxiety were front and center. Since, as I said, I didn't realize how rare it was for HR to present to the committee, I didn't understand her level of emotions. I watched in amazement while this brilliant subject matter expert and eloquent speaker gave her best while the refinery executives ignored her, talking about football, stocks, and children. The apparent rudeness was stunning. But I didn't know that the refinery executives did not believe HR could contribute strategic value. In their world of blowing up small cities, no room existed for "soft" conversations. HR didn't very often talk strategic business, and, in their eyes, HR "shouldn't" talk strategic business.

As I stood up to present to the committee, the members' constant conversational rumblings did not subside in the least. I had only one slide to present. It was a large table of data from an Excel worksheet. As I began to speak, they paid no more attention to me than they had to my HR organizational development cohort. It was like talking into the wind. Then out of the clear blue, from the very back of the room, came a stern voice asking in jest, "Is this some HR weenie talking stats?"

I took the chance to get their attention and responded rather loudly, "Yes, sir! This *is* an HR weenie talking stats!" All of a sudden, the room was dead silent as they all gazed at the data slide being projected—not one set of eyes on me, just on the data on the screen. One of the GMs asked, "So what are you trying to tell me with this data?"

"Sir, what this data says is that if Valero's stock keeps rising at the same pace it has for the past twelve months and the average age of retirement for our engineers drops from 59 to 55, which is the actual retirement age our predictive models forecast, you will have a shortage of senior engineers of at least 20 percent on average in the next two years. Might that cause you any operational problems?"

The mood in the room changed instantaneously as we, the HR weenies, handed out packets of spreadsheet printouts. The plant executives rapidly circled around two tables, examining the printouts, talking among themselves.

Then the salvo began. "If we give you other critical positions, can you do the same analysis?" "Can you extend the projections beyond two years?" "What's your standard deviation?" "Can we send one of our analysts down to examine the data and formulas?"

I did not know that HR weenies shouldn't talk statistics to business leaders. I did not know that HR shouldn't use modeling and forecasting programs linked to multiyear capital expansion projects and correlations to retirement projections based on rising stock prices. My entire career had been in business leadership and revenue production. So I ignorantly, and luckily, went into HR thinking that everyone at a company should discuss, and should be encouraged to discuss, any sound business process that might deliver valuable business results with the highest-level business leader who could be reached. Three years and sixteen HR awards later, the rest is history.

To those of you who come from financial modeling, supply chain management, IT, or other mission-critical management, monitoring, and optimization systems, the following will be second nature and easily comprehended. For those who have little to no background in software system management, these processes may be challenging, so wherever possible, I will try to use common and hopefully somewhat familiar analogies.

The first two key terminology phrasings to grasp are:

1. *Human Capital Business Impact Correlation (HC-BIC)*. This first concept is exactly similar to the financial term *ROI*. Instead of referring to financial return on investments in capital projects, new services, securities, or other forms of typical financial investment products, the investment here is in human capital (HC).

2. This is not a "soft," "touchy-feely" conversation in the least. To make sure this is clearly understood for finance, operations and strategy executives, board members, and the C-Suite, *these are not soft values*. These are as measureable as nearly all financial investment assets and even more mathematically straightforward than capital amortization or derivatives. And most human capital drivers are much more easily manageable than security investments.

A few weeks ago, one of our new healthcare clients was trying to create the value proposition with its finance executives. Having had more than a half-dozen CFOs work for me, I like finance executives, particularly the hard-nosed, no fluff, I've-pretty-much-seen-it-all attitude generally accompanied by a wee touch of sarcasm (or maybe even a heavy dose of sarcasm). I just had to have fun and couldn't stop myself, so I asked the VP of finance, "Would you be interested in decreasing bottom-line costs by 2 percent to 10 percent with little or no investment, with very minimal change management fees, and usually receive an increase in operational efficiency?" The normal answer is something like, "Is that a rhetorical question?" usually laced with a strong dose of skeptical sarcasm. But this time he came back with a hysterical deadpanned comment: "You sound like a used car salesman!"

THE FACTS ARE SIMPLY THE FACTS

And the facts are simply the facts, and these facts were true for that organization. And after fifteen minutes, my somewhat cautious and quite droll VP of finance asked, "Will this be finished by the end of February? We start the strategic planning process then and I want this data for the planning."

And the facts are simply the facts. Because this is based on new data repositories and correlated in new ways to business, it can sound new or unbelievable. But here it is, strange or not.

Our experience with more than seventy-five global companies with workforces ranging from 600 to 72,000 employees has shown that strategic human capital management can deliver these levels of earnings improvement, and there is every reason to believe that the results to date can be bettered.

Strategic human capital management addresses the workforce at all levels as a core asset of the business, ensuring that the performance of this "asset" can respond to demands of the business or organization while mitigating workforce-related risks to the business.

One common thought that must be noted and cannot be stressed strongly enough: *Human capital management is NOT human resources.* Because of the criticality of this dimensional view, we stress it again: Do not correlate human capital management (HCM) with human resources (HR).

Here are the facts: 2 percent to 21 percent of earnings—LOST, unnecessarily—annually! The majority of companies unnecessarily lose in the range of 3 percent to 8 percent annually, including companies that rank in the upper quintiles of total shareholder return (TSR).

This is a massive business problem and opportunity that has largely been ignored because what you can't see is what you miss. Leadership has been blind to these drivers and correlations. *And it's not the visible tip of the iceberg above the water that sinks a ship. It's the unseen mass of ice below the surface.*

OrcaEyes now has data sets on more than seventy-five global companies. Here are a few of the facts represented from these data sets:

▶ The average company loses .09 percent to 12 percent of earnings completely from unnecessary mishandling of overtime positions.

- The median is 1.88 percent.
- One Fortune 50 company was losing 14.5 percent of earnings from unnecessary OT (overtime) of truck drivers. *Yes! 14.5 percent!*

▶ The average company loses .84 percent to 14 percent of earnings from unnecessary loss of top performers and time-to-fill of revenue-producing positions.

- The median is 2.1 percent.

▶ More than 70 percent of the companies have severe labor supply gap problems now and over the next three years in at least seven critical positions.

- However, only two industries have systemic labor supply problems: healthcare and energy.

▶ Companies that handle PerformanceTurnover™[1] effectively generate 20-plus percent better TSR.

▶ Flight loss risk of top performers can be predicted with 75-plus percent accuracy up to three years in advance with specific, preventable reasons.

▶ Specific levels of overtime over defined periods of time of hourly employees result in increased accidents, errors, and lost customers and higher legal costs.

   • These "high-risk" thresholds can be predicted from weeks to months in advance before becoming serious business problems.

▶ More than 67 percent of U.S. companies have at least one area of high "class" risk EEO liabilities. More than 51 percent have at least three areas of class liability risks.

▶ Lack of required skilled labor, timely delivery of this skilled labor, and retention of employees in critical positions negatively impacts more than 40 percent of strategic plan projects and major contracts.

▶ The average company loses 1.1 percent to 3.8 percent of earnings as a result of ineffective appropriations of labor across different business entities and even departments: employees being laid off and paid severance when another business unit is paying agency fees for the exact same skills.

▶ Aging demographic retirement loss is not going to be the disaster for businesses as predicted. The impact will be more than Y2K but far less than a labor experience shortage and supply disaster.

   • However, in healthcare, energy, and utilities, more than 61 percent of companies have severe aging demographic problems in at least five critical position groups today. The majority of these at-risk positions require "localized" skilled labor.

   • This is defined as at least 40 percent of workers in a critical position being 55 years of age or older, and the two levels of feeder pools below have less than 50 percent of required talent to account for the coming loss,[2] with external talent pools insufficient to meet the gaps.

For the ten "Human Capital-Business" correlations listed above, more extensive analysis can be undertaken, providing at least thirty different measures relating to business risk and performance. In addition, there are a further number of industry-specific metrics that we have and expect to continue to evolve. This is not a static approach; rather, it is an evolving body of work responding to the dynamics of the business world.

In my dealings with finance executives, I learned to appreciate and value that top finance executives need to measure the size of the iceberg under the water, the speed and direction of movement, and a risk damage assessment. To top finance and business executives, it's not the tip of the iceberg they see above the water that concerns them. The first step for business leaders is transparency—making what were perceived as unquantifiable and undefinable issues into clearly identifiable and quantifiable action items. The second step is statistically and financially providing leadership with the quantifiable drivers to change lost earnings, costs, and revenue into competitive advantages. And the majority of HCROIs (human capital returns on investments) are absurd. I hesitate to mention normal HCROI ranges because I fear executives will immediately dismiss this. Even to me—someone who has lived in the area more than any other human on the planet in the last decade—they still seem incredulous. Businesses often invest large sums of money to get a "hopeful" five-year average rate of return of 15 percent. So I dare say that most HCROIs return over 100 percent in the first year. Actually, I would be straying from the facts. The facts are that the first-year returns usually exceed 200 percent.

In early January 2012, I had my first conversation with the VP of finance at a major healthcare system. I said "Hello!" Without a bit of emotion, he immediately replied, "I don't understand why we bought this software. We do nearly all of this in other financial programs we developed. I have no idea what we will gain from this except higher labor and software costs." If I hadn't had some understanding of senior finance executives, this would have been one of those movements when I thought about cutting my wrists with a butter knife.

Instead, I asked a simple question: "If you could reduce labor costs by 4.9 percent, overtime costs by 21 percent, and unplanned contract labor by 15 percent in the first twelve months with minimal investment and minimal political headaches, would you be interested?" Knowing I was from New Orleans, he jokingly replied, "Sounds like Mardi Gras math!" I couldn't help but bust out laughing and retorted, "I do *not* do funny tricks for beads. So please bear with me before we both make an assessment of my suspect math logic!"

"Are you aware of your full cost of turnover?" I asked. He shot back, "$6,700 for professional positions, $4,900 for skilled labor, and a couple of grand for everyone else!" I then asked, "Loaded or unloaded?" to which he replied, "What do you mean by loaded recruiting costs?"

"Recruiting software, performance review software, fully loaded recruiter costs including their management, association, and SHRM certification costs," I told him. "These are factored into G&A and amortization costs," he answered.

Trying to get to what I thought was a slam-dunk strategic HCM win, I offered, "Let's just forget those for now since they are buried. And please don't answer until I ask my brief questions. How many positions turn over a year? How many lost work hours are related directly to refilling these turnover positions? How much is the average 'premium' being paid for overtime and contract services while these full-time employees are being replaced?" Since we had access to their data, we had a pretty good idea at least within a few percentage points.

I continued, "How about 2,900-plus replacements per year with an average time-to-fill of sixty-nine days? The average 'premium' hourly cost is between 69 percent and 72 percent. This translates into more than 1.6 million hours paid at an average of 70 percent higher labor costs. What happens if the time-to-refill is reduced ten days on average?" This was a real sharp professional. He needed no more prompting. His first reply was, "This is not a way we were taught to view labor spend. But this is bottom-line reducing nearly 400,000 hours at 70 percent or more labor cost per hour." He then asked me, "Where did you get the time-to-fill data? From the recruiting system?" When I answered, "Yes," he immediately jumped in and said, "But this is not accounting for the time it takes to get a requisition approved, priced in compensation, then posted. Nor does it include the time it takes the average employee to start once the offer is accepted—on average more than two weeks."

I told him that there was not always a one-to-one correlation between an employee turnover and a premium paid replacement. And he jumped back in, saying, "This does not include the cost-to-fill per position that will be eliminated. If we change the performance review structure and add $5 million in bonuses for managers with low turnover, the return is likely more than 400 percent. It shouldn't be that straightforward." I laughed to myself, remembering my recent mental conversation on the back porch: "I wouldn't be here today if I didn't know what 'shouldn't have ever been done'!"

But it is. And it's measureable fact, and it's another of those major business successes right underneath the corporate offices that just *shouldn't be that way*. And that is just the tip of the iceberg—literally, when it comes to labor costs, lost revenue, and business operational risks.

And at the end of the day, once again, the facts are the facts and these are the facts. Previously hidden or inaccessible data about mission-critical processes, entities, and functions are competitive game changers, especially when it relates to the highest business cost—usually by far.

THE HUMAN CAPITAL BUSINESS IMPACT CORRELATION METHODOLOGY

The Human Capital Business Impact Correlation (HC-BIC) methodology is a four-part management system for discovering, diagnosing, and measuring business impact; defining business risks; performance optimization modeling; implementing and managing performance enhancement; and ongoing monitoring of HC drivers that impose risk on financial, operational, and strategic performance.

The first key understanding is that this is:

▶ Not rocket science
▶ Technically not new to businesses at all
▶ Typical in management of nearly all other mission-critical business functions
▶ Not time-consuming or disruptive

For companies that utilize supply chain management methodologies, this will be readily apparent. For companies that use network management, plant management, financial modeling, load balancing, or transportation management software, this will also be readily apparent. For all of its other claims, Google is essentially a network management company. Walmart, Dell, and HP are supply chain companies. These are dominant companies based on software modeling and software management systems.

Can you imagine for one second what Michael Dell would say if he were told, "We just ran out of LCD displays for our highest-selling laptops. We don't know why. We have no idea where we are going to get more, or when." Tar and feathering would be gentle. And imagine if someone told the CEO of Google, "We ran out of electricity to support our networks. We have lost 30 percent functionality, and response time has increased by 370 percent. We don't know why, when, or how we will fix this!"

However, in the domain of human capital, this is not only acceptable—it's the norm. The results are staggering financial and operational losses and increased strategic risks. There's no one to blame. It's no one's fault. Until recently, the methodology, data, and technology did not exist to deal with these issues. As you will see, though, this model is sound, based on proven processes and technologies.

Step 1: Resource Planning—Demand Forecast

It's literally unimaginable for transportation companies to not perform sophisticated resource planning. Do we have the trains, planes, and trucks to meet the demand of our customers and new strategic initiatives?

Can you imagine retail stores not performing sophisticated resource planning to ensure that they understand the projected buying patterns of their customers?

Or hospitals not performing resource planning to ensure they have an accurate estimate on the number of procedures that will have to be performed?

And what about . . .

➤ Planes for the Air Force?

➤ Buyers for automobiles?

➤ Semiconductors for customers?

➤ Money required for capital expansion?

➤ Electricity required to run a city in the heat of the summer?

➤ Budget to meet operational needs?

In the context of the HC-BIC methodology, we are *not* talking about traditional workforce planning as the answer. In HR, workforce planning means at least a half-dozen different processes and outcomes. To some it's headcount planning, to others it's financial arbitrage, to others it's budgeting, and to still others it's call center management.

It's quite interesting and revealing that the definition for Enterprise Resource Planning (ERP) in Wikipedia makes no mention of labor, workforce, or HC:

> **Enterprise Resource Planning** . . . systems integrate internal and external management information across an entire organization, embracing finance/accounting, manufacturing, sales and service, customer relationship management, etc. ERP systems automate this activity with an integrated software application. Their purpose is to facilitate the flow of information between all business functions inside the boundaries of the organization and manage the connections to outside stakeholders.

Including human capital planning in resource planning does not have to be a complex process. The most effective and familiar way to begin resource planning is just like budgeting. Managers submit a human capital requirements analysis to their superiors for approval. As long as management is included for all existing operations, strategic plans, future growth, new products, and services, this will be sound start. The key components are:

1. Projected need by individual position for each quarter for at least the next three years
2. Some sort of notation to indicate "critical" or essential positions

This is not to be confused with headcount planning. HC resource planning links the human capital variable to the strategic and operational business components.

Mark DeYong is the CEO of ATK, one of the largest U.S. defense contractors, annually consistent in delivering TSR in the top market quintile. Once he saw the power of this model, Mark insisted that the business unit leads at ATK update their human capital demand forecast quarterly in their quarterly operations report. Mark clearly understood that an accurate, dynamic HC plan that adjusted to changing business conditions was the essential first component of business-driven strategic human capital management. A proactive human capital demand forecast was the first vital step. Mark told me that he's wanted to do this type of strategic human capital planning for twenty years, "but the technology and data was not there."

Step 2: Supply Forecasting

Human capital supply forecasting is not complex. It can be performed systematically. With Step 1 in place, the demand forecast is aligned directly and dynamically to the business. Supply forecasting can also be dynamically aligned to the business.

The two primary components of human capital supply forecasting are (1) internal resource projections and (2) external supply availability.

Internal Supply Projections. Historical employee data is used to analyze and forecast through predictive modeling that projects the actual company headcount over the next three to five years. The key variables by position, business unit, and location are:

► Current headcount
► Historical turnover
► Historical fill rates
► Projected retirement

The #1 objection is "Our data is terrible." There's no question some company data is cleaner than others. The real answer is this: Have you been paying your employees? Do you have a payroll system with records? Then you have enough data. If this data is bad, you really need to know because it likely means your employees are not being paid accurately. As with all data, simple analysis tools can be used to assess accuracy, so that the accuracy of the projections is understood—exactly how most of the rest of the business works.

Recently, sophisticated employee flight risk prediction software has enabled companies to predict who will leave, when, and why with stunning accuracy. One of our clients uses it to assess the impact of bids in union negotiations. This client was able to analyze who would leave if certain benefits were changed. The results were clear that the loss of critical employees would be severe, so this intelligent information empowered the client to shape its bid to achieve the desired outcomes.

External Supply Data. This is another area where technology has just emerged, especially in North America, and where a lot of guesswork has been removed. Business leaders no longer have to guess about the availability, cost, and trends of external labor.

Intelligent data empowers intelligent decision for leadership:

► How large is the supply in the required location?
► How big is the gap or surplus right now?
► Is the gap or surplus going to get better or worse over the next five to six years?
► What is the actual cost in the market today?
► Is it going to increase over the next five to six years, and how much?

Critical HC business questions no longer have to put financial and operational performance at risk.

With precision, leaders can know:

▶ Is there enough affordable talent in the critical positions at the right locations to support ongoing turnover?

▶ Is there enough of this talent to support growth?

▶ How bad is it going to get?

▶ Where can I find the largest available pools of skilled labor at the best costs to expand or consolidate?

▶ Do I need to adjust my strategic plans as a result of the labor supply?

Other external variables to be monitored are general economic conditions or specific industry factors that will increase HC demand and, thus, the actual supply.

A perfect example of no supply demand forecasting occurred at one of the major insurance companies. The director of organizational development had built a superb management training program. On multiple occasions, the CEO suggested that the director not focus so much energy on one business unit. He didn't listen to the CEO. A few months later, it was announced that the business unit was sold. As a result, a good deal of time and resources were expended to train leaders for another company. And, yes, the director was among the ranks of the unemployed shortly thereafter.

Step 3: Monitoring—Problem Determination.

If any of you have ever been into the NOC (network operating center) at a major company, you have witnessed an exceptional implementation of advanced technology. Literally thousands of global servers, PCs, bandwidth, switches, and routers can all be monitored, diagnosed, managed, and optimized from a single set of color-coded monitors.

The monitoring need for strategic human capital management is no different. Strategic human capital management without effective monitoring is an oxymoron. It's impossible. It's like throwing darts blindfolded at a moving target.

First and foremost is the supply of required labor meeting the demand today and over the next few years. As with all critical business elements, proactive discovery of business risk is always preferred so the potential problem can be corrected before it manifests into a business problem. Monitoring supply and demand with a good system is quite easy. Does a green icon turn yellow or red? When does it turn red? How big is the potential gap? In what positions? Where is it? Why is it occurring? What is the potential risk on business performance?

It's essential that leadership is aware of supply–demand imbalances. It's also essential to understand the root causes so that corrective and effective actions can be implemented. The answer is in the HRIS and external labor data.

As strategic human capital management systems evolve, financial, operational, accident, and performance data is added in short order. The sophistication and power of the monitoring increases exponentially, as do the measureable benefits.

Monitoring and effective problem determination are essential for high-performing organizations. In fact, many of the soft points made by HR that incessantly drive business leaders crazy can now be quantified in terms of business performance:

- Do we really have aging demographic problems?
- Is turnover in our sales staff really impacting revenue?
- What levels of OT cause accidents and customer complaints?
- Is leadership training delivering any measureable business results?
- If we spend a few million dollars on a talent management system, what business benefits will we realize?
- Is paying certain employees more or increasing benefits across the board really in the best interest of the business?
- Is there really a talent crisis that will impact the business?

We met the CEO of what became a major client. When the subject of aging demographics arose, he boldly and proudly stated, "We don't have any aging demographic problems. The average age of our workforce is 29.7 years old." I asked if we could get the HRIS data needed and promised him an analysis. Having spent the past four years living inside the data of more than twenty energy, utility, and mining companies, we were pretty sure the company in question had aging demographic problems someplace.

After loading the data, we called the CEO back and told him, "We have never seen so few aging demographic problems in an energy firm. We found only one area of concern: 39 percent of your sales staff is 62 years of age or older, and from the limited amount of sales data we have, it looks like more than 50 percent of annual sales are at risk." We signed a contract in less than a week.

Step 4: Risk Management and Performance Optimization— Human Capital Business Impact Correlation

Relatively simple correlations can each increase earnings by 2 percent or more:

- Performance turnover to earnings
- Time-to-fill of revenue billing positions
- OT levels to accidents, customer service complaints, and thefts

- ➤ Leave levels to accidents
- ➤ External labor supply and costs to success of strategic plan initiatives
- ➤ Aging demographics to fulfillment of multiyear contracts
- ➤ Loss of top performers due to duration in a position
- ➤ Optimal levels of FTEs and temporary labor
- ➤ Human capital performance compared to industry competitors
- ➤ Time-to-fill of OT positions to earnings
- ➤ Actual ROIs of leadership training
- ➤ Top management importers and trainers of talent
- ➤ Worst management at retaining top talent
- ➤ Optimal layoffs
- ➤ Significant reduction in training and recruiting costs while improving workforce performance

Once the demand, supply, and business variables are into the strategic human capital management system, the amount of low-hanging fruit is unbelievable. Actually, it's not unbelievable at all. It's simply new usage of mature data correlated with intelligent decisions measurably linking human capital to business—predictively. However, by traditional thinking, "It just simply shouldn't be viewed or work like that!"

Last year, we did an assignment for one of largest transportation companies in the United States. Our staff always studies annual reports of publicly traded companies before visiting a prospective client. We noticed that the company's margins were below those of its competitors. Within two hours of getting the data into the system, we called the CEO and asked him why the company was paying $182 million in OT to truck drivers. He explained that $60 million of the OT was part of the business model for certain trucks requiring advanced certifications. That still left about $120 million. We accessed the company's recruiting system data and discovered that the average time to fill was sixty-one days, and the average manager was sitting on resumes for forty days before responding. We used our external market intelligence products and discovered there were ample supplies of certified eighteen-wheel drivers in the majority of the company's major locations. We recommended a recruiting outsourcing firm that guaranteed thirty-day fills as long as the managers responded to their resume submission in seven days. The recruiting firm simply started to pipeline driver candidates.

As ridiculous as this may sound, this one simple process added $63 million in first-year earnings.

The risks and opportunities abound simply because system management, resource planning, monitoring, and performance tuning have not been applied to strategic human capital management.

WHERE WILL STRATEGIC HUMAN CAPITAL MANAGEMENT RESIDE?

We were recently engaged as the principal external consultant on a futures project for one of the major HR software vendors. As part of the assignment, we participated in a focus group of elite analysts and thought leaders. More than 80 percent believed human capital management was too strategic to reside in HR.

Our company, OrcaEyes, has as its primary message "Translating Human Capital into the Language of Business," but the reality is that strategic human capital management is the language of business and is much broader than the traditional HR function, requiring significantly greater skill sets.

In some organizations, the HR function may well step up and grab what would clearly be a transformative opportunity to become intimately and significantly involved in key strategic decision making in a measurable way. The alternative position is that once business leaders see the value of what can be provided to them, they sensibly will require direct reporting and be in a position to take specific action themselves, through their HR department or through external service providers.

AT THE END OF THE DAY

A number of major takeaways can be realized from this fact-based methodology. Every company is losing stunning amounts of earnings, experiencing unnecessarily high costs, dealing with numerous serious business risks, and losing strategic competitive advantages. But the "soft" side of this transformative new methodology is that "sometimes being unaware of what we shouldn't know" and being allowed or empowered to examine what unspoken corporate culture normally prevents are the platforms for industry-leading companies.

Notes

1. Simple ratio for the number of low performers who leave an organization to each top performer who leaves.
2. This does not include projected normal attrition of the feeder pools, further exacerbating the business risk.

Dan Hilbert is Global Talent Acquisition and Planning Lead at Valero Energy Corporation. Recognized by Jobster as the "Bill Gates of Workforce Planning," hailed as the workforce planning industry "Trailblazer" by *HR* magazine, awarded the Optimas award for innovation by *Workforce Management* magazine and industry leader of the year by IQPC and ERE, Dan Hilbert is considered the undisputed leader and pioneer in strategic workforce planning. His fifteen years of successful experience leading early-stage, venture-capital-backed software companies as both chairman and CEO provide him with the vision to clearly see workforce and talent management strategically, through the eyes of business leaders.

His ground breaking work in the areas of workforce supply chain management, predictive workforce modeling, quantifiable workforce to business value chain correlation analysis, talent acquisition process mapping, and workforce performance metrics resulted in over a dozen industry awards in 2006—record-setting.

He holds a bachelor's degree in business from Belford University, General Management certification from the McCombs School of Business at the University of Texas, and Advanced Process Engineering certification from the University of Texas.

SECTION 3

Analytics

Rob Tripp

ONCE UPON A TIME, back in the days of expensive mainframe computers, we were so pleased when we developed a cohort-based analyses of attrition (we used to call these Markov models, a simplification of the statistical underpinnings of the models of the time) and the aging workforce and found a way to use those tools to tell compelling stories about the workforce. Today, we have effective and sophisticated prediction models for both organizations and individuals on our desktops or even "in the cloud." Although the term *workforce analytics* is still new to many people, as with the term *workforce planning*, thirty practitioners will have thirty definitions!

Routine reports and metrics, even embedded in colorful dashboards with awesome "wow" factors, can take you only so far. And having access to high-quality data about your workforce is only a starting point. Today, many of the really important questions about the workforce require the power of statistics, operations research, and game theory applied to "big data" involving not just traditional employee demographic data, but also employee and customer surveys, financial data, economic and business data, education and global political data, cultural norms, and on and on.

In today's increasingly complex world of global competition for talent, you need people who can translate business issues into workforce questions, use those powerful tools and approaches to develop deep and actionable insights about the workforce, and tell compelling data-based stories that lead to action.

The line between workforce planning and workforce analytics is sometimes artificial: Where workforce planning at its core deals with matching the demand for talent with the supply of talent, workforce analytics can take you into a deep understanding of your workforce that can enhance your workforce planning efforts.

The next several chapters in this short section will give you more insight into the scope and breadth of workforce analytics and the tools, skills, and competencies needed to be successful.

Jeremy Shapiro and **Tom Davenport**, two of the leading writers and speakers about the expanding use of analytics in business, have given us "The Rise of Talent Analytics," a high-level overview of business and HR leaders who are learning to use analytics to make better decisions. As they state, "Great HR leaders never worry about having a seat at the table . . . . Talent analytics . . . create a quantifiable difference in . . . the execution of their strategies."

With a bit more detail into the "how" as well as the "what," **Leo Sadovy** and **Christian Haxholdt** from the SAS Institute, in "Workforce Analytics," deepen our understanding of the approaches and tools that help us gain deep insight into our workforce, helping the HR leader add "value to the strategic decisions that can make or break an organization."

"Predicting Analytics" by **Amit Mohindra** and **J. Allan Brown** gives us a tour of the breadth, promise, and perils of predictive workforce analytics. As in many other activities, predictive analytics in HR is the wave of today. Let's get on board!

The Rise of Talent Analytics

Jeremy Shapiro and Thomas H. Davenport

WHEN A SENIOR MANAGER suddenly announces her resignation at your organization, what typically happens next? A panicked call to human resources? Emergency meetings on how to handle the transition? A hasty phone call to your favorite headhunter on speed dial? Some organizations still panic when a senior leader leaves. But many do not because through analytics, they know more about their people than their competitors do. These companies not only know exactly how much the departed senior leader was contributing—they also understand what internal relationships the leader depended upon to get the job done, what five other people could do the leader's job just as well as she could, and the value of the job at the company. These companies are able to sustain the good work of the departed employee and increase revenue without missing a beat.

Companies like Lowe's, Comcast, Google, and Caesars Entertainment have adopted talent analytics. They use data about their employees to find new insights that link people decisions to organizational performance. Some companies have transformed themselves through the use of these approaches. Many, like Caesars (formerly Harrah's) Entertainment, are in service-intensive businesses.

TALENT ANALYTICS AT CAESARS ENTERTAINMENT

Caesars, the global operator of more than fifty casinos, is a well-established analytical competitor. The company employs analytics across the business in areas including marketing, pricing, and employee/customer interactions. It turns out that in the controlled environment of a casino, where privacy is assumed to be almost nonexistent, the thousands of cameras installed to stop fraud and theft can also observe how customers react in different situations. Caesars paired industrial psychologists and casino veterans to examine thousands of hours of footage from the casino floor. What did they find? That customers, win or lose, stay longer in the casino if they are made to feel welcome there by casino employees. And apparently, as customers, we need this reinforcement about every ten minutes.

Every interaction with a customer is under scrutiny at Caesars. Take, for example, the length of the hotel check-in line and staffing for it. On a Friday night, how much does a long wait impact revenue? Friday is a popular night to check in since people are starting the weekend. Each moment someone is standing in line, he is not doing what he is eager to do, whether it's shopping, gambling, or seeing a show. Caesars was interested in learning more about what the optimal staffing level would be for the hotel front desk and the impact on revenue from optimizing staffing levels. To find out, Caesars turned to its data. Cameras could capture wait times, and the company has the ability to see how customers interact with different games and attractions through customer loyalty cards that patrons insert into slots to get "comped" rewards from the casino later.

Crossing data from camera observations and loyalty cards with staffing plans and financial measures, Caesars changed the way it recruited, staffed, and trained employees. The company focused specifically on fifteen key positions with a direct impact on customer loyalty and revenue. For these positions, Caesars could define the impact of optimal staffing on its profit and loss statement. Caesars made full use of its data to change the way it deployed its talent, measured the impact, and optimized operations for the right customer experience. Ultimately, this lifted the company's top and bottom lines.

ANALYTICS AND THE SERVICE/PROFIT CHAIN

Organizations are beginning to make connections between people performance, customer satisfaction, and profitability. One common approach to that relationship is called the *service-profit chain*, which specifies that as employee engagement and satisfaction rise, customer satisfaction and spending also increase. One reason that Caesars exploits this relationship is that Gary Loveman, the company's CEO, was a coauthor of the published research on the service/profit chain.[1]

However, you don't have to coauthor the research to employ the ideas. A variety of other companies have adopted the approach, including retailers like Sears and Lowe's. Sears dramatically improved its performance in the mid-1990s through what it called the "employee-customer-profit model."[2]

While most organizations run some type of employee opinion survey, home improvement giant Lowe's has studied the exact impact of employee engagement at its stores. It turns out that the difference between its most highly engaged and lowest engaged store, all other differences boiled out, is $1 million a year in sales. And what does it take to achieve that $1 million? Better leaders who know how to engage employees, great hiring practices, and better functioning teams.[3] Other companies, including Limited Brands, Best Buy, and General Mills, have done the same types of analysis—with similar benefits.

THE OVERALL RISE OF ANALYTICS

Talent analytics are just one example of the increasingly widespread application of metrics and analytics to key business processes. From finance to supply chain management to marketing, managers are increasingly making decisions on the basis of data and analysis rather than intuition or experience alone. Data of various kinds—from enterprise systems transaction data to Internet data to sensors of all kinds—have proliferated throughout organizations. Virtually every industry has experienced this transformation, and even those once reliant on intuition—the entertainment and retail industries are good examples—have begun to embrace more science-based decisions.

After mastering the transactions and getting data in order, executives begin to explore how they can make better decisions using the data. This is exactly the state of human resources and talent management. Most organizations now have basic HR transaction systems and databases in place. The function is poised on the edge of a dramatic change in decision making about people.

OF WHAT ARE TALENT ANALYTICS CAPABLE?

It turns out that converting data about your talent into actionable insights can have big impacts no matter how advanced your organization's capabilities are. To illustrate, consider the hierarchy of talent analytics that ranges from HR facts at its most elemental up to sophisticated talent supply chain analyses, as shown in Figure 1.

FIGURE 1. THE HIERARCHY OF TALENT ANALYTICS.

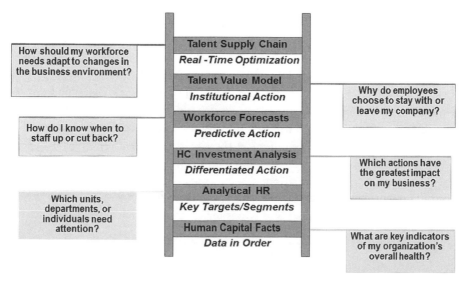

Human Capital Facts

The foundation of talent analytics are *human capital facts*—a single "version of the truth" regarding individual performance and enterprise-level data such as head-count, performance levels for each employee, contingent labor use, turnover, and recruiting. Companies need to think carefully about what facts they need to get that baseline.

Particular metrics can be identified through general logic (the employee engagement or satisfaction score, for example, seems an obvious metric for many companies) or specific analyses that show that a metric is important to some other performance measure. For example, Caesars found through research that a key factor in customer satisfaction was the extent to which front-line service employees smiled at customers (which, like customer behaviors, could be measured through ceiling cameras). The company doesn't measure smiles for every employee every day, but it did embark upon a program to remind employees to smile at the start of every work shift.

Google, whose strategy relies heavily on hiring high-quality employees, devotes considerable effort to determining who the best people actually are, both before and after they are hired. Employees are scored on twenty-five performance metrics, from how frequently they have hosted "tech talks" to the variance of the assessments given potential recruits after interviews. For more detailed analyses, Google gathers up to 200 "biodata" metrics on samples of employees to determine what factors might be correlated with performance.

For some companies, there may be one or two unique data points that indicate overall health of the employee relationship. For example, JetBlue created a new employee satisfaction metric around the willingness of employees to recommend the company as a place to work. This "crewmember net promoter score"—modeled after the metric used for customer satisfaction—has been used to understand the impact of compensation changes, to predict operational and financial performance, to evaluate the impact of employee training programs, and as a factor in executive bonuses. JetBlue also asks employees if they'd recommend the company each year on their hiring date, so effectively the company has a 1/12 sample of all employees' opinions every month, which is used to monitor employee engagement.

JetBlue and other successful organizations are completely transparent with end users on the common definitions of these facts; any manager or employee can see how the data was collected, what formulas are being used, and importantly, why the data matters to the operation. For example, Caesars provides management-friendly documentation in its HR scorecard to ensure that all readers understand how "facts" are created and why they matter to their daily management responsibilities.

Analytical HR

Analytical HR takes metrics to the next step—not simply reporting on past outcomes but analyzing the relationships among HR and other variables. Companies displaying analytical HR approaches would also be likely to group together HR data or segment the data to gain insights into specific departments or disciplines—allowing a manager, for example, to see if staff turnover intervention is needed within the East Coast sales team but not the West Coast team. Analytical HR integrates individual performance data such as personal achievement of key result areas with HR process metrics (such as cost and time) and outcomes metrics (engagement, retention, and nonfinancial business outcomes).

For example, Lockheed Martin built an employee performance management system with the ultimate goal of measuring each employee's performance and linking it to organizational objectives. The process is continuous throughout the year and uses an automated system to collect timely employee review data. This data can then be compared to learning management information. Lockheed Martin not only understands who has undergone formal training in specific areas, but it then identifies and monitors areas for improvement. Through these analytical tools, the company more clearly understands employee performance and can identify its highest performers and highest potentials for special programs.

Human Capital Investment Analysis

Human capital investment analysis allows an organization to understand what knowledge, skills, abilities, and connections matter most to the business and allows decision makers to understand what kind of recruiting or learning and development investments create the biggest payoff. Companies practicing this approach analyze their talent DNA to replicate and grow to their strategic objective.

For example, General Mills had been running an employee opinion survey for years. At the end of the survey, the company did what most organizations do: thanked employees for being forthright, pointed out areas the organization can improve upon, and handed managers an analysis of their own populations along with employee comments. Then, the company took a second look at its analysis regarding an employee's willingness to put in an "extra mile" effort at work. It turns out that the employees of the top managers were twice as willing to go the extra mile at work compared with the employees of the second-best rated managers. For General Mills, excellence in management pays off in big ways. The company told everyone about what had been learned and embedded the most effective managerial behaviors into the executive learning program, which was named the "Great Managers" program. The company literally intended to understand what makes a great manager at General Mills and embed those qualities into as many managers as it could.

Workforce Forecasts

Workforce forecasts may use turnover, succession planning, and business opportunity data to create pipeline analyses identifying shortages and excesses of key capabilities long before they happen. The analyses can work off internal plans and forecasts to ensure alignment with the enterprise.

Valero Energy, an energy company with the largest number of oil refineries in the United States, is one of the most aggressive adopters of this idea. The company needed to grow in an environment of critical skills shortages within its industry. Its model analyzes historical employee records for turnover patterns and creates three-year forecasts by position, location, level, division, department, and salary—and relates them to talent supply for key job categories. The model also incorporates talent needs for future capital projects and new systems, services, and projects.

Talent Value Model

Talent value models seek to answer questions like, "Why do employees choose to stay with a company?" One way to answer that question is by using analytics to calculate what employees value most, and by using that data to create a model that will boost retention rates. For example, a value model can help managers design a personalized set of performance incentives or to assess whether they should match a competitor's employment offer to retain an employee or decide when it is time to promote an employee.

Google, for example, uses employee performance data to determine the most appropriate intervention to help high- and low-performing employees succeed. Laszlo Bock, vice president of people operations at Google, told us, "We don't use performance data to look at the averages, but to monitor the highest and lowest performers of the distribution curve. The 5 percent of our lowest performers we actively try to help. We know we've hired talented people, and we genuinely want to help them succeed." The hypothesis was that many of these individuals might be misplaced or poorly managed. A detailed analysis of them found that this was often the case, and many difficult situations have been addressed by understanding what each individual's needs and values are. Google also used similar approaches to learn which employees were likely to leave the company.

Talent Supply Chains

Finally, with *talent supply chains*, companies can quickly make decisions about any number of talent demands—from optimal hiring techniques based on up-to-the-minute data to workforce forecasts integrating new data in real time. This is at the top of the ladder because it requires high-quality human capital data, effective analytics, and the integration of broad talent management and other organizational processes. We're not sure that any organization has yet mastered this level of talent analytics, but many of those we've already described are moving toward it.

GETTING STARTED WITH TALENT ANALYTICS

The DELTA model is an approach for understanding and prioritizing how to build analytical capability within an organization. It, or a similar model, is critical for organizations wishing to build their talent analytics. DELTA stands for Data, Enterprise Thinking, Leadership, Targets, and Analysts.[4] Each of these key components of an analytical orientation is described below.

Data

Without acceptably clean data, analysis is impossible. Identifying what data should be captured in a defined and repeatable way is core to competing on talent analytics. If you dislike your organization's data quality, you are not alone. Many people are frozen into inaction by data problems. Consider, however, the vast quantities of people data we do have access to that is useful. People generate huge quantities of data simply by doing their jobs and through the basic systems that support them. And with modern HR transaction systems and databases in place within most large corporations, there is better data available than ever before to feed analytics initiatives. Data is important, but equally important is the ability to understand what raw measurements are critical to organizational results. Think back to Caesars; measuring the number of smiles a customer receives is data, too.

The data category also includes analytical technology. It is necessary to have technology to solve business problems using talent analytics. However, the bar has never been lower to acquire the right technology for the job. Options range from hosted business intelligence solutions that will start your journey in talent analytics within a week to enterprise systems that are more powerful than ever. You may find that the greater challenge is capturing the data you want—not reporting on it.

Enterprise Thinking

Silos are the enemy of analytics. The most effective analytics cut across HR, finance, marketing, and customer service in order to find the nugget of insight that could create new revenue or unlock the potential of a team. It's common to combine something as mundane as employee transfer data with customer satisfaction, gross sales, and employee performance data to find departments that are creating pools of your best salespeople and which have a negative impact on customer satisfaction. Some organizations have also suggested to us that the reason they do not pursue service/profit chain analysis is because there is no one function within the organization that controls all the necessary data.

Leadership

Don't projects always run more easily when they are supported from up above? This holds particularly true for insights regarding talent analytics. Managers are prone to trust their gut when it comes to managing their own people. The truth is, unsurprisingly, that our instincts often mislead us. For example, while most managers believe they are exceptional interviewers, 50 percent of hires by managers using pure gut instincts do not quite work out according to executive hiring experts Geoff Smart and Randy Street.[5] That fact does not tarnish a manager's belief that when it comes to people matters, the gut rules.

When leadership (within and outside the HR function) believes in the power of data, you can create a better result—and the organization can dissolve old assumptions about how to make talent decisions. A clear, actionable set of analyses that help grow the top line or yield savings will do the trick nicely.

Targets

A key aspect of succeeding with talent analytics is a clear sense of an organization's targets or objectives for analytics. Are you attempting to improve recruiting, retention, or customer service? It is difficult to do everything at once. Google, for example, had a strong target on recruiting when it was hiring 100 people a week. When its growth subsided somewhat, it switched its primary target to retention.

Analysts

What kind of people do you need to create talent analytics? Do they all need to be math geniuses? In short, no. The most successful companies certainly do have their fair share of statisticians, business intelligence gurus, visualization experts, and even Hadoop-capable data scientists. However, we would trade most of those skills for a team of people who understood their operations, could think creatively, and told a good story with data.

A FINAL THOUGHT ON TALENT ANALYTICS

Great HR leaders never worry about having a seat at the table in their organizations. Increasingly, the stack of paper or iPad they bring to meetings is data. But the data they are bringing are not plain old headcount data or other traditional HR information. They are bringing insights to leaders to help improve operations, fuel innovation, or execute an organizational goal. Talent analytics have helped many leading companies to create a quantifiable difference in their management of people and the execution of their strategies, and it can for your organization as well.

References

1. J. Heskett, T. O. Jones, G. Loveman, E. Sasser, and L. Schlesinger, "Putting the Service-Profit Chain to Work," *Harvard Business Review* (March–April 1994).
2. Anthony J. Rucci, Steven T. Kirn, and Richard P. Quinn, "The Employee-Customer-Profit Chain at Sears," *Harvard Business Review* (January–February 1998).
3. C. Coco, F. Jamison, and H. Black, "Connecting People Investments and Business Outcomes at Lowe's: Using Value Linkage Analytics to Link Employee Engagement to Business Performance," *People and Strategy*, 34 (2011), p. 2.
4. T. H. Davenport, J. Harris, and R. Morison, *Analytics at Work* (Boston: Harvard Business Press, 2010).
5. G. Smart and R. Street, *Who: The A Method for Hiring* (New York: Ballantine, 2008).

Jeremy Shapiro is an HR executive at Morgan Stanley, responsible for its data and analytics function. He speaks and writes frequently on HR analysis, and is the co-author of *Harvard Business Review*'s October, 2010 cover story, "Competing on Talent Analytics" with Tom Davenport and Jeanne Harris. Jeremy serves as the Metrics and Measures taskforce chair for the Society of Human Resource Management, developing HR metrics standards certified by the American National Standards Institute.

Prior to Morgan Stanley, Jeremy worked at the Omnicom Group consulting with organizations such as GE, Motorola, KPMG, and BAE Systems. He was an early influencer in developing online recruiting practices in the 1990s, and co-founded Hodes iQ, a leading online applicant management system in 1999.

Jeremy is a teacher within Cornell ILRs continuing education program on analytics. He holds an M.S. in information systems from NYU's Stern School of Business and a degree in economics and history from Rutgers University

Tom Davenport is a visiting professor at Harvard Business School. He also serves as the President's Distinguished Professor of Information Technology and Management at Babson College, is co-founder and research director of the International Institute for Analytics, and is a senior adviser to Deloitte Analytics. He pioneered the concept of "competing on analytics" with his best-selling 2006 *Harvard Business Review* article (and 2007 book). His most recent book is *Analytics at Work: Smarter Decisions, Better Results*, with Jeanne Harris and Bob Morison. He has written, or edited, twelve other books, and has written over 100 articles for such publications as *Harvard Business Review*, *Sloan Management Review*, the *Financial Times*, and many other publications. In 2003 he was named one of the world's "Top 25 Consultants" by *Consulting* magazine. In 2005 *Optimize* magazine's readers named him among the top three business and technology analysts in the world. In 2007 and 2008 he was named one of the most 100 influential people in the information technology industry by Ziff-Davis magazines.

Workforce Analytics

Leo Sadovy and Christian Haxholdt

HR EXECUTIVES, ON THE WHOLE, are well equipped to competently manage the basics—recruiting, hiring, onboarding, payroll, benefits, training, etc.—and operating unit general managers are satisfied with the results. The missing link for HR executives is often their ability to help general managers with the more strategic issues they grapple with, like:

- Are we better off keeping our geographic sales structure after the acquisition, or do we now have sufficient critical mass and concentrations of expertise to take an industry-centric approach?
- Can we predict how the increased average age of our skilled workers, their upcoming retirement, and the massive replacements by inexperienced workers will affect the business?
- The increased production and sales capacity is going to make R&D the bottleneck. What are the critical technical skills we're going to need, and what is the optimal mix of hires, layoffs, and retraining to counteract that bottleneck?
- In order to meet the increased seasonal demand from new customers, should we build inventory early, run additional shifts, or outsource some of our production needs?

As an HR executive, how do *you* feel about your ability to respond strategically to such requests? If you are like most, the desire and skills to respond are there, but the information, tools, and systems are not. The problem often starts with the basics. To paraphrase the public service announcement "It's 9:00 AM Monday morning; do you know where your employees are?" After all, you pay them every week, so of course you know where they are, right? In a majority of businesses, that question would go to the finance department, not HR, because finance has the required data collection and consolidation systems. Financial systems may collect headcount data from 2,000 different cost centers, eighty different countries/business units/subsidiaries, and forty separate payroll systems, along with month-end closing or forecast data—but only at a very high level. The granular detail you need to contribute strategically to the operating units (e.g., permanent versus temps, salaried versus hourly, managers versus individual contributors) is not there. Three primary resources—people, money, and technology—make up every organization. Of these, it is invariably the human factor that is the most difficult to manage. In addition, for most businesses (except, perhaps, the resource extraction and heavy manufacturing industries), employee-related expenses—salaries, benefits, taxes, training—represent the single largest cost category. Many healthcare and public sector organizations have no significant physical or direct material components whatsoever (outside of facilities). For financial institutions, employee costs are the largest noninterest expense item. For airlines, they are the largest costs after equipment depreciation (even larger than fuel costs). For telecommunications companies, they are the largest costs after the physical network.

In spite of this, most companies have more system and IT resources invested in tracking office supplies and spare parts than they do in managing their critical human resources. Your company probably has more than $10 million invested in an ERP (Enterprise Resource Planning) system that tracks every single physical part or SKU (stock-keeping unit) from when it first appears on a purchase requisition, through receiving, production, and inventory, out the door, and to each customer location. And that information is often retained for years for warranty or defect recall purposes.

ERP systems can tell down to the SKU level how many left-handed widgets of each color are available right now in eleven different warehouses across the planet, but not how many synthetic chemists, C++ programmers, turbine-rated mechanics, OB-GYN nurses, or Series 7 brokers are on the payroll *anywhere*—let alone how many have between five and ten years of experience, combined with expertise in a particular industry, and reside within 200 miles of your potential client's headquarters location. This institutional legacy from the prewar industrial era should have been put to rest by the mid-1980s at the latest, but it has somehow lingered on well beyond what should have been its expiration date.

Companies such as Google, Microsoft, SAS, Amazon, eBay, and Facebook like to say that their most important assets walk out the door at 5:00 PM every day, but do they act like they really mean it? Or do they still have more invested in an ERP system that tracks copying paper and yellow highlighters than they do in an HR system designed to get the most value out of those assets? If you base your answer on what you know about the success of these companies, you'll probably guess that they *do* really mean it. So what do companies like these have that sets them apart from others in this area? The answer is workforce analytics.

WORKFORCE ANALYTICS 101

Every workforce consists of four factors: skill, numbers, time, and location. An organization's success depends on having the right number of workers with the right skill levels at the right times in the right locations, with the flexibility to make appropriate, timely changes as conditions dictate. To achieve this, the workforce needs to be managed proactively. Both a shortfall and a surplus of human capital can be costly and inefficient, and preventing such difficulties requires forecasting future workforce needs well in advance while also adopting corresponding strategies for identifying, acquiring, developing, and retaining talent.

Today's workforce is large and diverse, and it exists in a highly competitive, rapidly changing global environment. As such, the tactical and strategic management and planning of the workforce is enormously complex, which makes it perfectly suited to the application of advanced analytics—or, more specifically, workforce analytics. The workforce analytics approach can be broken down into three steps:

1. Forecast *workforce demand*, based on business expectations.
2. Predict *workforce supply*, based on history, the current workforce, and various economic factors.
3. Calculate the *workforce gap* between demand and supply, and address that gap.

We will examine these steps more closely in the context of the components that make up workforce analytics.

THE COMPONENTS OF A WORKFORCE ANALYTICS PROGRAM

In order to fully participate in strategic discussions about issues like those raised at the beginning of this chapter, HR executives need two primary types of knowledge: knowledge of business operations and knowledge of their human resources. When it comes to the business itself, HR must become fully engaged with operational personnel, markets, customers, and products and understand the business processes that support the strategies. On the human resources side, however, workforce analytics can play a key role in creating an HR organization that adds real value to strategic issues. Workforce analytics span a wide range of capabilities, but the basic components of a workforce analytics program include:

▶ *Business intelligence.* Business intelligence capabilities, including an information delivery portal and/or dashboard, get you the information you need when you need it, in your preferred format. If your organization uses scorecards, you can adapt them to align HR initiatives with broader corporate objectives, including key performance indicators (KPIs) and other metrics.

▶ *Data mining.* Data mining tools can help you identify, break down, and summarize the key business drivers affecting your workforce (e.g., voluntary terminations, age and gender distribution, and skill sets by function, geography, and pay grade). You can use data mining to estimate, at the individual employee level, the likelihood that an employee will leave voluntarily and likely causes of his departure.

▶ *Forecasting.* Forecasting software lets you analyze and predict workforce demand or workload so you can plan for the type of workforce your company will need to meet future business demands and carry out strategic objectives under various business scenarios. Forecasting can help you determine what critical roles need to be filled with the best talent in both the near and long term, given the business strategy and market conditions.

▶ *Simulation and optimization.* Simulation and optimization tools are used to evaluate alternative scenarios, such as potential future workforce profiles, so you can determine which business strategies will best align your human resources supply and demand. Using simulation and optimization, you can gain insight into how external events or factors will affect workforce demand and what the financial ramifications will be.

The benefits of investing in workforce analytics do not depend on specific industry segments, as organizations spanning public and private sectors can attest. Here is a look at some industry-specific and non-industry-specific issues where investing in workforce analytics have had a quick and clear payback. As you read these examples, keep in mind the scale involved, as most organizations in these industries employ thousands or even tens of thousands of people.

▶ *Healthcare organizations* need to forecast the various wellness, disease, and disability trends across their aging and changing clientele demographic, and then they must match those results with continually scarce clinical nursing and physician skills.

▶ *National, state, and local governments* need to match human capital with the direct needs of their constituency as well as the changing directives and dynamics of their associated executive and legislative branches.

▶ *Major energy companies* need to explore how rising energy demands and the increasing cost of finding and extracting raw materials from new sources will be affected by the significant turnover in their workforce, which is dominated by aging baby boomers—many of whom have hard-to-replace skills and training.

▶ *Financial services businesses* need to optimize the skill sets of their branch personnel and match those skills with the varying market demands across different metropolitan areas.

▶ *Global enterprises of all types* need to optimize their call center staffing, perhaps in several 24/7 call centers on different continents and in different time zones across the globe.

▶ *Companies in all industries* are employing a varied combination of offshoring, onshoring, and outsourcing of IT skills, making the management, coordination, training, recruitment, and retention of those capabilities much more challenging than when they all resided in one building at corporate headquarters.

▶ *Business systems and processes across industries* are becoming more complex, requiring extensive training that puts a premium on retaining key skill sets, not to mention key customer-engaged employees who would take valuable, hard-to-rebuild relationships with them if they left.

BUSINESS INTELLIGENCE

Now let's tackle some issues more directly, starting with the question we posed earlier—"It's 9:00 AM Monday morning; do you know where your workforce is?"—and applying business intelligence (BI). What you need is an executive dashboard tailored to the specific needs of your HR function and including:

▶ Easy-to-understand visual displays that add context to the data (data + context = BI)

▶ Summary-level data associated with goals, thresholds, or benchmarks

▶ The ability to drill down into the detail from anywhere on the dashboard

It might look something like Figure 1.

FIGURE 1. HUMAN RESOURCES DASHBOARD. (SEE WWW.

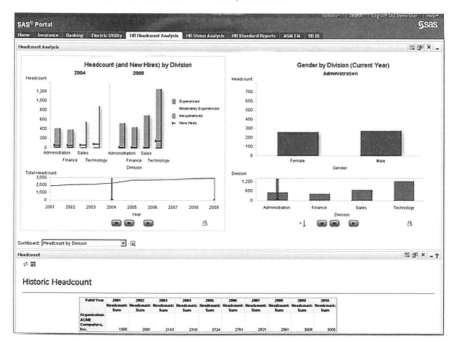

Information Management

The result is an easy-to-understand visualization of your workforce. All that visual data didn't just appear magically, however. The bulk of any significant IT project lies at the front end with information management—the collection, extraction, translation, and loading of the data in such a way that ensures data quality. This means collecting and consolidating human resources data from the myriad systems, subsystems, and geographies in which they reside, similar to the way your finance department collects and consolidates cost and revenue data for the monthly forecast.

Yet even after this effort is complete, the information is still not ready for consumption. Basic employee data residing on local payroll systems may still need to be matched with other types of data—e.g., training and education, skills and certifications, promotion history and succession planning, pay grades and career paths, performance evaluations—each of which may be stored in a separate corporate or department file. Getting this data quality aspect right, however, will have a huge payback in the long run, as we shall see shortly.

Context

The next step in the business intelligence process is providing context. Whether it's financial or employee data, raw numbers provide only part of the story. The rest comes from targets, budgets, benchmarks, thresholds, goals, objectives, metrics, and measures. You might say that the purpose of the dashboard is to interpret the numbers within the appropriate context, so that when you see the numbers, they are telling you a story: Are we ahead, behind, or on target? Are we too high or too low compared with budget/forecast/last year/year-end/industry benchmarks/strategic objectives? Is the story best told as a trend? A percentage? An all-or-nothing win/lose proposition? Or perhaps a step-function, a cluster diagram, a bar or pie chart, or a histogram? The story the data tells depends heavily on which context is used.

Despite the apparent simplicity—just raw data, some context, and some basic arithmetic operators (i.e., addition and division)—having this information readily available is a major leap for most organizations: It *is* 9:00 AM on Monday morning, and you *do* know where your workforce is. Now you are ready for the next step—going beyond BI.

DATA MINING

Data mining is the process of selecting, exploring, and modeling large quantities of data to discover previously unknown patterns or relationships, with the goal of obtaining a clear and useful understanding of the information hidden in the data. Applying a data mining methodology means following a specific process that involves translating a business need (e.g., increasing revenue, cutting costs, or accelerating cash flow) into a properly defined problem statement. You then apply statistical techniques to the appropriate data in order to gain insight that you can use to inform strategic decisions and obtain desired results.

In the context of workforce analytics, data mining is where the story gets interesting, including things such as:

▶ Age, gender, and race distributions. A graphic example of the gender mix by age, often called a population pyramid by demographers, can be seen in Figure 2.

FIGURE 2. AGE/GENDER DISTRIBUTION.

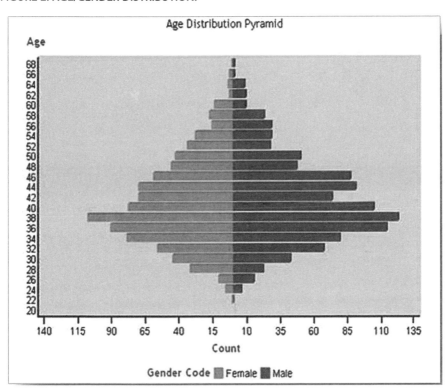

▶ Reasons given for voluntary terminations (e.g., retirement, better offer, promotion).

▶ Identifying other factors associated with voluntary terminations (e.g., last pay increase, position in salary level, training, length of service, time in current position), Figure 3 shows an example of the impact of these factors on voluntary attrition.

▶ Skill sets, clusters of skill sets, competencies, combinations of skill sets, experience, education, industry, and location

FIGURE 3. ANALYSIS OF THE IMPACT OF VARIOUS FACTORS ON VOLUNTARY ATTRITION.

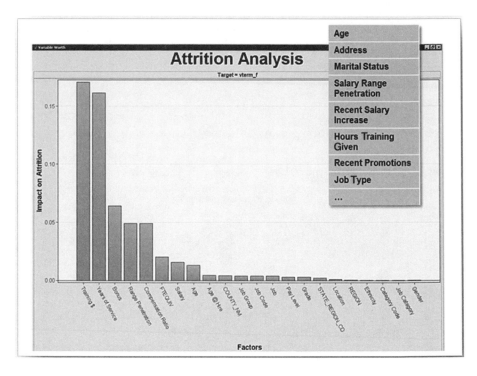

▶ Attributes of high achievers and high potential candidates

▶ Training, education, and certifications by job classification or management level

▶ Pay grades and cost-of-living adjustments across locations, geographies, and subsidiaries

▶ Most effective recruiting channels

▶ Productivity comparisons between similar departments, branches, regions, or subsidiaries, or between in-house and outsourced operations

Data mining techniques range from intuitive to reasonably sophisticated, but HR executives should not be intimidated by their seemingly daunting nature regardless of how sophisticated the techniques are—that's what software is for. No, the critical issue in any data mining venture is not statistical. Just as in our earlier business intelligence example, the critical issue is information management, and the success of a data mining venture—in HR or anywhere else—is the accessibility and quality of the underlying data. From that solid foundation, data mining software can sort and select for significant attributes, correlations, and causal relationships, then present the information in a readily consumable visual format, whether that be cluster graphs, trend lines, pie charts, tables, or histograms. (See Figure 4 for an example of a visual format of presenting information.)

After the data is gathered, context is added, and analytics are applied both by and for the business users, the resulting information can be put to use in a number of additional ways. Take, for example, the analysis described earlier to determine the causes and likelihood of employee attrition. Applying a model to predict the causes and drivers of voluntary termination can help you anticipate—and take measures to prevent—the departure of top talent. You can predict attrition by analyzing many years of historical data on employee movements and numerous other factors that can have an impact on an employee's desire to leave.

Some analytic techniques, such as forecasting, are best applied to groups of individuals. Other techniques, such as creating a "likelihood-to-leave" score (similar to the approach banks use to calculate individual customer credit scores), can be applied quite well on an employee-by-employee basis. By scoring the likelihood of each individual employee leaving, supplementing that information with a performance evaluation, and then clearly identifying the likely causes of attrition, managers can gain enough insight to take proactive measures—perhaps by adjusting working conditions—to prevent the departure of key employees! Imagine what a beneficial impact you could have on hiring and training costs, and loss of domain knowledge, by adopting a proactive approach with the information shown in Figure 5 at your disposal.

FIGURE 4. VOLUNTARY TERMINATION RISK ANALYSIS.

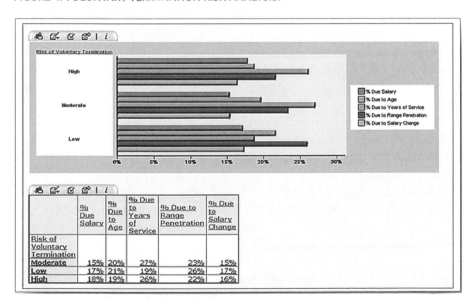

Risk of Voluntary Termination	% Due Salary	% Due to Age	% Due to Years of Service	% Due to Range Penetration	% Due to Salary Change
Moderate	15%	20%	27%	23%	15%
Low	17%	21%	19%	26%	17%
High	18%	19%	26%	22%	16%

FIGURE 5. EMPLOYEE ATTRITION SCORECARD.

Employee ID	Employee Name	Job Class	Department	LTL Score	Performance Score		Drivers
000912	Émile Bouchard	A37	Finance	95%	9.50	●	Bonus, Training, YOS
000794	Pierre Bouchard	B53	Sales	94%	9.40	●	Bonus, SRP, YOS
000786	Billy Boucher	A15	Marketing	94%	9.40	●	YOS, SRP
000534	Frank Boucher	A62	Sales	92%	9.40	●	SRP, Training, Location
000846	Georges Boucher	B85	Sales	91%	9.30	●	Bonus, Training, YOS
000154	Philippe Boucher	A11	Production	90%	9.20	●	Bonus, Training, YOS
000698	Robert Boucher	A69	Sales	89%	9.10	●	Bonus, Training, YOS
000661	Leo Bourgeault	B12	Finance	88%	9.09	●	Bonus, Training, YOS
000469	Bob Bourne	A36	Sales	87%	9.03	●	Bonus, Training, YOS
000386	Phil Bourque	A6	Sales	86%	8.96	●	Bonus, SRP, YOS
000782	Ray Bourque	B67	Sales	85%	8.90	◐	YOS, SRP
000327	Paul Boutilier	A47	Production	84%	8.84	◐	SRP, Training, Location
000782	Johnny Bower	A1	Finance	83%	8.78	◐	Bonus, Training, YOS
000256	Ralph Bowman	B48	Sales	82%	8.72	◐	Bonus, SRP, YOS
000446	Scotty Bowman	A20	Marketing	81%	8.66	◐	YOS, SRP
000108	Stan Bowman	A64	Sales	80%	8.60	◐	SRP, Training, Location
000603	Nick Boynton	B31	Sales	79%	8.54	◐	Bonus, Training, YOS
000878	Doug Brennan	A74	Production	78%	8.48	◐	Bonus, SRP, YOS
000892	John Brenneman	A38	Sales	77%	8.42	◐	YOS, SRP
000975	Tim Brent	B84	Finance	76%	8.36	◑	SRP, Training, Location
000566	Carl Brewer	A82	Sales	75%	8.30	◑	Bonus, Training, YOS
000376	Frank Brimsek	A23	Sales	74%	8.24	◑	Bonus, SRP, YOS
000206	Rod Brind'Amour	B14	Sales	73%	8.18	◑	YOS, SRP
000410	Patrice Brisebois	A85	Production	72%	8.11	◑	SRP, Training, Location
000698	Punch Broadbent	A9	Finance	71%	8.05	◑	Bonus, Training, YOS
000231	Turk Broda	B17	Sales	70%	7.99	●	Bonus, SRP, YOS
000822	Connie Broden	A39	Marketing	69%	7.93	●	YOS, SRP
000789	Martin Brodeur	A78	Sales	68%	7.87	●	SRP, Training, Location

HIGH-PERFORMANCE FORECASTING

Forecasting is the one area where the recent advances in technology have enabled sophisticated statistical techniques to be packaged in business-user-friendly, highly visual, wizard-driven applications that run in seconds rather than hours (*that's* high performance!). If you view the essential workforce planning approach as forecasting demand, predicting supply, and addressing the gap between the two, then high-performance forecasting is where you should turn first.

High-performance forecasting enables you to *better understand workforce demand* by analyzing the work-to-workforce relationship. Workforce analytics help you better assign skills, thus increasing the efficacy, quality, and efficiency of the workforce. You develop forecasting models to accurately predict workforce demand given demographics and business projections for hundreds of skill sets and geographies. Workforce analytics help you automate the complex processes of forecasting a large volume of data across multiple dimensions by finding the patterns and proposing the best-fit model.

This is where recent advancements in state-of-the-art forecasting technology really come to the aid of the business user. After analyzing the historical input data, the software automatically chooses the most appropriate model from an extensive model repository, optimizes model parameters, and then runs the forecast at the employee/cost center/job code level for hundreds of thousands of employees in mere seconds. And to top it all off, it's all wizard-driven, which means you don't have to be an analytics wizard yourself in order to use it.

To look at state of the art from another angle, consider this: Approximately 80 percent of all time series data can be forecasted using automated techniques, and the tools are advanced enough to analyze the historical data and extract the best-fit model using automated approaches. Around 10 percent of the data cannot be forecasted at all by any technique or approach, generally because it is completely random, and another 10 percent lies between those two extremes, requiring the assistance of statistics professionals—an unlikely state of affairs for workforce data.

WORKFORCE SIMULATION

The next step is to project the current workforce into the future via simulation. Simulation is the process of building or designing a behavioral model of a specific real-world system, often with a significant random component. The simulation model tracks changes in individual profiles over time (i.e., each resource has a profile that can include many attributes, such as competencies, job classification, salary level, age, gender, race, location, and educational level), and integrates these profiles with organizational factors such as recruitment policies, attraction and retention programs, attrition, and employee movement within the organization.

Many real-world systems include not only complicated mathematical and logical relationships, but also a significant random component. For example, one can model and simulate a manufacturing process by incorporating the relationships among production times, inventory lead times, demands, breakdowns and changes in the workforce, including the random nature of each factor. For such systems, a simulation model can numerically generate data to cultivate a better understanding of the behavior of the system.

By making virtual changes to any factor in the model, one can estimate the impacts of the changes and analyze the consequences of different scenarios in financial planning, marketing, and workforce strategies.

Incorporating uncertainty into the model will make analyzing the output from simulations more difficult, requiring advanced statistical methods to formulate valid conclusions about the behavior of the system under such conditions.

The advantage of simulation is, of course, that it gives decision makers the ability to evaluate different scenarios; however, there are significant limitations to attempting such an exercise manually, since only a fraction of the entire range of options could be assessed. This would make the goal of identifying and evaluating the best option—or even a few good ones—practically impossible. Clearly, a more disciplined approach is needed. Identifying best options falls within the domain of optimization, which we will examine after calculating the workforce gap.

FIGURE 6. WORKFORCE GAP.

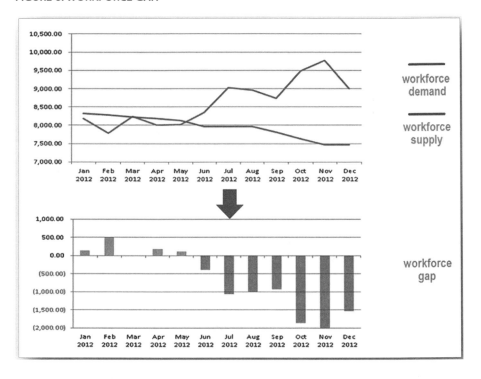

CALCULATING THE WORKFORCE GAP

The difference between workforce demand and supply is the workforce gap, as depicted in Figure 6.

High-performance forecasting enables the HR executive to *anticipate potential workforce gaps* and take proactive steps to *promote workforce optimization*. By merging workforce supply and demand information into one integrated planning offering, you can identify and anticipate potential workforce gaps by geographies and skill sets, then propose actions (hiring, training, relocations, etc.) to alter the undesirable situation before it becomes reality.

The information derived from applying advanced analytics (data mining, forecasting, and optimization) must be brought together in a coherent planning engine that business users can interact with easily. Because of the multidimensional nature of the data, using office automation software such as spreadsheets to do this can lead to an unsecure, complicated, and error-prone system that is difficult to maintain—as has been proven time and time again in organizations spanning all industries.

It is also important to add financial data, such as standard costs, to the planning engine in order to accurately predict what financial impacts any workforce

FIGURE 7. DETAILED WORKFORCE GAP ANALYSIS.

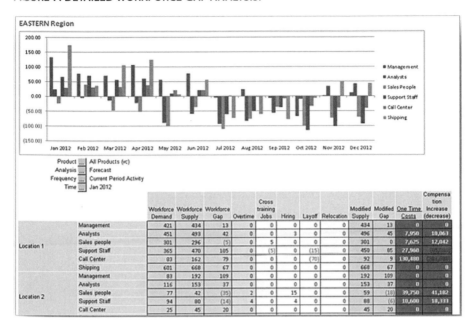

planning scenarios may have. The planning engine should be tightly linked to both HR and the financial systems to avoid any lag times caused by slow turnaround in the finance department that would delay getting results from the scenarios you run.

Don't let the simplicity of the workforce gap graph shown in Figure 6 fool you; there is a lot more analytic power behind the scenes than just the two supply and demand trend lines that you see there. In recent years, technology and analytics have progressed in their behind-the-scenes contributions to accuracy and effectiveness. Shown in Figure 7 is a detailed regional breakdown of required position categories by month.

Identifying the gap at this level of detail is most of the battle but not all of the value. There's more than one way to bridge a gap, and a scenario planning approach (see Figure 8) allows you to develop, compare, contrast, and evaluate the various roads that may lead to your goal. All of this harkens back to the point made at the very beginning of this chapter: Workforce analytics can give you, the HR executive, the tools you need to sit across from business unit operations managers and add value to ongoing strategy discussions. They want analysis and options, recommendations, and risk assessments—proactive engagement on your part. While workforce analytics isn't the whole answer, it is a significant part of it.

FIGURE 8. WORKFORCE SCENARIO ANALYSIS.

WORKFORCE ANALYSIS - GLOBAL 2012 PREDICTIONS SCENARIOS SUMMARY	SCENARIO 1 No Hiring	SCENARIO 2 No Layoffs	SCENARIO 3 Balanced
Forecasted Revenue	659,760,078	659,760,078	659,760,078
Prediction - Workforce Supply - **Initial**	93%	93%	93%
Re-Forecasted Revenue (based on initial Supply)	612,109,986	612,109,986	612,109,986
Prediction - Workforce Supply - **Modified**	95%	102%	97%
	626,772,074	659,760,078	637,822,540

	SCENARIO 1	SCENARIO 2	SCENARIO 3
Total Cost of Workforce Movement:	4,895,685	5,754,520	4,777,085
Increase (Decrease) in Workforce Compensation	6,211,546	37,895,632	14,052,624
TOTAL FINANCIAL IMPACT: (no regard to business demand being met)	11,107,231	43,650,152	18,829,709
Forecasted Increase (Decrease) in Revenue	14,662,088	47,650,092	25,712,554
NET ROI	3,554,857	3,999,940	6,882,845

WORKFORCE OPTIMIZATION

We are nearing the end of our journey through workforce analytics. After introducing and discussing the uses and benefits of business intelligence, data mining (*What happened?*), forecasting (*What* will *happen?*), and simulation (*What* could *happen?*), we are left with one remaining analytical powerhouse, perhaps the strongest contributor to gaining a competitive advantage: optimization (*What is* the best *that could happen?*).

Simply put, optimization is the process of choosing the permissible actions that will result in the best outcome given certain constraints. This is the basic concept, no matter how complex the means by which optimization is implemented. Optimization helps determine the best combination of resource profiles within a given set of constraints, such as how to allocate merit increases to maintain the best internal and external pay equity, or how to best distribute the workforce to achieve a certain performance level, cost, and geographic spread. Advanced mathematical optimization can support strategic and tactical decision making for

FIGURE 9. 24/7 CALL CENTER OPTIMIZATION.

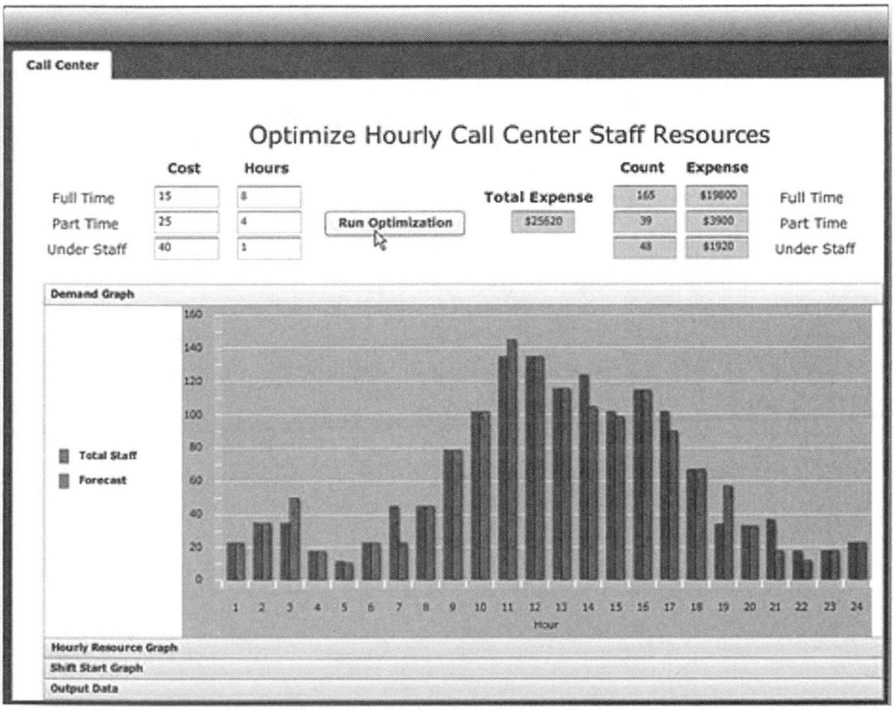

organizations with a large, complex workforce. (See Figure 9 for an example of such optimization.)

SCORECARDS

The analytical journey has now come full circle with a return to BI, where there is still the matter of ensuring that all of these insights and tactical actions agree and align with top-level corporate strategy. Whether your organization uses the balanced scorecard approach or one of your own designs, the HR executive is responsible for aligning and managing the organization's workforce objectives in accordance with its other strategic goals, such as those for revenue, customer satisfaction, quality, innovation, or time-to-market. Human capital strategy maps and HR scorecards (see Figure 10) can help you accomplish this by measuring, monitoring, and managing workforce plans in support of organizational goals, including:

► How managing talent, and the entire workforce, supports organizational goals

FIGURE 10. TALENT SCORECARD.

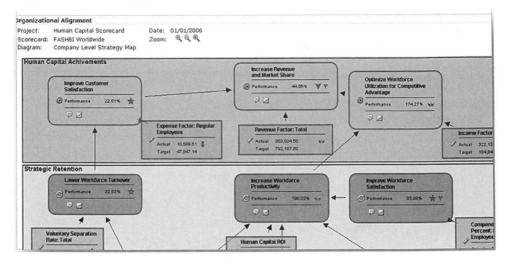

> Setting and viewing business strategy and seeing cause-and-effect relation-ships and leading and lagging indicators
> Engaging in a larger enterprise approach to performance management

WORKFORCE ANALYTICS IN PRACTICE

There's an old saying: In theory, there is no difference between theory and practice. But in practice, there is. So what have we at SAS learned about putting workforce analytics into practice? Here is a brief survey of use cases and objectives achieved by just some of SAS's workforce analytics clients:

☐ U.S. Air Force Personnel Center (which oversees 400,000 active-duty U.S. Air Force members and 185,000 civilian employees)
  • A web-enabled personnel data system delivers lifecycle demographic data (such as promotions, compensation, benefits, and retirements) to author-ized users worldwide.

☐ Finmeccanica (a global aerospace, defense, and transportation holding company headquartered in Italy, with 100 companies and 70,000 employees)
  • An intuitive HR dashboard provides quick and easy access to KPIs and key human resources data across the organization, helping it gain better in-depth knowledge of the company's situation and significantly reduce deci-sion times.

☐ Regione Umbria (a public agency in central Italy with 11,000 healthcare workers)
  • Implemented a solution that provides an integrated, strategic view of human resources—including payroll, attendance, personnel data, and sub-

contracts—that has helped lower labor costs, enabled strategic data control, and provided efficient personnel management.

☐ Public Service Commission (an independent agency and Canada's largest employer)

- Uses a customized online reporting application that analyzes trend and demographic data for every position, combined with twenty years of historical data.

☐ A major American airline

- Saves millions in overstaffing costs by better matching staff by skill with locations/airports and routes served.

☐ A healthcare management service provider

- Has cut from weeks to hours the amount of time it takes to forecast the labor needs of more than twenty hospitals down to the specific clinical skill set required.

☐ A U.S. federal organization

- Plans workforce demand for more than 100,000 employees and uses workforce analytics to identify staffing shortages and manage across workforce trends, including the increased diversification of the American population, changing expectations of a multigenerational workforce, and shortages of available skilled labor.

☐ A leading European energy company

- Uses workforce analytics to optimize and manage the allocation of personnel (150,000+) to Individual projects.

☐ A European federal organization

- Uses workforce analytics to gain process efficiency by monitoring HR behavior with a special focus on staffing.

CASE STUDY: North Carolina Office of State Personnel

Situation

The state must meet the needs of a growing population in the face of an impending state worker shortage. Of 90,000 current employees, more than 58 percent are baby boomers; 10 percent are currently eligible to retire, and that number will jump to 38 percent by 2015. The Office of State Personnel (OSP) needed to forecast the eligible supply of candidates to fill openings for an anticipated state worker shortage.

Solution

SAS provided the OSP with a solution that includes:

- A single repository (North Carolina Workforce Outlook and Retirement Knowledge System, or NC WORKS), which combines multiple workforce data sources
- Advanced business analytics that let the state predict employee turnover and the availability of qualified candidates needed to fill openings

Results

- Overall performance has improved since NC WORKS provides the workforce intelligence needed to proactively respond to changing workforce demographics.
- Agencies can access predefined and ad hoc analysis, forecasts, and predictions of human capital needs to support strategic decision making for current and future talent needs.

CLOSING THOUGHTS ON WORKFORCE ANALYTICS

With workforce analytics, you can analyze what *has* happened, forecast what *will* happen, explore what *could* happen, determine the *best* that can happen, and select and execute the next best action to take. But in the end, any business proposition worth its salt has to pass the "so what" test: *"Yeah, so what if I do all this? What will I gain?"*

For starters, you'll get answers to questions like those raised at the beginning of the chapter. You will gain insight. You will be able to anticipate opportunity. You will be empowered to take action. And you will get tangible results. But perhaps the biggest net gain from workforce analytics is its ability to put the HR executive in a position to offer proactive business advice to the executive board as an effective partner to business unit general managers—one who adds value to the strategic decisions that can make or break an organization.

Leo Sadovy handles marketing for Performance Management at SAS. Before joining SAS, he spent seven years as VP of Finance for Business Operations for a North American division of Fujitsu. During his years at Fujitsu, Leo developed and implemented the ROI model and processes used in all internal investment decisions. Prior to Fujitsu, Leo was eight years at DEC, and also at Spectra-Physics and General Dynamics . He has an MBA in finance and a bachelor's in marketing.

Christian Haxholdt works in the Professional Services and Delivery, Global Forecasting Solutions Practice at SAS. Before joining SAS, he spent three years with Arthur Andersen Business Consulting and two years with Deloitte, and was a professor at the Copenhagen Business School, Department of Statistics. He has been a visiting professor at George Washington University, Massachusetts Institute of Technology, and University of Wisconsin. Christian holds an M.A. in management sciences and a Ph.D. in mathematical modeling.

Predicting Analytics

Amit B. Mohindra and J. Allan Brown

INTRODUCTION

THE IMPORTANCE OF MEASUREMENT and analytics in the practice of human resources has grown apace since Jac Fitz-enz's pioneering work in the 1970s. Further contributions have been made over the years by academics, consultants, and HR practitioners. The literature now includes numerous articles that recount how companies are beginning to reap a competitive advantage through the adroit use of human resources data, analysis, and insight. There is also a handful of recent books that serve to provide a framework for the application of human capital analytics.

Human capital analytics has evolved with the growth in sophistication and importance of the HR function.

Through the 1980s, HR was largely an administrative function (called personnel), and measurements were transaction-based and largely unremarkable—for example, how many people were hired last month or how many performance review forms have been submitted. These were descriptive measures and primarily backward looking. Since HR was not considered a strategic function at the time, there was no urge to project measures forward or to consider alternative scenarios. The focus—as Fitz-enz often recounts—was on building a conceptual measurement framework and getting HR itself to take metrics seriously.

As business conditions changed in the 1990s and resources were stretched in economic downturns, HR turned inward to focus on measuring its cost and efficiency and comparing these with industry benchmarks to which it aspired. As companies competed in the war for talent, the complexity and vitality of human resources—by now called *human capital*—became apparent. Thinking of the workforce as an asset rather than a cost implied the connection between human capital activities and business performance. It became incumbent upon HR to characterize and understand this asset using approaches established to manage other corporate assets. HR co-opted accounting terms and frameworks to ascribe a return on investment in HR programs and in the HR function itself.

The 2000s saw the emergence of human capital analytics, defined more specifically as the use of data, analysis, and systematic reasoning to make human capital decisions. HR data were more readily available with the emergence of ERPs and the associated move toward data warehouses; business intelligence software could as easily be applied to HR data; and business conditions required further optimization of companies' investment in human capital. According to one head of HR at the time, "Analytics is the next evolution. If HR wants a seat at the table, analytics is going to become table stakes. If you can't talk in your business leaders' language, you won't be invited into the conversation."[1]

The publication of the first "handbook" of HR analytics[2] signaled the arrival of analytics on the broader HR stage. All of a sudden conferences devoted entirely to human capital analytics were organized, and companies began to establish analytics teams and departments within their HR functions. It is now rare to encounter an HR department that does not apply at least some sort of quantitative approach to its operations or to meet an HR practitioner who is not intrigued by the latest application of human capital analytics. The quantitative and visual output of current HR analytics teams is a far cry from the transactional HR reports of a couple of decades ago.

By all accounts, the next big thing is *predictive* human capital analytics.

Human capital analytics has progressed in sophistication. Evidence is increasingly required to support decisions about the attraction, motivation, and retention of talent. In leading analytical companies, data have become invaluable, disparate claims are framed as hypotheses, models are built to test the hypotheses, and statistics are used unabashedly. Analytics allows all factors—employee attributes, operational parameters, and business results—to be examined and correlated. Data from employee engagement surveys provided the missing link of employee mindset and attitudes, enabling connections to be made between HR investment, employee perceptions, and business outcomes.

In the last few years, there has been an interest and growing demand for "predictive" human capital analytics along the same lines as predictive analytics conducted elsewhere in the business. For example, the marketing department constructs models to forecast revenue in different scenarios, based on integrated data on customers and their behavior, external economic indicators, and actual purchasing outcomes. The increasing amounts of data on consumer behavior available via web-based transactions and social media activities allow for richer predictive models. Business leaders expect these sorts of models from their organizations, are increasingly familiar with the models' premises, and employ such models in strategic decision making.

It does not take a huge leap of imagination on the part of HR to wonder about the possibility of playing in this arena. Jac Fitz-enz's most recent book challenges HR to do just this.[3] Presentations and comments at HR conferences as well as recent human capital measurement and business analytics group discussions on LinkedIn all hint at this new frontier for HR. Indeed, once companies have a handle on their employee data and connect it to other enterprise information and business performance, the next logical step is to use the implicit models to make predictions about human capital as well as business outcomes. The ability to look ahead and "place bets" on human capital investment and practices with some degree of confidence in their effect on business outcomes is a powerful and attractive proposition. More and more companies will attempt to harness this capability as they progress along the human capital analytics continuum (Figure 1).

FIGURE 1. THE HUMAN CAPITAL ANALYTICS CONTINUUM.

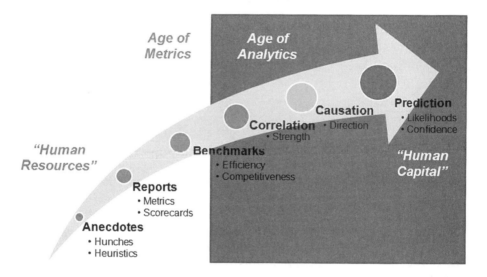

PREDICTIVE ANALYTICS

Wikipedia defines predictive analytics very broadly as an endeavor "encompassing a variety of statistical techniques from modeling, machine learning, data mining, and game theory that analyze current and historical facts to make predictions about future events."

Make predictions about future events! It's no wonder then that HR professionals, being mortal, are interested in predictive analytics. Instead of just reporting what has happened to employee longevity, engagement, performance, turnover, or any other human capital variable, you can now predict what will happen next. What is often lost in the fervor, however, is how predictive analytics is actually constructed—using statistics, data mining, and game theory. It is worth summarizing these three key approaches to predictive analytics.

Statistics

Statistics is a branch of mathematics that is concerned with the collection and study of data. One aspect of statistics that is well known within HR is descriptive statistics—measures that describe a set of data. These include measures of central tendency (for example, average and median) and dispersion (for example, variance and standard deviation). Predictive analytics necessitates the use of another aspect of statistics—inferential statistics. Inferential statistics allows for modeling the randomness or uncertainty underlying a set of data with a view to drawing inferences—that is, predictions. Statistical models, therefore, are at the heart of predictive analytics.

Regression Models. Statistical models include simple correlations and regression analyses of various types and a wide variety of other techniques. Most HR practitioners are familiar with correlations and linear regression involving two variables. Relationships between two variables are convenient to depict via a scatter plot and to model via a regression line. It is easy to represent the correlation—either visually or in terms of the regression's R-squared (also known as the coefficient of determination) value. The following figures, 3 and 4, represent a statistical model that tries to capture the relationship between years of experience and compensation. The first model is linear; the second model is nonlinear—it attempts to capture the slowdown in compensation with increasing years of experience. The equations are used to predict compensation, given years of experience.

FIGURE 2. A STATISTICAL MODEL THAT TRIES TO CAPTURE THE RELATIONSHIP BETWEEN YEARS OF EXPERIENCE AND COMPENSATION—LINEAR.

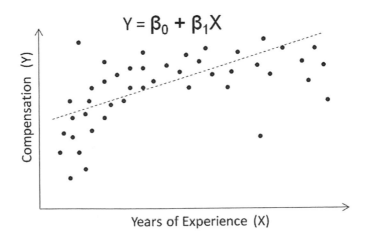

$$Y = \beta_0 + \beta_1 X$$

FIGURE 3. A STATISTICAL MODEL THAT TRIES TO CAPTURE THE RELATIONSHIP BETWEEN YEARS OF EXPERIENCE AND COMPENSATION—NONLINEAR.

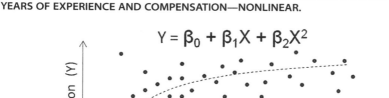

$$Y = \beta_0 + \beta_1 X + \beta_2 X^2$$

Compensation (Y)

Years of Experience (X)

However, the real world involves multiple variables (compensation is affected by many things, not just years of experience) and complex, nonlinear relationships. These are best modeled using multiple regression. However, multiple regression, especially nonlinear multiple regression, is not widely used in HR. One reason is that interpreting and explaining the outputs and statistical significance of the results often presents a challenge, since there is no visual analog of a scatter plot or regression line.

Logistic Regression. A very special type of multiple regression—logistic regression—is seldom used in HR even though it is arguably one of the most powerful weapons in the predictive human capital analytics armory. Logistic regression allows for a dichotomous dependent variable (i.e., a variable that has only two possible values), and its results are easily characterized as probabilities or odds that allow for easy and direct interpretations in a predictive model.

HR-related variables are often dichotomous or categorical i.e., having discrete rather than continuous values. People either participate in a program or not; they either receive a salary increase or not; they are either male or female; etc. They can be characterized as one of five race/ethnicity categories; as having four levels of education; as being rated high, solid, low or nonperformer; etc. Logistic regression can combine dichotomous, categorical, and continuous variables (e.g., tenure in the company) into powerful models.

Logistic regression analyses have been used to predict turnover and success. These traditional models' predictive power can be enhanced by incorporating data from engagement surveys and learning program participation, among other things. With adequate individual profile information, it is possible to predict the nature of a candidate's fit with the department or company and the quality and effectiveness of teams in which employees participate.

Consider a logistic regression attempting to explain what drives turnover. Avoiding the complexities of modeling for the moment, let's take a look at the output of such a model. In Figure 4, the regression coefficients are reported as likelihood ratios—the impact of each variable (in isolation, controlling for all other variables in the model) on turnover in terms of the contribution to the odds of turnover. Only a few variables are shown; the model can be enriched by including geography and business unit to capture variations across the company. The interpretation of each likelihood ratio is described. Note that the model can include multiple years of data; the more data, the more robust the model.

FIGURE 4. OUTPUT OF A LOGISTIC REGRESSION ATTEMPTING TO EXPLAIN WHAT DRIVES TURNOVER.

Factor	Likelihood Ratio	
Experience	1.02	Each additional year of experience has no impact on likelihood of exit, *all else equal.*
Graduate Degree	1.25	
...		
Female	1.82	Women are 82% more likely to exit, *all else equal.*
Minority	0.95	
Top Performer	0.75	Top performers are 25% less likely to exit, *all else equal.*
<Business Unit>	...	
<Geography>	...	

Survival Analysis. Turnover gets much attention in HR, yet few companies employ survival analysis to model turnover. Survival analysis is used in a number of fields. Engineers refer to it as *reliability analysis* (where they would predict, for example, when a component would likely fail), and economists refer to it as *duration analysis* (where they would predict, for example, the duration of unemployment spells). It can be used in HR to predict tenure in a job or longevity with a company. Data needs for survival models are very modest; all you need is a start date (for everyone) and an end date (for those who have terminated), and the output is the probability that someone will terminate at any point in time. You can add covariates—i.e., variables that you think impact a person's decision to resign—and build a more complex model that conditions the probability on these factors.

The mathematics underlying the model is quite complicated, but most statistical packages produce tabular and graphical output for survival models. Another variant of the model allows for "tenure tables" along the lines of demographers' life tables that insurers use for pricing life insurance. The key point is that the probability of an employee exiting the organization at time X is conditional on the probability that they have not terminated until time X—just as the probability

FIGURE 5. WHAT CAUSES THE SPIKE IN PROBABILITY OF EXIT FOR WOMEN AFTER THREE YEARS OF SERVICE?

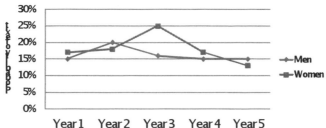

that a person will die at age Y is conditional on the probability that they have survived until age Y.

Markov Models. HR practitioners often have to determine the strength of the leadership bench or the overall size and shape of a "pyramidal" organization. These kinds of population dynamics are best analyzed using what are known as Markov models. For example, Ward et al. include an application of Markov analysis in forecasting human resource requirements.[4] In general, Markov analysis is associated with situations in which there are a number of "states," there are known probabilities of moving from one "state" to another, and you are interested in what happens over time.

Think of the states as levels within an organization. In financial services organizations, levels (from junior to senior) could be analyst, associate, vice president, senior vice president, and managing director. Movement into states, between states, and out of states represents hiring, transfers, or promotions and terminations. You can then apply Markov analysis to predict the shape and size of the organization over time. You can plug in historical rates of hiring, transfers, promotion, and termination and then model what happens to the people in the organization as they move into, up, or out of the career ladder.

Markov models have been used for workforce planning since the days of "manpower planning" and may come back in vogue. Again, the underlying mathematics is complicated, the model requires certain restrictive assumptions in order for the math to work, and you need reliable historical data. An example of the successful use of a Markov model in a commercial setting occurred in 1999 when one of the authors employed a Markov model to adjust the size and shape of a global financial services firm's investment banking division. The model enabled the division to control headcount moves in anticipation of changes in the underwriting, securities, and mergers and acquisitions (M&A) market and competitors' hiring strategies.

Statistical models, useful though they may be in making predictions, are demanding tools. They need to be understood thoroughly in order to be applied appropriately. Their results need to be considered very carefully, and one must not fall into the trap of assuming that there is a causal relationship when there is a correlation among variables. The results also need to be qualified in terms of whether the model explains the data—i.e., whether there is a good fit between what the model predicts and actual outcomes—and whether the results are statistically significant. Last but not least, you need rich data to compute complex models. These data have to be relevant, accurate, and complete. They can be compiled manually from forms or extracted from the HRIS system, or even better, from an enterprise data warehouse that contains HR, financial, and operational data that have been "scrubbed" for use in developing metrics and analytics.

Data Mining

Data mining is considered by some as an alternative to statistical modeling for the purposes of prediction. It refers to the process of looking at vast amounts of data and identifying strong patterns. These patterns can then be used to make predictions. Economists are typically disdainful of data mining; they prefer to construct a model, test its validity using real-world data, and then either refine the model or discard it and start anew. The better the model and the better the data, the better the predictive power. Data miners trawl through real-world data, looking at variables in all sorts of combinations to extract a reliable relationship that is strong enough to warrant a prediction. Data mining has acquired a wide following through its discoveries using sophisticated statistical software and large quantities of data—e.g., customer behavior based on web activity. The important thing is to establish a strong enough relationship among variables that forms the basis for predicting a value for one variable based on the value(s) of the other variable(s). There are a wide variety of data mining techniques, each of which is suited to a particular situation or need.

Game Theory

Game theory is the science of strategy and, generally speaking, deals with "strategic" situations that are characterized by five elements:[5]

1. Strategy becomes necessary when your actions affect others' well-being and their actions affect your well-being. If there were only one firm in the world, it would not need to engage in strategy. The first element of strategy is the notion of *players*—people or entities who interact and whose actions have consequences for each other.

2. Strategy becomes relevant when there is *competition* among the players. The players are rivals in some sense or another. Players are trying to outdo their

adversary, who is trying to do the same to them. It is important to keep in mind that strategy allows room for cooperation and collaboration as well.

3. Strategy becomes interesting when there are *choices* and those choices involve *trade-offs*. It's worth remembering that economics is all about choice—allocating scarce resources among competing ends.

4. Strategy becomes complex when there is *uncertainty*. Players don't know what the other player or players want or what they will do. There may be uncertainty about the state of nature—will it rain today? Will interest rates be high? Will unemployment be low?

5. Connected to the element of uncertainty is the notion of a future, or in other words, a *time horizon* or time frame. Your actions will likely be different if you are going to be in business for just one fiscal year or in perpetuity.

What does all this have to do with predictive analytics? When you need to model the behavior of an individual (say, an employee in the situation of a performance management discussion with a manager) or a group of individuals (say, workers intent on unionizing) to predict how they will behave in response to a situation or an offer, it is often useful to turn to game theory. When the situation is properly characterized in terms of all the elements at play, game theory provides a range of possible solutions. Some of the solutions are win-win and some are not. By addressing the right items, it is possible to move toward more preferable solutions.

PROMISE AND PERILS OF PREDICTIVE HUMAN CAPITAL ANALYTICS

Predictive human capital analytics fits right into the HR function's need to be strategic and to be a recognized business partner. Successfully deploying predictive human capital analytics arms HR with confidence and credibility in a number of ways. HR models can incorporate financial, operational, and external market data, allowing HR to offer a more integrated view of the enterprise than other functions (arguably, finance could do the same, but let's assume for now that HR has a competitive advantage with respect to understanding HR data). With the help of predictive analytics, HR can make more than just educated guesses about a host of business outcomes. Assuming a reasonable understanding of business and industry conditions, HR can comfortably participate in strategy and planning.

Becoming familiar with the methods and application of predictive analytics requires a way of thinking that lends itself to a strategic, enterprise-wide view of the world. You need to understand the data that you are using, particularly the data that reside outside HR's purview in the finance, strategy, and operations departments. Detailed knowledge of this information and how it ties together will arm HR leaders with the confidence and credibility to go "toe-to-toe" with other leaders during business discussions. On the flip side, understanding the limitations of the data (since you know how they are collected, cleaned, and maintained) will give you a balanced perspective to differentiate between *bona fide* arguments, educated guesses, wild gambles, dissembling, and blatant falsehoods. Predictive analytics models require a "systems" way of thinking: What are all the factors involved? What are all the connections both internal and external? What are the feedback mechanisms at play? What are the current and future impacts? And so forth.

HR owns a rich data set—information on applicants, new hires, employees, and ex-employees. The information includes personal characteristics, employment history, pay and performance histories, promotion and other organizational move histories, learning interventions and outcomes, engagement scores and histories, and the like. Armed with this information and the appropriate statistical models, HR can get a complete grasp of what works and what doesn't with respect to recruitment, motivation, compensation, engagement, and retention by examining cross-correlations (i.e., considering all factors at once, not just a single variable) and dynamics over time.

It would be possible to make predictions on any or all of the following. Note that the predictions are stated in terms of likelihoods (i.e., probabilities).

▶ Likelihood of an offer being accepted
▶ Likelihood of a candidate's success in a division or in the company
▶ Likelihood of an HR program's success
▶ Likelihood of a new hire's longevity with the company
▶ Likelihood of an employee voluntarily terminating at any point of time in the future

Predictive analytics is a powerful tool, but one should be careful to not get carried away by the hype. Virtually all descriptions of predictive analytics have dwelled only on the positive—i.e., that you act on the output of some predictive analytics work, the business wins, and HR's stock rises. People seem to forget that there is a possibility of making an incorrect prediction. What would happen to the unfortunate analytically armed, newly strategic, soothsaying HR leader whose brilliant models just happen to spit out three dud predictions in a row? This possibility is all too real even with the best minds and models at work.

The emergent predictive human capital analytics movement can sometimes seem a little disparaging of traditional HR approaches and practices. Predictive analytics is viewed as the vanguard of a new kind of HR—smarter, more sophisticated, scientific, and way cooler than their non-numerate and less analytically inclined colleagues. What is often forgotten is that a great deal of judgment is necessary to formulate useful models and interpret the results. One CEO cautioned his analytically eager head of HR that if you take the judgment out of human capital decision making, HR is scarcely distinguishable from the finance department.

A case in point is the recent financial crisis, whose roots can arguably be traced to the creation and indiscriminate spread of complex, derivatives-based financial instruments that seemed so brilliant and cutting-edge that people no longer questioned their validity. The so-called "quants" gained ascendancy, but their models were unable to account for human behavior. In a *Harvard Business Review* article entitled "The Big Idea: The Judgment Deficit," Amar Bhidé concludes that statistical models "reveal broad tendencies and recurring patterns, but in a dynamic society shot through with willful and imaginative people making conscious choices, they cannot make reliable predictions."[6] He makes a number of arguments for caution in predicting human behavior based on statistical patterns without complementary case-by-case judgment.

When intelligently formulated, predictive human capital analytics can be very persuasive. However, not everyone is wired the same way to respond to predictive models. Ultimately, the executive decision is predicated on confidence in a stated probability. People have different degrees of comfort with uncertainty and risk, different appreciations for probabilities, varying levels of understanding vis-à-vis the power of test statistics. The decision maker could disagree that a 60 percent probability is good enough or that a 95 percent confidence limit is powerful enough. The characterization as a probability may actually defeat the whole argument if the decision maker has a strong hunch about an alternative. It is not always prudent to discount the subject matter expert's or executive decision maker's gut instincts if they do not align with a model's prediction.

Executives don't always have the patience to buy into a solution that doesn't fit onto a PowerPoint slide. If executives like the answer and the analysis is supportive, chances are they will move forward with the recommendation and thank the team for a job well done. But if the recommendation is counterintuitive or countercultural, the data need to be combined with judgments about the non-quantitative aspects (like desired behaviors or values) and wrapped into a solution that suggests that the leap of faith is worth taking. When asking a CEO to make a decision "against her better judgment," HR needs data to support the path and the likely result.

On balance, the promise of predictive human capital analytics is compelling, and HR ought to harness its power. Companies that position themselves to take advantage of predictive human capital analytics will have a head start in terms of HR having a direct impact on business strategy and decision making. They will also inculcate a broad and deep culture of analysis within HR and beyond. In the best of all possible worlds, assertions will require evidence; alternative strategies will be evaluated based on careful analyses; and decisions will be made based on all available information. Decision makers will understand the likelihood of success and be able to make strategic plans and decisions. Of course, predictive analytics offers the possibility of all these things, but things such as leadership and culture will influence its actual impact.

BARRIERS THAT HAVE HINDERED HR'S ANALYTICS INITIATIVES

In the enthusiasm around analytics that pervades the HR function today, the question of why HR arrived so late to the game is seldom asked. After all, in a very general sense, it has always been recognized that "people are a company's most important asset" and often its largest expense; that employee-related data or at least the means to collect and organize such data have typically been in HR's hands; that quantitative analysis has been applied to business by management consultants since World War II, and the popularity of business analytics has grown exponentially with the emergence of the Internet in the early 1990s; and that the basic statistical tools and models applicable to human capital analytics have been available for decades.

However, if we press on without some appreciation of why the adoption of analytics has taken so long in HR, we risk losing the opportunity to learn from our mistakes. Indeed, learning some of the lessons may speed up the adoption of predictive human capital analytics.

Despite how wonderful the techniques and models of predictive analytics may be and how powerful their influence might seem, they are neither new nor especially remarkable from a technical standpoint. HR's delay in adopting predictive analytics mirrors in some ways its delay in adopting analytics in the first place—HR capability, HR's credibility with the business, and data integrity. In particular, successful development and deployment of predictive analytics needs formidable data requirements, deep training in statistics and preferably in econometrics, and the judgment to apply the right model to a situation. Perhaps most importantly, it also needs the ability to succinctly and accurately describe a model's prediction with all the requisite qualifications.

The fundamental hurdle in the adoption of analytics by HR has been its capability with respect to analysis and modeling.[7] Other than compensation professionals, traditional HR roles have not required these skills and as a result have not attracted individuals who are numerate and analytical. Said one HR professional: "I didn't join HR to become a spreadsheet jockey." Even master's level programs in HR have fairly modest quantitative course requirements, and from a cultural standpoint within HR, there is an aversion to getting too much into analytic detail. When was the last time you attended an HR conference presentation or webinar where the presenter voluntarily delved into some mathematics or the audience asked him or her to talk a little about the technical underpinnings of the presentation? HR audiences typically enjoy hearing about survey results and then begin relating their own anecdotal evidence. Seldom does anyone question the survey methodology and the potential consequences of small samples, sample selection bias, and measurement rigor.

As a result of this capability gap and the resultant lack of quantitative analysis or argument from HR, the field has had to wage an uphill struggle to be taken seriously when it has finally produced metrics and analytics. HR's credibility in this area is not helped by the lack of HR equivalents to standards like generally accepted accounting principles (GAAP) around data and metrics. The Society for Human Resource Management (SHRM) is currently addressing this gap in conjunction with the American National Standards Institute (ANSI). The standards they develop can be used by companies in sharpening their HR metrics and analytics and by investors examining the quality of human capital management in the company.

By far the most challenging impediments have been the availability and quality of data. Absent a demand for data to feed metrics and analytics, there was no urgent need to ensure that HR data were captured universally, accurately, and systematically. In the past, HR data were stored in different locations and systems that didn't necessarily talk to each other, immensely complicating the task of creating a comprehensive, live employee database. Even when databases were available, there were issues with the quality and reliability of the data. Data privacy regulations that limited the storage and spread of data across geographies created additional challenges. As a result, initial steps toward creating metrics and performing analytics had to be careful and tentative at best. Anytime holes were poked in an argument due to poor data, HR took two steps back in terms of credibility.

Even when HR has developed analytics that are inserted into reports and dashboards, a frequent complaint is that the information is not always actionable. The charts and numbers look lovely and are sometimes even compelling, but unless there is a clear and visible cycle of discernment, action, and results, the HR data ends up being window dressing to the "hard" numbers on revenue growth, customer satisfaction, market share, and the like. The need to generalize the information for the top-line view that dashboards require takes the focus away from identifying issues within segments of the company or certain topical areas. Drilling down from the top-line view uncovers messy details that require a lot more attention than the nice round macro numbers on top.

As a result of one or more of these factors, HR's ability to capitalize on analytics is either stymied at the outset or stalls earlier in the evolutionary path than desired. It is important to note that the requirements for successful predictive analytics are even more stringent across all the factors. Data needs are greater, more sophisticated software is necessary, and specialized skills are required to build predictive models.

Typically, predictive analytical models require rich data sets. This entails large volumes of data—more data on more individuals over multiple time periods. More data on individuals, including performance histories, learning interventions, and career progression allows for more complex modeling that incorporates all the relevant information for the issue being studied. The quality of the data is important, too. There can't be too many systematic gaps in the data since those observations will have to be thrown out, resulting in skewed estimates. The large number of observations also helps to improve the statistical results in the sense that tests of significance have more "power." The ability to track cohorts of employees over time allows for the creation of so-called "panel" data, which facilitates dynamic modeling, that is, modeling changes over time. Of course, the nature of the "sample" (it's not really a sample in the true sense, since there is no random selection; it's typically the employee population or a defined subset of it) is important to understand so that appropriate adjustments can be made to the analyses and results can be interpreted properly.

Constructing predictive analytical models requires specialized training and skills. Prerequisites are an interest in and mastery of basic statistics at the level of a junior- or senior-level undergraduate course. But statistical training and propensity are not enough. Some training in econometrics, biometrics, or psychometrics is useful for an effective human capital analytics shop that builds predictive models. Econometrics is the field of study that applies quantitative and statistical models to economics and other fields (econometricians are known as biometricians in the health sciences area, for example). Econometricians are able to build models and test them using real-world data (known as the parametric approach, since the intent is to estimate the value of the model's parameters) and also to examine data to unearth patterns and relationships (known as the non-parametric approach, where the data is unencumbered by structural constructs). Econometrics is taught at the undergraduate level with a handful of courses, depending on the size of the institution and its economics department. One or two years of graduate training in economics provides the necessary econometric skills and insight to comfortably apply the skills to a corporate setting.

Microsoft Excel has been the weapon of choice for most analytical work, and successive versions have incorporated more and more useful tools. However, performing predictive analytics requires more sophisticated software that manages data, runs predictive models, and outputs customizable charts for import into presentations. There are a number of packages available, but the best are SAS, Stata, SPSS, and S-Plus. An open source alternative called "R" is gaining traction as a result of its cost-effectiveness and charting flexibility. SAS has been used by corporations for some time, and it's likely that companies already have a license that can then be extended to the HR or analytics team. Stata is very user-friendly, but it is not geared toward a corporate environment. It is most popular in health sciences and economics research. SPSS is a recent entrant into business analytics. S-Plus is very powerful, but it is also relatively more complicated to use.

There are ways to overcome these barriers, as demonstrated by some leading-edge companies. The challenges suggest that the speed with which HR adapts analytics and moves into the predictive phase will depend on how well HR organizations can do the following:

➤ *Shift the mind-set with talent from outside HR.* When two engineers educated in operations research and management science interviewed for intern positions with Google's People Operations group, several HR professionals suggested that their skills were better suited to marketing or web analytics and wondered what they would do for HR. By the end of the summer, the application of their skills was clear. They weren't doing deep analytics yet, but with a ready supply of work that went beyond data compilation the stage was set for building on the capability and executive buy-in soon followed.

➤ *Start a data quality program.* Delving into analytics with a focus on data integrity may seem like a foregone conclusion, but it takes only a few mistakes in this area to set back credibility or give the impression of a false start. It is surprising how many HR organizations don't have a data warehouse or "single version of the truth."

➤ *Build on the analytics capability over time.* The promise of analytics and Google-like success with talent management might lead some organizations to make the leap to predictive models. We shouldn't discourage that work, but time is often needed to bring together data that works into the right combination of analyses, some of which have already been bought into. Too much complexity at once, even if done accurately, may not be bought into by senior management. More often these approaches are viewed as an attempt to "boil the ocean."

➤ *Allow for missteps within the analytics function.* Let them make mistakes. Nearly every analytics exercise is interesting; not every model will be useful or relevant. Choose carefully the work you put forward to ensure it has an actionable outcome or suggested path.

➤ *Prioritize the work toward critical pain points relevant to the business and define the questions you hope to answer.* Start with a thrust in one or two areas to build the capability and organizational learning. If, for example, growth is a strategic priority, then the appetite for staffing analytics may be high.

There has been some interesting work done in predictive human capital analytics. Google in particular has been at the forefront recently and has a number of advantages in its favor, including management appetite and expectation, thoughtful HR leadership, availability of data, and skilled resources to conduct research and develop predictive analytics. Other companies, such as Morgan Stanley, have recently established human capital reporting and analytics functions. Still other companies dabble with predictive human capital analytics where there is a happy convergence of demand for such work and supply of internal talent and resources. In some cases external consultants fill the void as well as develop off-the-shelf approaches and analytics, such as Mercer's internal labor market and productivity suites.

PREDICTIONS ON PREDICTIVE HUMAN CAPITAL ANALYTICS

Given what we now know about predictive human capital analytics—what it is, what its strengths and weaknesses are, and what resources are needed to develop and use them—we can turn our attention to thoughts about how its advent might play out in the next few years. At the current time, it is reasonable to say that there are only a few companies that employ predictive human capital analytics, the applications are limited, and the modeling expertise is in relatively short supply.

A few companies will remain in the vanguard (Google comes to mind immediately). These will be larger companies with diverse business footprints—both geographic and product. The argument for investment in predictive human capital analytics is that understanding the relationships between various inputs, assets, and outputs allows them to make optimal decisions in each segment as well as reap advantages through scale. Investment is possible because the HR leadership team is business-oriented, numerate, and willing to hire nontraditional HR staff that have analytical backgrounds. Business leadership has high expectations of its ROI on human capital investment and is willing to let HR "experiment" and work toward optimality.

It is safe to say that predictive human capital analytics will be used more and more. On the one hand, more companies will begin to experiment with and ultimately use these models, and those companies that have already adopted them will begin to apply them to new situations. Consultants will emerge in the marketplace who specialize in developing customized predictive human capital analytics. Some products will become standardized, and there will be some benchmarks created. Companies will hire consultants or develop in-house capabilities. The in-house capabilities may either grow organically as demand for analytics is met through hiring specialist staff or may be purpose-built and staffed as a centralized unit.

Some companies will focus on so-called macro-analytics that attempt to model the entire enterprise. These will be akin to the computable general equilibrium (CGE) models so popular among economists in the latter part of the last century. The data, technology, and capability exist, so why not try and model the entire workforce or, for that matter, the whole company? These, like the CGEs of yore, will likely fall apart under their own weight. The real treasure will be in the micro-analytics that help a company understand its myriad internal dynamics, incorporating people, operations, and financial perspectives. Analytics will best be applied on almost a project basis to "get under the hood" of an issue, process, or outcome.

Specialists in predictive human capital analytics will begin to emerge as a formal job description. Initially, there will be a bimodal distribution of talent. On the one hand, there will be the technically adept analysts who can build the models and run the numbers. These individuals will initially come from graduate programs in economics and industrial psychology with formal training in statistics and econometrics as well as consulting companies. On the other hand, there will be more experienced, more senior managers and executives who understand the power of analytics and which situations are amenable to modeling. These more senior people understand the business context for analytics and the specific needs vis-à-vis predictive human capital analytics. Over time, the technical specialists will get some practical experience under their belt and through their experiences will develop the judgment necessary to properly apply their models. They will become a new generation of highly quantitative HR leaders with an innate strategic instinct. The seat at the table will have been warmed up for them and they will take the HR function to new heights.

CONCLUSION

Human capital analytics have come a long way. Their sophistication has grown and their rate of adoption has accelerated in the last few years. As more companies adopt analytics and more success stories are publicized, the interest and investment grow will grow further. Many companies are now engaged in predictive human capital analytics. These statistical models allow users to make inferences about future outcomes and therefore participate more confidently in business strategy, a realm that HR has always aspired to.

As companies develop human capital centers of excellence (COEs), they should be mindful not to wring all the analytical work from the rest of the company, nonintuitive though this might appear. The centralized resources are a good way to attract and develop talent, create quality standards, and come up with solutions across the enterprise. However, in the long term, companies can truly harness the power of analytics via its dispersion throughout the company. What is to be avoided is a tendency toward central planning and all data flowing to the central body that makes decisions and issues orders for execution. Just like the Soviet planning committees, centralized organizations cannot know everything and take everything into account. Decisions that drive the business are made every day by employees and managers, and it is as important for them to see the analytics so that the right decisions can be made.

While the possibilities are large and exciting, some words of caution are in order. First, predictive analytics can do only so much. It's sobering to keep in mind that no one really understands the macroeconomy or the market, even though the best and brightest minds in the world have been designing and applying predictive analytics to make an academic reputation or a business fortune. Second, no matter how good a model is, it is still a representation of reality built upon assumptions and past facts. Unpredictable things can happen and models may never be able to account for these events. Third, the importance of the judgment of seasoned HR professionals cannot be underestimated.

Note: The views expressed in this article are the authors' personal opinions. The authors are grateful for fruitful discussions and insightful comments from Jamie Herslow and Lawrence Gallant.

Notes

1. Bill Roberts, "Analyze This," *HR Magazine*, October 2009.
2. Laurie Bassi, *HR Analytics Handbook*, Reed Business, 2010.
3. Jac Fitz-enz, *The New HR Analytics*, (New York: American Management Association, 2010).
4. Dan Ward, Thomas P. Bechet, and Robert Tripp (editors), *HR Forecasting and Modeling*. The Human Resources Planning Society, 1994.
5. Amit B. Mohindra, "Closing the HR Capability Gap," *HR Executive Magazine*, September 2010.
6. Amar Bhide, "The Big Idea: The Judgment Deficit," *Harvard Business Review*, September 2010.
7. Mohindra, "Closing the HR Capability Gap." Thomas H. Davenport, Jeanne Harris, and Jeremy Shapiro, "Competing on Talent Analytics," *Harvard Business Review*, September 2010. Alexis A. Fink, "New Trends in Human Capital Research and Analytics," *People & Strategy*, 33, no. 2 (2010).

Amit B. Mohindra is the founder and managing director of Nelson Touch Consulting, LLC. The firm was established in 2008 and advises clients on HR strategy, incentives, and analytics. In 2011, Amit served as research director at the Institute for Corporate Productivity (i4cp). He has worked in economics research, compensation consulting, and corporate human resources for organizations that set the agenda in their industry: the World Bank, Towers Perrin (now Towers Watson), Lucent Technologies (now Alcatel-Lucent), IBM, and Goldman Sachs.

Amit received a master's degree in economics from Brown University, where he specialized in labor and development economics, and undergraduate degrees in economics and business (AB) and electrical engineering (BS) from Lafayette College, where he was a McKelvy Scholar and a member of the varsity crew team. He has written articles on HR capability, workforce analytics, and workforce planning in publications such as *HR Executive Magazine*, *Talent Management*, *Training & Development*, and *Chief Learning Officer*.

Jeffrey Allan Brown is vice president of human resources for Marvell Semiconductor. Allan joined Marvell in May 2008 as the director of compensation and benefits and assumed leadership of worldwide human resources in January 2012. Prior to joining Marvell, Allan was Google's first director of recognition and HR systems, where he led the development of reward practices and productivity systems that supported the culture and helped grow Google from 3,000 to 22,000 employees during his tenure. Allan's experience also includes leading the HR analytics team at Microsoft, compensation consulting with Towers Perrin and Mercer, and financial analysis with Wells Fargo Bank. He holds an MBA from Rice University and an AB in economics from the University of California, Berkeley.

SECTION 4

Future Directions

Dan L. Ward

THE FINAL SECTION OF THE BOOK focuses on future directions in SWP, both from an organizational perspective and for the individual practitioner. **Jac Fitz-enz** is recognized as the person who has done more than anyone else to shine a light on workforce data. His pioneering efforts led to the creation of the Saratoga Institute and a new generation of human capital specialists who embraced the quantitative aspects of what was traditionally considered a "soft" field. I vividly remember some of the older "personnel" executives in the early days of my career who firmly believed that personnel administration was just one of those things that had to be done and should be accepted as part of the cost of doing business: Minimize the cost as best you can, and don't waste time trying to analyze it too deeply. Jac's efforts showed not only that these things could be measured, but that comparative data could establish reference points, benchmarks, and milestones for improvement.

In "Disrupting the Future," Jac notes that times have changed, and he challenges even some of the paradigms he helped establish. He references a comment from a CIO (chief information officer) that information technology has shifted from a focus on control to a focus on risk management. He talks about some new types of metrics, such as Talent Development Reporting Principles (TDRP), which fly in the face of conventional wisdom that the results from training investments cannot be effectively quantified. While Jac has done more than anyone else to bring discipline to the ability to measure the characteristics and investments in the workforce, he reminds us that how, where, and when we work is changing rapidly, and the way we measure and evaluate workforce data will have to evolve and do so quickly.

In "Workforce Planning Across the Great Divide," **John Boudreau** and **Ian Ziskin** remind us that workforce planning exists within the context of a whole resource environment. The organization structure, the reporting relationships, and the physical and mental aspects of social networks are all critical aspects of any organization. Unless the workforce planning mind-set is balanced within a holistic perspective, it will be as shortsighted as some of the purely mechanical workforce forecasts of thirty years ago. Some of the traditional analytical tools, such as detailed analysis by functional job categories, may become less valuable, perhaps even a waste of time, as more roles become cross-disciplinary. The generation that grew up using Google has never had to accept "I don't know" as a legitimate answer to a question. Google can always find an answer. The challenge currently is deciding which one of the million answers is actually relevant.

Steve Arneson's "Plan Your Own Development" may at first seem a bit unusual for a book focused on SWP because most of us spend our careers focusing on the growth and development of hundreds or thousands of employees at a time. This piece challenges us to step back for just a minute and look at how we should manage our own careers while working in SWP. What do we really want to accomplish? How can we more effectively work with others? Too often, like the cobbler's children, SWP practitioners are so busy serving the needs of a community that their own individual needs are left behind. We must include our own growth and development or risk becoming out of touch.

The final chapter, **Dave Ulrich**'s "The Future Targets or Outcomes of HR Work," provides insights from the individual widely regarded as our foremost thought leader in business. Dave reminds us that effective SWP must recognize that ability is measured at the individual level, while capability is a function of aggregated ability aligned by effective leadership. We must learn new ways to work and to think about work. Increasingly, we must learn to refocus on capabilities that may only via temporary virtual relationships. We must remove the narrow vision blinders created by the constraints of outdated mind-sets if we are to imagine and design effective approaches for getting resources when and where they are needed.

Disrupting the Future

Jac Fitz-enz

RECENTLY, I WAS INVITED to a CIO (chief information officer) meeting in Silicon Valley to discuss how to manage people and information in the constantly changing global marketplace. Two statements were made there. One was a somewhat surprising admission. The other was astounding.

First, it was acknowledged that IT is overwhelmed by advances in personal information hardware and software—i.e., social networks, tablets, and smart phone apps. It seems that the issue of central management of information is now moot. One CIO noted that his job has shifted from control to risk management.

Second, several executives stated that incoming employees, age 20 to 25, work differently than older ones because they take for granted the new information channels and tools. As an example, one CIO remarked that his company no longer gives PCs to 20- to 25-year-olds because they don't want them. The "kids" operate with tablets and smart phones.

Clearly, disruptive change is upon us. Social networks are rapidly and dramatically changing the world the post-30s grew up in. The twentieth-century people management systems are as outdated as the horse and buggy that ushered them in and the landline phones that carried them out. No one could argue that tomorrow will be the same as even today.

RISK MITIGATION

Management is a combination of the art of persuasion and the science of analytics to influence behavior. A month before I wrote this, a strategy magazine interviewed me about the future of talent management. My reply was that, basically, it is risk mitigation. Now, I am absolutely certain it is. Due to the rate, scope, and depth of change, every decision carries with it potentially significant risk. Planning, hiring, developing, and engaging talent has become an almost mystical exercise. I can't think of many companies I know that are not struggling over managing human capital. If we can't control the situation, all we can do is minimize the risk.

Risk management starts with Strategic Workforce Planning and runs from talent acquisition all the way to talent retention. In between are the decisions about where to invest in human capital. The two most effective ways to handle them are to upgrade workforce planning and incorporate predictive analytics.

Fortunately, developments in management software and statistical analysis have given us the power to leverage human capital now. As Naomi Bloom put it: "We have some really fantastic automation tools. If HR people had started using them [several years ago] instead of asking for a seat at the table, they would have owned the table."

On the other hand, customers of almost all large HR software products complain about the promise, cost, and difficulty of implementation. If you can't afford or don't want to spend a lot of money for a large-scale system, there are a number of solutions available from small vendors that are leading-edge applications. This chapter highlights products already in the field that are more than tools. They threaten to disrupt the way we manage talent.

FROM ACQUISITION TO PERFORMANCE

The hiring process has made advances in the past thirty years primarily through applicant tracking and assessment systems. Unfortunately, companies have not made use of the intelligence embedded in these systems during and after the hire process. Now there are tools being developed that capture data for selection, deployment, and performance management all in a neat, inexpensive, easy-to-implement package. One case is Wentworth Recruiting's talent analysis system. On the front end, the value of a good hire is judged not only by the initial cost, but by the long-term performance of the employee. Then, with the system's graphic layout, managers can carry hiring criteria through deployment and on to performance management. See an example in Figure 1.

Given the many job requirements and the applicant's strength on each criterion, a manager can compare the numeric profiles of the new employees when they were candidates to later job performance, thereby developing a success profile. A feedback loop can be created so that the profile is continually updated. Selection has now expanded through deployment and job design to performance analysis and consultation services.

Granted, a similar system can be built around a pre-hire psychological screen-

FIGURE 1. HIRING CRITERIA. (REPRINTED BY PERMISSION OF JOHN WENTWORTH, THE WENTWORTH COMPANY.)

SAMPLE COMPANY — INFRASTRUCTURE MANAGER	Goal	Jill	Mary	Joan	Harry	Lee	Sean	April	Bob	Jim
Job-Related Has demonstrated effective management of i-Series servers.	3	1	3	3	4	2	3	1	3	2
Has demonstrated effective management of PC hardware with Windows XP operating system and MS Office Suites in an IT environment of the size of our client.	3	4	4	3	3	4	3	3	3	3
Has demonstrated competence in upgrading infrastructure-focused software.	3	4	3	3	4	3	3	3	3	2
Has demonstrated effective oversight of vendor-managed networks.	3	5	3	4	3	3	3	3	2	3
Has effective experience managing Win 2003 infrastructures (or newer).	3	4	4	3	3	3	3	3	3	2
Has demonstrated the ability to develop and deploy comprehensive infrastructure-focused security applications (principally, firewalls).	3	4	4	3	3	4	3	3	3	3
Has demonstrated effectiveness in Unix-based operating systems.	3	4	3	3	1	3	2	3	2	2
Has demonstrated effective management of back-up and business continuity issues.	3	4	4	4	3	3	3	3	3	2
Has demonstrated competence in describing complex technical issues in clear and understandable lay language.	3	3	3	4	3	3	3	4	3	3
Has demonstrated sufficient familiarity with methodologies for configuring, deploying, and maintaining telecommunications (phone systems, cell phone and PDA devices).	3	3	4	3	4	2	3	3	3	1
Has degree in computer science or related field, or comparable experience.	3	3	3	3	3	3	3	3	2	3
Job-Related Average	**3.0**	**3.5**	**3.5**	**3.3**	**3.1**	**3.0**	**2.9**	**2.9**	**2.7**	**2.2**

Legend: ■ =Less than goal-0.5   ■ =Goal +0.5 - goal-0.5   ■ =Greater than goal+0.5

ing instrument. The only drawbacks with such assessment packages are that they take at least a year to validate and can be very expensive to maintain.

GAAP REPORTING FOR LEARNING AND DEVELOPMENT

Most organizations lack standard performance measures to quantify learning effectiveness. Even when metrics exist, they focus on activity or cost. In short, although many companies spend 3 to 5 percent of payroll on employee development, there has never been a standard return on investment accounting for that expenditure. It is difficult to make a case for learning management when there is no generally accepted method to account for it.

In 2010, Kent Barnett, CEO of KnowledgeAdvisors, and Tamar Elkeles, CLO of Qualcomm, recruited a group of thought leaders along with representatives from Fortune-listed companies and major vendors. The goal was to design and develop Talent Development Reporting Principles (TDRP).

What TDRP Aims to Do

In concise terms, TDRP is a set of guidelines to provide practical and relevant reporting using standard measures and definitions along with standard reports.

Organizations are now adopting TDRP because it provides clarity around learning measurement and can provide comparisons across the L&D (learning and development) profession.

TDRP is a phased implementation. Phase I focuses on basic L&D reporting. Phase II is more advanced reporting, while Phase III is an expansion to other areas of talent management.

TDRP provides guidance similar to what GAAP (Generally Accepted Accounting Principles) offers. Like GAAP, TDRP has templated statements and defined guidance to help in populating the statements.

The Barnett and Elkeles group has built templates for three statements that show last year's actual, plan (or goal) for the year, and year-to-date results. Standard measures are suggested, but organizations can add their own as well. The three statements and templates are:

1. Business outcomes
2. Effectiveness
3. Efficiency

TDRP also provides operating tools such as:

▶ Guiding principles for reporting
▶ Standard measures and definitions
▶ Standard statements
▶ Executive reports

In the end, TDRP benefits organizations by:

▶ Providing industry standards on tracking and reporting
▶ Supporting better ROI management of the function
▶ Supporting benchmarking and cross-company comparisons

While this effort may not seem to qualify as disruptive technology, one must keep in mind that the training discipline has never had any consistent form of performance measurement or ROI reporting. In short, training was administered but not managed. Now, for the first time, L&D can provide valid and reliable decision-making data for enterprise management.

ACCELERATING CAREER DEVELOPMENT

With the market moving as fast as it is and change being broader and deeper than ever, we need to develop talent much more quickly than before. The old talent model took several years of planning, developing, testing, and review. This won't satisfy the market today or tomorrow. We need a real-time career development system.

A recently constructed predictive analytics system by Human Capital Source is being applied to workforce planning and career development with amazing results. The model starts with a scan of market forces and a review of internal factors. The scan covers the interdependence of human, structural, and relational capital—all forces outside and inside that could affect how we manage and develop talent. Top management is engaged in this market review. Once the forces and factors have been agreed upon, the system is ready for liftoff. This phase is programmed so as to lay out a workforce plan within a matter of days. By using the querying technique built into the system, it sets up a process for developing essential capabilities for the near future.

Capability is different from competence. Competence is about current skills. Capability is about future human capital or talent needs. We know two things. One is that tomorrow's capabilities will be somewhat different from today's competencies (e.g., digital versus analog). Two is that we need to anticipate from whence the changes will emanate. Change can be driven internally by management's decision to transform the enterprise to deal with the new marketplace. In addition, change can come from outside economics, technology, customers, competitors, regulators, or the communities/countries in which we will do business. The scan will have surfaced projections of change source, direction, and scope. From there, we can launch a workforce planning and career development system to generate tomorrow's capabilities.

The speed with which this system works is attested to by one of the user companies. The company has more than 35,000 employees operating in a dozen countries. Within six months of the initial market analysis session, the chief human resources officer said:

> We have successfully implemented our management evaluation program through which we identified our high potential employees. We developed their career paths and determined their training and development needs. We were also able to identify potential successors, and now we are working on their development needs. The best thing we achieved after the session was change in mind-set of our business area heads.

Most companies of that size would be struggling for six months to get line managers organized around an agreeable model. Most important, the last statement about changing the mind-set of a company of engineers to acknowledge the power of talent management is a remarkable achievement. This is a lasting benefit that transformed the culture of the company.

EAST MEETS WEST

Almost forever, finance and human resources have stood on opposite sides of the management field. The so-called hard and soft sides of the business have had a difficult time finding a mutually respectful accommodation. Now, at last, this is changing.

Jeff Higgins, CEO of HCMI, is a former finance executive who found himself in HR through the workforce planning path. He has developed an objectively based system for connecting people and profitability. This system rides in a series of instruments called Human Capital Financial Statements. Regulatory securities commissions, such as the Securities and Exchange Commission (SEC) in the United States, require extensive disclosure regarding all major assets, including financial, physical, and technological/intellectual property. However, they do not require disclosure of what is, for most organizations, their largest annual operating expense.

I believe these new Human Capital Financial Statements will lay the groundwork for closing the historic gap between money and people. They consist of the following:

1.	Human Capital Impact Statement
2.	Human Capital Asset Statement
3.	Human Capital Flow Statement

Each statement quantifies the value of human capital from a different dimension, much as traditional financial statements do for financial results. Together, these statements provide:

▶	Greater transparency into an organization's greatest asset
▶	A method to value knowledge capital
▶	Standards for human capital measurement and reporting
▶	True linkage of human capital to financial results

Figure 2 shows one outcome. It is a Workforce Productivity Impact schedule, the overall summary of the Human Capital Impact Statement. It is similar to a summary profit and loss statement versus the detailed profit and loss statement that provides far more detail across the entire talent management lifecycle.

Human Capital Financial Statements provide greater transparency and a method to truly value knowledge capital in the twenty-first-century marketplace. Now, knowledge capital drives market valuation far more than financial or physical capital. These statements are a standard with which to measure, report, and disclose a company's human capital.

FIGURE 2. HUMAN CAPITAL FINANCIAL STATEMENT. (REPRINTED BY PERMISSION OF JEFF HIGGINS, HUMAN CAPITAL MANAGEMENT INSTITUTE.)

Workforce Productivity Impact

Revenue	Prior Year	Current Year	Variance	% Chg
Net Operating Revenue (Current Annual)	$1,400,000,000	$1,540,000,000	$140,000,000	10.0%
Total Headcount (FTE)	15,000	16,400	1,400	9.3%
Revenue per FTE	$93,333	$93,902	$569	0.6%
Costs				
Total Expenses	$1,170,000,000	$1,285,000,000	$115,000,000	9.8%
Total Operating Expense	$725,000,000	$795,000,000	$70,000,000	9.7%
Total Cost of Workforce (TCOW)	$779,950,000	$861,000,000	$81,050,000	10.4%
TCOW Percent of Revenue	55.7%	55.9%	0.2%	0.4%
TCOW Percent of Expenses	66.7%	67.0%	0.3%	0.5%
TCOW Percent of Operating Expenses	107.6%	108.3%	0.7%	0.7%
Profit				
EBITDA	$310,000,000	$340,000,000	$30,000,000	9.7%
Net Operating Profit	$143,750,000	$159,375,000	$15,625,000	10.9%
Profit per FTE	$9,583	$9,718	$135	1.4%
Productivity and ROI of Human Capital				
Total Market Capitalization [1]	$2,156,250,000	$2,390,625,000	$234,375,000	10.9%
Average Market Capitalization Value per FTE	$143,750	$145,770	$2,020	1.4%
Human Capital ROI Ratio	1.29	1.30	0.00	0.1%
Return on Human Capital Investment	18.4%	18.5%	0.1%	0.4%
TOTAL WORKFORCE PRODUCTIVITY IMPACT:	**$34,570,000**	**$41,294,200**	**$6,724,200**	**19.5%**

CONCLUSION

Disruption can be defined by words such as *distraction, interference, disorder,* and *disturbance.* This is clearly what is happening within talent management with the latest hardware and software apps. The future configuration of talent management is being defined by the new analytic and measurement programs coming online. By the time you read this, many new apps will be available. The question is: Are they better ways to administer an HR process, or are they going to help you leap the curve and disrupt your competitor's market? We need models underlying the apps if we are to truly and positively disrupt the twentieth-century talent management system.

Jac Fitz-enz—or Dr. Jac, as he is known—is acknowledged as the father of human capital strategic analysis and measurement, having developed the first HR quantitative reporting system in 1978. He has published 12 books and more than 350 articles, reports, and book chapters on HR topics, and has trained more than 90,000 managers in 46 countries. Jac has received numerous awards, including from SHRM, IHRIM, and *HR World.* He can be reached at jac@drjac.com.

Workforce Planning Across the Great Divide: Redefining the Professional Boundaries of HR

John Boudreau and Ian Ziskin

THE FUTURE WILL REQUIRE that Strategic Workforce Planning (SWP) define its questions at multiple levels, that it draw on disciplines well beyond its traditional expertise, and that it be prepared to accept that the HR profession may or may not be the primary leader in these significant issues. It may instead be the orchestra conductor charged with bringing together world-class capabilities to create a more integrated and harmonious set of solutions.

HR's reason for being is to make people and organizations more effective. This will not change in the future, but HR must work faster, with less bureaucracy and more business relevance. At the same time, we must also acknowledge that the bar keeps getting raised: HR is indeed improving and developing its capabilities, but the expectations about what HR can and should deliver are also getting bigger, in possibly unrealistic ways. In addition, the consequences of not delivering are also getting tougher and less forgiving.[1]

SWP plays a vital role in meeting these challenges. Many of the chapters in this book attest to the current reality and future potential for SWP to provide sophisticated insights into the predicted supply and demand for talent, the anticipated risks and gaps that result, and the optimal investments to address them. Even today's most sophisticated SWP systems often focus solely on the workforce, using frameworks and tools that are largely in the domain of human resources management, and often provide the majority of their information about the HR function and its processes and activities. To be sure, information from strategy and business processes is used to extrapolate workforce demand and supply, and information is often gathered through econometric modeling to describe likely future trends in worker supply across regions and skill categories. This is important, but in this chapter, we want to draw attention to the untapped potential for

SWP, and HR generally, to look beyond the boundary of the HR profession. The boundary of HR in the future will be far more permeable than it is today or has been in the past. This offers both significant challenges and opportunities for the profession and has placed SWP squarely as a key factor in its future evolution.

Perhaps most important, this broader lens on SWP requires that we view it as a strategic organizational capability, rather than as a functional discipline within HR. As we will argue, Strategic Workplace Planning, at its very best, is an amalgamation of capabilities drawn from multiple disciplines such as statistics, demographics, labor economics, geopolitics, anthropology, sociology, finance, marketing, supply chain management, communications, and HR. This construct places HR and SWP experts in the role of orchestra conductor, harmonizing different instruments that all play a vital part in the performance. It is time that SWP and the HR profession span the "great divide" that has long defined the boundary between HR and its context.

MULTIPLE LEVELS AND MULTIPLE CONSTITUENTS

While the future of HR will certainly be defined in part in terms of questions that exist within the domain of today's HR discipline, we increasingly find that the most significant and important issues will require that HR professionals look beyond the traditional boundaries of their function. HR's future role and its effectiveness will typically be defined through multiple levels and in terms of issues and standards that will span multiple constituents.[2] Figure 1 portrays this idea graphically.

FIGURE 1. MULTIPLE LEVELS THAT DEFINE THE FUTURE OF HR. (FROM J. W. BOUDREAU AND I. ZISKIN, "THE FUTURE OF HR AND EFFECTIVE ORGANIZATIONS," *ORGANIZATIONAL DYNAMICS,* 40 (2011), 255–267.)

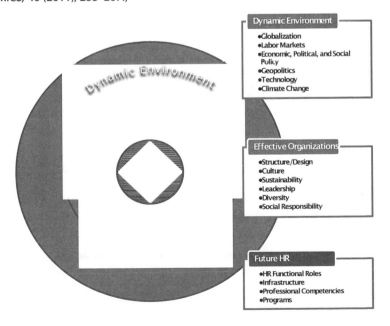

The centermost circle, "Future HR," is meant to capture those issues that are primarily focused at the level of the HR function itself. Thus, this involves important questions about the design of HR functions, HR's professional roles and competencies, how HR uses infrastructure like information technology and process delivery systems, and the specific programs and practices that HR enacts. Much attention to HR and SWP has rightfully focused here. It is important to ensure that the HR function, its processes, its competencies, and its role are aligned with organizational strategy. Yet our view is that as important as such issues are, they must be embedded within a broader perspective to fully understand the challenges and opportunities facing the future of HR and SWP.

The middle circle, "Effective Organizations," is meant to capture the reality that HR must exist and optimize its role within a surrounding organizational context. HR will influence and be influenced by organizational elements such as structure and design, culture, and leadership, as well as such organization-level issues as sustainability, diversity, and social responsibility. This reality has not been lost on those who study the profession and its future. Indeed, the HR profession is often centrally involved with—and even a primary driver of—organizational success in areas such as diversity and leadership. SWP increasingly incorporates outcomes related to diversity and has long attended to projecting the supply and demand of future leaders. That said, we and our colleagues at the Center for Effective Organizations often find that HR's involvement and leadership in these organization-level issues varies considerably. The evolution of HR's role in these areas will significantly define the evolution of the professional elements in the centermost circle.

For example, it is still common, though our experience suggests less so than in the past, for the functions of OD (organization effectiveness, design, and development) to be separate from the HR function. Indeed, it is not unusual to find professionals in the OD area who are quite insistent that they are not a part of HR, noting that they address more "strategic" issues of organization design and effectiveness, while HR addresses more tactical and administrative issues that support the strategy. It has been noted that such a stark separation can create serious and important limitations for organizations and for both the OD and the HR professions,[3] and that OD competencies are vital for HR and vice versa.

For SWP, the question is how much the systems and frameworks draw upon and influence questions of organizational design and development. Are organizational structures, reporting relationships, informal networks, and social structures explicit parts of strategic workforce plans? Often, they are determined apart from the SWP process and serve as boundary conditions on the plan, as when the organization structure is taken as a given in projecting future workforce flows. The future will require that alternative formal and informal organization designs become an integral part of strategic workforce plans, not simply a boundary constraint.

In arenas such as social responsibility and sustainability, the evolution of SWP is even less advanced. We see many organizations where there are significant initiatives in these areas, but little presence of HR in formulating the agendas or implementing the key initiatives. Rather, the role of the HR profession seems to be more reactive, awaiting resolution of the thorny questions and then being ready to implement the requested HR programs and practices.[4] That said, there is an upwelling of books and articles suggesting a more central role for HR in defining such issues and their strategic role in the organization.[5] The implication is that SWP will increasingly be called upon to have deep and sophisticated points of view on these issues to answer questions like these: *When does diversity create innovation versus confusion? How can we align the workforce to the right balance between financial, social, employment, and environmental considerations? When do we risk the sustainability of our employment relationships by pushing too hard on our employees? Where is the critical inflection point between buying and building talent?*

Finally, the outer circle of Figure 1 reflects the "Dynamic Environment." These are the trends and influences that will span organizations and affect entire industries, regions, and economies. Like the issues in the center circle, these broader environmental trends are sometimes a central concern of SWP, but more often they appear only in the broadest context statements and are not specifically a part of planning forecasts and scenarios. Perhaps more important will be the profession's ability to pick its spots to engage on such issues. It is not yet clear that the HR profession must play a leadership role in such issues as climate change and geopolitics, but what is increasingly clear is that HR leaders must understand such trends well enough to help their organizations craft strategic responses. In this case, functions such as strategy and government relations might take the lead and then look to SWP to play more of an implementation role in defining the workforce characteristics necessary, forecasting supply and demand and crafting programs to create the necessary workforce.

Will SWP go beyond this implementation role? Often, these trends manifest themselves primarily through the employment relationship, and thus thrust HR and SWP into a central role. Global collective employment action is often the organization's first tangible globalization challenge. Employment unrest or HR's role in crisis management and evacuating employees and their families can often be the first challenges that require significant attention to geopolitics. Thorny issues of employee behavior in technologically enabled social networks and forums may often be the organization's first tangible challenges that require a considered position on emerging technology and the power of social influence. So, the role of SWP in the outer circle of Figure 1 may be more prominent than many planners think and require answers to questions like these: *Where will political or economic unrest make us most vulnerable to work stoppages or labor shortages? Where would a change in legislation about collective voice at work potentially constrain our flexibility or raise our employment costs? Who are the key opinion leaders on climate change, and should we create roles for them within our organization to prepare us for future strategic opportunities and challenges?*

For example, an item in the *New Yorker* magazine of May 16, 2011, described PepsiCo's efforts to position itself to benefit from future demand for foods that are not only tasty, but also healthy.[6] For PepsiCo, traditional talent such as manufacturing, supply chain, marketing, and branding will of course be important for this or any strategy. However, the greatest improvement in PepsiCo's future readiness to achieve this strategy will come from human capital that has never existed in the company before. A key talent acquisition for PepsiCo was Derek Yach, PepsiCo's director of global health policy. In 2002, as a leader at the World Health Organization (WHO), he drafted new dietary guidelines that were circulated among the member states of the United Nations. They were resisted by food industry and government leaders, and little progress was made. By 2006, Yach had left the WHO, and PepsiCo's CEO, Indra Nooyi, asked him to join her company and "do exactly what you were doing at the WHO here at PepsiCo." The pivotal talent for PepsiCo's future strategy lay in a job that had not existed before, and in a person, Yach, who might seem an unlikely member of a snack food leadership team.

As Figure 1 shows, the future of HR will be defined in large part by how well the HR profession spans boundaries that have in the past been unaddressed or seen as outside the domain of SWP. We must avoid the temptation of the comfort zone, where we focus solely on the HR function and its programs (the center circle) to solve gaps and problems at a broader level. Some of the most important defining elements of HR's future will reflect how the profession navigates the multilevel challenges of the future.

IMPLICATIONS OF THE MULTILEVEL PERSPECTIVE ON THE FUTURE OF SWP

The boundary-spanning perspective of Figure 1 suggests at least three implications for the HR profession and the role of SWP within it:

1. HR and SWP success will incorporate other disciplines.
2. HR and SWP success will rely on boundary-spanning.
3. HR and SWP success will require accepting diverse definitions of the role of HR and SWP.

Incorporating Other Disciplines

Challenges such as diversity, sustainability, and socioeconomic disparities require approaches that draw on disciplines well beyond the traditions of the HR profession. Traditional HR disciplines such as industrial and organizational psychology and labor economics are valuable, but increasingly we see HR organizations reaching beyond these traditional areas in an effort to address thorny but important challenges. Google employs analysts in its People Analytics (HR) organization with disciplinary backgrounds including operations, politics, and marketing.[7] Human capital planning and strategy is increasingly carried out with the assistance of those with deep training in competitive strategy and scenario planning, whether they exist within the HR function or in a separate strategy group. We have long seen examples of HR process excellence being achieved with the involvement of operations management experts, or even by placing responsibility for HR processes within the operations management group itself.

The disciplines needed to take SWP systems to the next level may well reside outside traditional HR. When IBM's HR organization wished to design its talent management system using the logical principles of a supply chain, it engaged its top experts in operations management to assist and help lead the project.[8] The employee value proposition and employer brand were defined using tools from the disciplines of consumer behavior and marketing. In some cases, those efforts are contained within marketing organizations with deep expertise in branding and consumer research. At Starbucks, Melissa Graves, an I/O psychologist, is the director of Partner Insights, which brings the best tools possible to questions about partners, stores, customers, and financials.[9] Prasad Setty of Google and Juha Äkräs of Nokia are two additional examples of non-HR professionals who came into the function to become effective HR leaders.[10]

An understandable reaction from HR professionals might be that the HR profession is losing "turf" to other disciplines and is in danger of being hollowed out unless it reclaims areas such as strategy, branding, and process excellence—or worse, that HR leaders see incorporation of capabilities and disciplines external to HR as a sign of failure to adequately define and protect the boundaries of the HR profession. Yet perhaps the most successful future HR organizations will be those that accept the permeability of functional and disciplinary boundaries as holding the promise of a richer discipline, even if the HR functional boundaries are less clear.

For SWP, this means that the planning process and planning teams will include experts from functions such as operations, marketing and finance, statistics, demographics, labor economics, geopolitics, anthropology, and sociology, but not just for their ability to validate data on their workforce needs. Rather, future planning systems will actually reflect the logic, measurement approaches, and decision rules that those professions have long used to optimize other resources in the spirit of creating a true strategic organizational capability—not merely a function—SWP.

The answer is unlikely to be the same for all organizations. Sometimes this trend will mean expanding the role of HR, such as when HR's effective handling of employment issues relating to communications and corporate social responsibility leads to giving HR leaders expanded responsibility for all these areas. In other organizations, it may mean that things like strategy, process excellence, and employment branding primarily reside in functions such as corporate strategy, operations, or marketing. The question in the future may be less about "What competencies must we in HR develop in order to address these multidisciplinary challenges within our own function?" and more about "What competencies exist among the best and brightest in any discipline that HR can skillfully draw upon to best address these challenges?" It's world-class orchestra conductor rather than world-class violinist.

The challenge for SWP is whether to adopt an open-systems approach that is capable of incorporating the best thinking from other disciplines, when such thinking may require radical changes in traditional planning approaches. For example, when IBM shifted its planning to a supply chain framework, it meant requiring all businesses to adopt strictly compatible definitions of jobs and competencies, so that the supply chain of talent was commonly described and "visible" throughout the organization and across its boundaries.[11] This goes far beyond planning that projects headcount gaps based on existing work descriptions, and it may accept "blind spots" in units or regions that don't join the common system. Is SWP prepared to analyze when the payoff from a common approach outweighs the desire for regional or unit customization?

Spanning Boundaries

Closely related to the idea of incorporating other disciplines is the idea that HR will increasingly need to span boundaries of all types to be effective. Certainly, boundaries between disciplines and functions will need to be more permeable, as noted above. However, HR will also likely need to span the boundary of the organization itself. Issues of sustainability often require considering organization designs that demand interorganizational cooperation, resource sharing, and decisions.[12] One can foresee that such solutions will be necessary for virtually all of the issues shown in Figure 1.

The "collective" is increasingly defined without the necessity of an organization boundary. Disciplines such as marketing and research and development routinely draw ideas from the "crowd" around the organization, and they consider engaging that "crowd" to be as vital to their mission as engaging the employees within their organizations. Focus groups are widely employed to elicit opinions and feedback from customers (and potential customers) about a whole host of issues, including products, services, new product development, and advertising.[13] The Mattel Imagination Center brings in children to play with, test, and comment on new toys not yet on the market.[14] Emerging markets increasingly require engaging constituents such as NGOs, governments, local collectives, and others that may exist both within and outside the organization. Joint industry and regional efforts to address diminishing U.S. student interest and capability in science, technology, engineering, and math (STEM) is another vivid example of how HR and SWP leaders are collaborating across organizational and societal boundaries.

Can future SWP systems include in their forecasts the potential for social networks, online gaming communities, and customers to augment employees in accomplishing organizational goals? Can strategic workforce planners incorporate the trade-offs, costs, and benefits of make-or-buy decisions that include options that don't even involve employment? For example, a recent article published in *Nature Structural & Molecular Biology* provided authorship to the Foldit Contenders Group and the Foldit Void Crushers Group, which were groups of online gamers playing a game called Foldit.[15] In three weeks, the gamers solved a thorny retrovirus enzyme structure problem that had eluded scientists. This human capital is not firm-specific, let alone immobile, as the gamers are not even employed by a specific company. This goes beyond just forecasting and planning for the employees who will engage crowds, customers, and gamers. The thorny issues will be to decide when crowds, customers, and gamers can actually replace employees for certain key tasks.[16]

Expanding the Meaning of SWP and the HR Role

Traditional debates about the role of HR have focused largely on its capability to influence and affect organizational outcomes and its role in influencing constituents such as line leaders and employees. Discussions about roles like strategic partner, change catalyst, trusted adviser, employee advocate, and process architect remain important. Still, the discussion about such roles has been largely within the center circle of Figure 1. We envision a broader definition of HR that will more directly account for the white spaces that are created by the multilevel issues and approaches of the future. When is the role of HR to support the initiatives of other departments, leaders, business units, and so forth, with strong traditional human capital programs and processes? When is the role of HR to be the "face" of the organization on significant issues such as sustainability and environmental responsibility? When is the role of HR to be the disciplinary expert on issues such as emerging social networks and harnessing the power of the crowd? When is the role of HR to provoke new ways of thinking and to surface and address unpopular truths?

For example, when Bill Conaty was at General Electric and wanted an executive to head up his new function of corporate responsibility in 2004, he reached out to Bob Corcoran, the head of GE's learning center at Crotonville, New York.[17] Bob soon found himself traveling the globe on projects such as bringing advanced healthcare to Ghana as part of GE's Developing Health Globally initiative. GE had no business interests, offices, or facilities in Ghana at the time.[18] In his new role, would we say that Bob Corcoran is still in HR? Is corporate social responsibility still a separate function from HR? In the future, these questions will probably be less important than the questions of how HR leaders can best leverage their capabilities to make the biggest impact, regardless of the boundaries they must cross.

At Gap Inc., HR professionals take assignments directly working with business owners in emerging economies, helping those leaders apply the basics of motivation, performance assessment, training, and communication. These HR assignments cross the boundary between the HR function, the organization, and the economic context. Traditionally, the role of HR and workforce planning might be to anticipate and create the capabilities of those outside the profession who would eventually work with these business owners. Yet Gap put HR leaders in a direct position to carry out the boundary-spanning activity. It was the HR expertise on motivation, performance assessment, and other areas that was so vital to improving the performance of the vendors and eventually contributing to lower costs, higher quality, and better employment relationships for Gap.

What are the implications for SWP? The Gap and GE examples show how the skills of HR leaders may directly apply to solving important business issues. In the same way, the disciplines of SWP may come directly into play in these issues. SWP has long drawn upon expertise about values, attitudes, engagement, and identification with the organization. Consider the strategic issues facing today's organizations. They involve the values, attitudes, engagement, and identification of a vast array of stakeholders. Can expertise from SWP about how employee engagement affects performance and retention also reveal how the engagement of customers or political groups will affect their reaction to organizational activities or initiatives? Can expertise from SWP about how capabilities develop and flow within the organization's internal workforce be used to understand how capabilities develop and flow externally through online or local communities? Can expertise from SWP about how the composition of teams enhances or detracts from performance be used to understand how the organization should forge broader alliances?

In other words, the door can swing both ways. Not only can the boundary of SWP become more open to receiving outside expertise, but the domain expertise that resides within SWP may well be essential to solving the broader strategic issues that organizations will face in the future.

CONCLUSION

In this chapter, we have purposefully tried to look outside the center circle of Figure 1 to emphasize how the future of HR and SWP will be defined and optimized through multiple levels, as well as at the value of looking beyond the HR function as the profession defines its future. Yet a significant purpose of SWP is to guide the activities, structure, and role of the HR function itself. How will that aspect of SWP change?

Today, the talent deliverable often refers to the processes that make up the talent lifecycle, such as sourcing, acquiring, deploying, engaging, and developing. In the future, this will be extended to include the quality of talent decisions made by leaders and others outside the HR function. Today, deliverables in the area of organization often focus on managing change from one organization design to the next. In the future, this will be extended to a capability to thrive on constant change and a concept of organization design that is more about the relationships embodied in formal and informal networks than about formal structures or matrices. Today, deliverables in the area of culture often focus on broad aspirations such as "high performance," "integrity," or "innovation." In the future, this culture deliverable will increasingly draw on anthropology, with a keen eye for myths, symbols, and unstated assumptions and will accept the idea of multiple organization cultures, approaching culture as a way to embed unique and hard-to-copy capabilities in organizational values and routines. Today, deliverables in the area of leadership often focus on preparing and developing the top executive cadre. In the future, this leadership deliverable will increasingly focus on leadership at all levels and in many different roles, defining leadership not as a set of generic competencies or development experiences but as the collective capacity of individuals to embody and encourage sustainable values and dynamic change in whatever position they occupy.

HR competencies will evolve. The traditional array of competencies focused on the technical capability to design and implement HR programs. The capability to understand and mitigate risks in areas such as legal and contract compliance will remain important, but both HR and SWP will draw upon competencies that are seldom or never currently used. We already see an expansion of these competencies to include elements such as analytics, measurement, and project management. We foresee a future in which competencies in areas such as storytelling, education, and the logical frameworks used by other business disciplines (e.g., risk management, supply chain, and market segmentation) will become more prominent. As we noted earlier, these competencies may arrive not through the development of HR professionals per se but through the inflow of leaders from areas such as strategy, marketing, and communication—as SWP matures beyond an HR function or discipline and becomes a strategic organizational capability.

Indeed, future strategic workforce planners might well seek out coaching from orchestra conductors.

References

1. J. W. Boudreau and I. Ziskin, "The Future of HR and Effective Organizations," *Organizational Dynamics*, 40 (2011), pp. 255–267.

2. Ibid.

3. E. E. Lawler and S. A. Mohrman, "HR as a Strategic Partner: What Does It Take to Make It Happen?" *Human Resources Planning Journal*, 26 (2003), pp. 15–29.

4. W. Brockbank, "If HR Were Really Strategically Proactive: Present and Future Directions in HR's Contribution to Competitive Advantage," *Human Resource Management*, 38 (1999), pp. 337–352; E. A. Hughes, "HR Professionals Struggling to Shake Off

'Pen Pusher' Image," *Personnel Today* (October 24, 2006), pp. 4–5; S. Meisinger, "Assessing HR: The View from the C-Suites," *HRMagazine*, 49 (2004), p. 1; Z. Zhonghai, "Overcoming the System-First Mentality in China HR," *China Staff*, 11 (2005), pp. 15–16.

5. E. Cohen, *CSR for HR: A Necessary Partnership for Advancing Responsible Business Practices* (Sheffield, UK: Greenleaf Publishing, 2010); P. Mirvis, B. Googins, and S. Kinnicutt, "Vision, Mission, Values: Guideposts to Sustainability," *Organizational Dynamics*, 39 (2010), p. 4; W. Wehrmeyer, *Greening People: Human Resources and Environmental Management* (Sheffield, UK: Greenleaf Publishing, 1996).

6. J. Seabrook, "Snacks for a Fat Planet," *The New Yorker* (May 16, 2011), p. 54.

7. A. R. McIlvaine, "The Innovator," *Human Resource Executive Online* (2010). Retrieved April 28, 2011, from http://www.hreonline.com/HRE/story.jsp?storyId=461233863; *People Analytics, PhD Intern—Mountain View* (2009). Retrieved April 28, 2011, from http://depts.washington.edu/hcde/2009/02/25/people-analytics-phd-intern-mountain-view/.

8. J. W. Boudreau, *IBM's Global Workforce Initiative* (Washington, D.C.: Society for Human Resource Management, 2010).

9. HR Analytics Summit. Melissa Graves (biography) (2010). Retrieved April 29, 2011, from http://www.hranalyticssummit.nl/sprekers/.

10. M. Coleman, "Most Important Function of the Future=HR," HRN Europe Blog (2011). Retrieved April 28, 2011, from http://www.hrneurope.com/blog/?p=3086.

11. Boudreau, *IBM's Global Workforce Initiative*.

12. S. A. Mohrman and A. B. Shani (editors), *Organizing for Sustainability* (Bingley, UK: Emerald Group, 2011).

13. C. Marshall and G. B. Rossman, *Designing Qualitative Research*, 3rd ed. (London: Sage Publications, 1999).

14. *Mattel Imagination Center* (2012). Retrieved February 17, 2012, from http://www.facebook.com/MattelImaginationCenter.

15. F. Khatib et al., "Crystal Structure of a Monomeric Retroviral Protease Solved by Protein Folding Game Players," *Nature Structural & Molecular Biology*, 18 (2011), pp. 1175–1177. Retrieved from http://www.nature.com/nsmb/journal/v18/n10/full/nsmb.2119.htm.

16. J. W. Boudreau, "Strategic Industrial-Organizational Psychology Lies Beyond HR," *Industrial and Organizational Psychology*, 5 (2012), pp. 86–91.

17. B. Conaty and R. Charan, *The Talent Masters: Why Smart Leaders Put People Before Numbers* (New York: Random House, 2010).

18. *GE in Africa* (2011). Retrieved April 28, 2011, from http://www.ge.com/gh/company/africa.html.

John Boudreau is professor and research director at the University of Southern California's Marshall School of Business and Center for Effective Organizations. His research illuminates the bridge between human capital, talent, and sustainable competitive advantage. His more than sixty books and articles include *Retooling HR, Beyond HR,* and *Transformative HR.*

Ian Ziskin is president of EXec EXcel Group LLC, a consulting firm that builds individual and organizational credibility through human capital strategy, leadership and talent development, and organizational transformation. He is executive in residence and adviser to the University of Southern California's Center for Effective Organizations at the Marshall School of Business. His recently published book is *Willbe:13 Reasons Willbe's Are Luckier than Wannabe's.*

Plan Your Own Development: It's Up to You to Build Your Leadership Skills

Steve Arneson

MUCH OF WHAT'S WRITTEN about leadership has to do with the leader getting the most out of other people. If you're a leader, you have to start with the basics of workforce planning: knowing how many people you need to accomplish your goals, what each person will do, and how your people fit into the larger organization. On a micro level, this involves figuring out whom to hire, how to define their roles, and how to organize their work. As the popular saying goes, you have to get the right people (with the right skills) in the right roles at the right time—that's how you win. This, in essence, is the leader's job—ensuring that the team is appropriately staffed, trained, and motivated to accomplish the mission.

But who is making sure that the leaders fit their role? Who is developing and motivating the leaders? Who is ensuring that *their* skills stay current, that they keep up with the constantly changing business climate? Some organizations do provide leadership development, but most don't. Even those that sponsor leadership training offer very little for senior leaders; it's a fact that the higher you go in any organization, the less likely you are to get any formal development. If your company does provide leadership development, it's typically offered in short bursts—maybe an executive coach or enrollment in the flagship leadership development program. Maybe the company moves you once or twice to new roles throughout your career. But even the best organizations don't plan or enable your everyday development. *This means that you have to be responsible for your own leadership improvement.* If you want to bring your best every day, you have to continue to learn and grow, and that means taking charge of your own development.

All leaders have the potential to improve—but you have to work at it. You have to *want* to get better if you're going to become a more effective leader. Why is this important? There are several reasons, of course, but perhaps the most important is your obligation as a people manager. As a leader, you have an opportunity to help people grow and develop so they can take their skills and contributions to another level. But to positively impact others, you have to be willing to keep learning and growing yourself. You have to model working on your own development.

Why lead at all? What's so cool about being a leader? There are a lot of ways to contribute in this world that have nothing to do with leading people. While that's true, there's something magical about being the driving force that helps a group of people accomplish something special. My philosophy on leadership is that it's all about the people, not the task. Yes, you're trying to get stuff done; that's why the team or organization exists. But leaders don't lead real estate, computer systems, or budgets: They lead people. Leadership is about helping others be the best they can be. Years from now, no one is going to remember your specific results; what people are going to remember is what it felt like to work with you. Don't believe me? What were you working on five years ago this month? How about two years ago? Does that contract, spreadsheet, or PowerPoint presentation jump right to mind? How about this question: Do you remember who your boss was two years ago? How about your teammates? The fact is most people will remember your leadership in visceral terms (what it felt like to work for you) rather than a list of specific accomplishments.

Here's an illustration of what I mean. When I facilitate leadership development programs, I ask the participants to go through a "best boss/worst boss" exercise. I put the participants in small groups and ask them to share stories about the best boss they ever had and how these leaders made them feel. Their answers are almost all about personal connections: how the boss challenged, coached, empowered, and enabled them to succeed. You can feel the positive energy in the room as people share stories of bosses who helped them grow and develop. The mood shifts, though, when they share stories of the worst boss they ever had; metaphorically, it's like a shadow has been cast over the room. I've heard some really depressing bad boss stories, and they mainly have to do with people being ignored, humiliated, or mistreated by their boss. The common denominator is clear: *They didn't care about me as a person.*

How do *you* want to be remembered by your direct reports? As one of their best bosses ever or as the bad punch line in a "worst boss I ever had" story? It's up to you. Are you establishing a compelling vision and creating a winning strategy? Are you setting a high bar for excellence? Are you challenging your people to grow and develop? Are you delegating effectively, so you can spend your time leading as opposed to doing? Are you stretching your leadership across the organization? If the answer is *not as well as I could be*—then that's your starting point for development.

Fortunately, it *is* possible to get a little better each day as a leader. If you're willing to put in the time, you really can learn, practice, and apply new skills on a consistent basis. And given today's pace of change, you can't wait for the organization to bring leadership training to you—you have to be willing to work on your own game. You can't rely solely on your boss for coaching and mentoring. You need to take charge of your own growth as a leader. You need a personalized learning strategy and a customized plan of action. And here's the good news: You don't need a big budget or an elaborate infrastructure to develop yourself. All you need is the willingness to seek and listen to feedback and the ability to be reflective about how you can improve. In short, you have to pull yourself up by your own bootstraps. Here are five ways you can make yourself a better leader.

HOW ARE YOU SHOWING UP AS A LEADER?

If you're going to improve your leadership, you have to get a sense of how others see you as a leader. How are they experiencing your leadership? What's working for them? What's not working? How do they feel about your ability to guide the team in the right direction? What do they think of your leadership style or your strengths and opportunities as a leader? How do they *really* feel about working for you? If you're sincere about working on your leadership game, you have to solicit and listen to feedback. The people around you know how you're "showing up" as a leader; if you ask them, they'll tell you what you need to work on. Listen carefully to the input, and then reflect on your own leadership brand. Where can you get better? Whether it's a formal 360-degree feedback assessment or simple conversations with your direct reports, peers, and boss, gather feedback about your leadership style and spend time reflecting on what you learn.

But it's not just others that you need to consult. You need to have a few honest conversations with yourself, too. Where has your career taken you? What have you learned along the way? What opinions have you formed that are helping you to succeed, or maybe, setting you up for a fall? What do you do really well, and what do you *know* you still need to develop? Can you trust yourself to diligently work on new behaviors, or are you going to need some assistance? What about the quality of your relationships? Where do you have opportunities to leverage the people around you for support on this journey?

It's been my experience that leaders really do know (in their heart of hearts) what skills they need to improve. What they don't always know is the extent to which their behaviors are positively or negatively impacting others. That's why it's so important to combine feedback from others with your own honest reflection to form a strategy for personal development. Take the time to gather input on how you're showing up as a leader—it's the first step to improving your influence and impact.

ADD SOMETHING NEW TO YOUR GAME

Next, if you're serious about developing yourself, you need to do more than just leverage your strengths and minimize your current weaknesses. Those are just the skills you have today. If you really want to improve, you have to continually add new elements to your leadership toolkit. After all, the leaders who stand still are destined to stay at their current level, which really means falling behind. If you're not constantly learning and adding new capabilities, your peers will leave you in the dust and you'll get passed by the group of managers coming up behind you.

The first thing you need to do is figure out and articulate what leadership means to you—your leadership philosophy. It's hard to chart a new course of skills development if you don't know the game you're supposed to be playing. And what about a specific plan for adding new skills: In what areas do you need to focus? Where do you need to learn some new leadership techniques? How about adding skills like coaching, leading change, fostering innovation, or broadening your peer leadership? What if you added great storytelling to your repertoire? Where can you leverage a learning opportunity that also benefits the company? Finally, what about creating some space for yourself by adapting some new time management skills? That would allow you time to actually think and reflect, which might lead to even more ideas for skills development. Now there's a cool concept—more time to explore new ways to develop yourself. Who knows, you might find that adding new abilities to your game is actually more fun than polishing your existing skills.

GET CURIOUS ABOUT THE WORLD AROUND YOU

Now that you've added some new skills to your game, it's time to branch out and expand your horizons. Developing yourself as a leader also means stretching your point of view and seeing beyond the borders of your office (and company). The world is shrinking, but you need to go the other way: You need to *broaden* your perspective. As you move up the ladder in your organization, you're going to be expected to see the world through a much wider lens.

Start with your general business acumen. Do you have a firm grasp of your organization's strategy? Do you know what people do in other parts of the company? Do you know how your company plans to innovate in the years ahead? How about your own discipline—how well are you staying up with new developments in your field of practice? How about your competitors—do you know who is winning and losing market share in your industry? What about looking beyond your industry—what's happening in organizations that look nothing like yours? What can you learn from them? Are you tapping into your suppliers or vendors or reaching out to (and expanding) your network to find and share best practices? How about learning about cultures? Do you know much about the values and principles of the people you manage?

The world may be shrinking, but you need to go the other way. You need to *expand* your perspective. Leaders who don't broaden their horizons are destined to live in a narrow world, and that's not a formula for success in today's global economy.

STEP OUT OF YOUR COMFORT ZONE

Once you've expanded your worldview and stretched the boundaries of your leadership, it's time to take some risks with your development. It's time to really step outside your comfort zone. How about taking a more proactive stance with your boss about your next assignment or role? What if you got more aggressive about what *you* want to do next? What about joining a professional network outside work or improving your speaking and presentation skills? After all, if you're like most leaders, you'll be making more and more presentations to senior management as you move up the organization. Do you have trouble admitting mistakes or seeing things from another perspective? One of the best skills you can master as a leader is seeing all sides of an issue. How about acknowledging that you don't know everything there is to know about how your organization really works or how it makes money? What if you asked others to review your team's strategy twice a year? As you can see, there are a number of ways that you can demonstrate vulnerability as a leader, pushing yourself to see things differently.

We all have certain fears as a leader, and we've worked around them for years. If you truly want to break out and move up, why not take your development to a whole new level? Challenge yourself: You have a lot to gain by stepping outside your comfort zone and adapting different leadership behaviors. Pick out the one thing that you've always avoided as a leader and bring it inside your core set of skills.

IT'S NOT ABOUT YOU

In the end, leadership is about the people you lead . . . it's not about you. Which begs the question: Is this how you define leadership? Is this how you prioritize your time? Are you focused on the right big things, and is one of those priorities people development? Are you going out of your way to raise the profile of your employees? Are you making it a priority to offer feedback and coaching to your direct reports and others? How well do you listen? What if you volunteered your leadership skills to a nonprofit organization? How about teaching a class at the corporate university? These last two suggestions are both great ways to "give away" your knowledge and expertise. Finally, what is your plan for succession—how are you preparing the leader who will come after you? These are the questions that will help you make the transition from "it's about me" to "it's about others." Ask yourself: If you were to adopt a servant-leadership philosophy, how would that change your enjoyment of the role, your impact, your legacy?

Leadership is a privilege. If you manage other people, you've been given a great gift—the opportunity to change people's lives. If you're going to make a difference, however, you need to keep taking your leadership skills to a new level. That means taking control of your own learning agenda. Start by creating a customized leadership development plan, one that says: *I care about becoming a better leader.* It's the right thing to do for your own leadership brand, and it's certainly the right thing to do for your team.

As a leader, you have certain obligations when it comes to managing talent. You have to hire the right people; get them in the right jobs; and motivate, coach, and inspire them to do extraordinary work. But you also have to manage yourself. You have to plan your own development so you can continue to stay relevant and open to change. Your people deserve a leader who's going to embrace new ideas, lead innovation, and promote learning and growth. The best way to role model that behavior is to demonstrate your own willingness to continually develop as a leader.

Steve Arneson is an executive coach and leadership consultant. He is a corporate speaker and the author of *Bootstrap Leadership: 50 Ways to Break Out, Take Charge, and Move Up*, a book about leadership self-development. Visit www.arnesonleadership .com or email Steve at steve@arnesonleadership.com.

The Future Targets or Outcomes of HR Work: Individuals, Organizations, and Leadership

Dave Ulrich

WHEN HR PROFESSIONALS PARTICIPATE in strategy or business conversations, what are the unique contributions they make? Imagine an HR professional who sits in meetings on emerging markets, managing costs, or increasing innovation. HR contributions in these settings are not just about the practices of HR (recruiting, paying, training) but about the outcomes of designing and delivering good HR practices. I like to think about three targets or outcomes of HR work: individuals, organizations, and leadership (see Figure 1).

FIGURE 1. TARGETS OR OUTCOMES OF HR WORK.

To deliver any strategy, individuals need to be more productive, organizations need to have the right capabilities, and leadership needs to be widely shared throughout the organization. In discussions on emerging markets, cost, or innovation, HR professionals might ask:

► *Individual:* What talent or human capital do we need to make this strategy happen?

► *Organization:* What organization capabilities do we need to make this strategy happen?

► *Leadership:* What do our leaders need to be good at to make this strategy happen?

Once these targets or outcomes have been defined, then the HR practices may be designed and delivered to accomplish these outcomes. Below we highlight some of the future thinking for each of the three targets of HR.

INDIVIDUAL ABILITY (TALENT OR HUMAN CAPITAL)

At the risk of grossly oversimplifying, let me suggest that there is actually a deceptively simple formula for talent that can help HR professionals and their general managers make talent more productive: Talent = Competence * Commitment * Contribution. Going forward, all three elements of this equation need to be considered and integrated to fully manage talent.

Competence means that individuals have the knowledge, skills, and values required for today's and tomorrow's jobs. One company clarified competence as *right skills, right place, right job, right time.* For example, an emerging trend in the workforce planning domain of competence improvement is to identify key positions and match people to positions. Competence clearly matters because incompetence leads to poor decision making. But without commitment, competence is discounted. Highly competent employees who are not committed are smart, but they don't work very hard.

Committed or engaged employees work hard, put in their time, and do what they are asked to do. Commitment trends focus on building an employee value proposition to ensure that employees who give value to their organization will in turn receive value back. In the last decade, commitment and competence have been the bailiwicks for talent. But we have found that the next generation of employees may be competent (able to do the work) and committed (willing to do the work), but unless they are making a real contribution through the work (finding meaning and purpose in their work), then their interest in what they are doing diminishes and their productivity wanes.

Contribution occurs when employees feel that their personal needs are being met through their participation in their organization. Leaders who are meaning makers for their employees help employees find a sense of contribution through the work that they do. HR professionals play the role of architects who design organizations that embed meaning throughout the organization. Organizations may be a universal setting where individuals find abundance in their lives through their work, and they want this investment of their time to be meaningful. Simply stated, then, competence deals with the head (being able), commitment with the hands and feet (being there), and contribution with the heart (simply being).

In this talent equation, the three terms are multiplicative, not additive. If any one concept is missing, the other two will not replace it. A low score in competence will not ensure talent even when the employee is engaged and contributing. Talented employees must have skills, wills, and purposes; they must be capable, committed, and contributing. HR leaders can engage their general managers to identify and improve each of these three dimensions to increase individual ability and gain productivity.

Going forward, there are a few likely implications of this formula. First, all three concepts (competence, commitment, and contribution) need to be managed together. It is not enough to have competent employees if they are not engaged and not feeling a sense of purpose. Second, competence definitions will likely be less about the skills of an individual and more about how those skills match the requirements of the position. Being the "employer of choice" is insufficient unless one is the employer of choice *of employees customers would choose*. Third, as employees increasingly seek purpose in their lives in general, they turn to work as a setting for finding meaning. Next-generation employees will be increasingly worried about finding meaning and purpose in their lives through social responsibility.

ORGANIZATION CAPABILITY (CULTURE)

Talent is not enough. Great individuals who do not work well together as a team or in their organization will not be successful. Some simple statistics show the importance of teamwork over talent:

▶ In hockey, the leading scorer is on the team that wins the Stanley Cup only 22 percent of the time.

▶ In soccer, the winner of the Golden Boot (the leading scorer) is on the team that wins the World Cup only 20 percent of the time.

▶ In basketball, the player who scores the most points is on the team that wins the NBA finals only 15 percent of the time.

▶ In movies, the winner of the Oscar for best actor or actress is in the move that wins the Oscar for best movie only 15 percent of the time.

Great individual talent may succeed 15 to 25 percent of the time, but teamwork matters most. In recent years, people have called for human resources to be relabeled as the talent or human capital function, with a focus on workforce, people, and competencies. Without attending to teamwork, workplace, processes, and culture, HR misses opportunities to have sustainable impact. HR professionals sitting in business discussions in the future need to offer insights on organizations as well as on individuals.

The organization of the future exists today, but not in the traditional sense. Generally, when thinking about an organization, we turn to morphology (i.e., the study of structure or form), and we define an organization by its roles, rules, and routines:

▶ *Roles* define the hierarchy of who reports to whom and who has accountability for work.

▶ *Rules* represent policies and prescriptions for how work is done.

▶ *Routines* reflect processes or cultures within the workplace.

Combined, these three traditional factors capture an organization's structure or shape. In the last decade, however, a lot of restructuring in organizations has been done to rightsize, reshape, reengineer, redesign, delayer, and rebuild organizations based on these three characteristics of morphology. Although this restructuring work encapsulates organization design, it is only a small part of the complete organization of the future.

When we work with executives to define an organization, we ask them a simple question: "Can you name a company you admire?" The list of admired companies varies, but it often includes such well-known businesses as Apple, Disney, General Electric, Google, Microsoft, and Unilever. We then ask the executives, "How many levels of management are in the admired business?" Almost no one knows.

More important, no one really cares—because we do not admire an organization because of its roles, rules, or routines. Instead, we admire Apple because it seems to continually design easy-to-use products; we admire Disney for the service we experience at its sites; we admire GE because of its capacity to build leaders in diverse industries; and we admire Google and Microsoft for their ability to innovate and shape their industry. In other words, organizations are not known for their *structure* but for their *capabilities*.

Capabilities represent what the organization is known for, what it is good at doing, and how it patterns activities to deliver value. The capabilities define many of the intangibles that investors pay attention to, the company brand to which customers can relate, and the culture that shapes employee behavior. These capabilities also become the identity of the company, the deliverables of HR practices, and the key to implementing business strategy. A Duke client study found that HR professionals today are "shifting their focus from individual competency to organizational capability."[1] McKinsey also looked to the future and found that capabilities will become more important than individual competencies:

Nearly 60 percent of respondents to a recent McKinsey survey say that building organizational capabilities such as lean operations or project or talent management is a top-three priority for their companies. Yet only a third of companies actually focus their training programs on building the capability that adds the most value to their companies' business performance.[2]

Competencies represent the abilities of individuals, while capabilities capture the organization's identity (see Figure 2).

FIGURE 2. DIFFERENTIATING COMPETENCE VS. CAPABILITY.

	Individual	Organizational
Technical	1 An individual's functional competence	3 An organization's core competencies
Social	2 An individual's leadership ability	4 An organization's capabilities

In this figure, the individual-technical cell (1) represents a person's functional competence, such as technical expertise in marketing, finance, or manufacturing. The individual-social cell (2) is about a person's leadership ability—for instance, the ability to set direction, communicate a vision, and motivate people. The organizational-technical cell (3) comprises a company's core technical competencies. For example, a financial services firm must know how to manage risk. The organizational-social cell (4) represents an organization's underlying DNA, culture, and personality.[3]

In the future, HR professionals will work to identify, assess, and build capabilities. Organizational diagnosis should focus less on redesigning structure and more on assessing capabilities. Some of the traditional and accepted capabilities that have been discussed extensively have included efficiency (e.g., lean manufacturing), globalization, quality, customer service, and speed of change or agility. Some emerging capabilities for organizations to succeed in the future might include:

▶ *Risk management.* In volatile and changing markets, organizations that can anticipate and manage risk will be more able to create sustainable change.[4]

▶ *Social responsibility.* With an increasing concern for environmental issues, organizations that have the ability to be socially responsible will attract employees, customers, and investors.

► *Simplicity.* As the business world becomes more complex, organizations that can remain simple in product design, customer interfacing, and administrative systems will be more responsive.[5]

► *Connection.* With technology being the workplace of the future, organizations that can form connections among employees, between employees and customers, and with partners will be more likely to have collaborative social networks around the world.[6]

► *Innovation.* While not a new topic, innovation will increasingly be broadened to include not only products, but customer interfaces or channels, administrative processes, and business models.[7] The targets or outcomes of HR may include individuals, organizations, and leadership. When sitting in business meetings, HR professionals deliver value when they offer insights on how each of these targets can be aligned to deliver business results.

When HR professionals see the connection of organization capabilities to individual abilities, they begin to make the whole (organization) more than the sum of the individual parts (individual talent).

In addition, in the future, HR professionals should begin to see the evolution of culture from events to patterns to identity. Events represent what happens in the company. Patterns represent norms, values, and expectations—who we are. We would propose that ultimately culture is the identity of the company in the mind of the best external stakeholders (e.g., customers). Apple's culture should be around innovation because innovation is Apple's core identity. Marriott's culture should be around service because Marriott has worked to build a service identity. When the outside expectations become the basis for culture and competencies, HR professionals become strategic positioners for their organizations.

LEADERSHIP BRAND

Ultimately, leaders bring together both individuals and organizations to solve customer problems. But there is a difference between leaders and leadership. *Leaders* refers to individuals who have unique abilities to guide the behavior of others. *Leadership* refers to an organization's capacity to build future leaders. An individual leader matters, but an organization's leadership matters more over time. Looking forward, HR professionals will need to not only help individual leaders be more effective through coaching, 360 feedback, and individual development plans—they will need to help build leadership depth by investing in leadership development.

In our studies of leadership, we have identified five things that HR professionals can do going forward to upgrade the quality of leadership.

1. *Build the business case for leadership.* HR can show that the quality of leadership will drive performance both inside and outside the organization. Organizations with leadership depth will have the capacity to respond to changing business conditions, execute strategy, increase investor confidence, and anticipate customer requirements.

2. *Define leadership effectiveness from the outside/in.* Consistent with the logic of creating value for external stakeholders, HR can help define what makes an effective leader from the outside/in. Often, leadership success remains either inside the company (leaders learn from other leaders in the company who have succeeded) or inside the individual. In the future, I think that the criteria of leadership should start with customers. In a number of companies, we start to define effective leadership by viewing the company's commercials or other media presentations. These externally focused broadcasts define the company's intended brand. We then identify the leadership behaviors consistent with this external brand. When leaders inside the company behave consistently with the expectations of customers (and other stakeholders) outside the company, the leadership will be more sustainable and effective. HR professionals who define internal leadership through external expectations will set more relevant and impactful leadership standards.

3. *Assess leaders.* Once leadership standards are set, leaders need to be assessed on how well they meet those standards. With an external view, leadership 360s may be expanded to 720s, where customers, suppliers, communities, regulators, or other external stakeholders may be included in assessing targeted leaders. In one company, the board of directors now regularly assesses the CEO's performance both inside the company with his team and among his employees and outside the company with key stakeholders. This type of assessment offers a more complete view of leaders who have roles with external stakeholders. Assessment also may help determine high potential and future leaders by looking at the extent to which they have aspirations to lead, ability to meet future standards, and agility to learn and grow. HR professionals charged with leadership assessment may monitor current and aspiring leaders' ability to serve customers.

4. *Invest in leadership.* The traditional formula for leadership investment has been 70–20–10. The logic is that 70 percent of learning and development is on the job, 20 percent is from feedback and observation of role models, and only 10 percent is from training. We think that this formula and should shift to something like:

- 50 percent of learning from job experience, including role models and coaching. Most learning still comes from doing and experiencing.
- 30 percent of learning from updated training. Traditionally, training is what we call a tourist activity where people visit the event, observe it, and may leave with a memento (the training notebook is the equivalent of a tourist's

pictures) but little impact. We suggest "guest training," where the participant in training is immersed in the business while in the training session. This means prework to know what the participant should leave with, learning solutions during the training, live and relevant cases and problems to be solved, customers as faculty and participants, and follow-up to ensure that ideas taught had real impact.

- 20 percent of learning from life experience. Many of us learn from experiences outside work, in families, social settings, social networks, volunteer work, reading, and traveling. When companies can encourage and access knowledge from these life experiences, leaders will broaden their repertoire. For example, one company uses its philanthropy efforts as development opportunities for high potential leaders.

This mix of leadership investments may be the basis for systematic development of leadership throughout an organization.

5. *Measure leadership.* Leadership investments have often been measured using Kirkpatrick's scale: attitude, knowledge, behavior, and results. This is an outstanding scale. I envision two changes in the future, both expanding on the results. First, in the case of leadership, HR professionals show how leadership will help an organization deliver value to its stakeholders. This value should be measured as an indicator of leadership success. Second, we have talked about a new ROI for leadership (and HR)—Return on Intangibles. As noted above, intangibles represent about 50 percent of a company's market value. When we can link HR and leadership to this market value, the issues become even more salient to line managers.

CONCLUSION

In the future, the targets or outcomes of HR may include individuals, organizations, and leadership. When sitting in business meetings, HR professionals who offer insights on how each of these targets can be aligned to deliver business results deliver value.

References

1. *Learning and Development in 2011: A Focus on the Future* (Duke Corporate Education Client Studies, 2008).

2. *Building Organization Capabilities*, McKinsey Global Survey. Retrieved from http://www.mckinseyquarterly.com/Building_organizational_capabilities_McKinsey _Global_Survey_results_2540.

3. The concept of capability is laid out in Dave Ulrich and Dale Lake, *Organization Capability: Competing from the Inside/Out* (New York: John Wiley, 1990). It is further

defined in Dave Ulrich and Norm Smallwood, "Capitalizing on Capabilities," *Harvard Business Review* (2005).

4. *Designing a Successful ERM Function: A Global Perspective on Risk Management Structure and Governance for the Insurance Industry*, Deloitte Consulting (2008). The work on managing risk is laid out in *Enterprise Risk Management—Integrated Framework*, Commission of Sponsoring Organizations of the Treadway Commission (September 2004).

5. See work by Ron Ashkenas, *Simply Effective:How to Cut Through Complexity in Your Organization and Get Things Done* (Boston: Harvard Business Press, 2009).

6. This logic is laid out in a PwC report, *Managing Tomorrow's People. The Future of Work to 2020*. Retrieved from http://www.pwc.com/gx/en/managing-tomorrows-people/future-of-work.

7. Excellent work on innovation is in Larry Keeley's work (www.doblin.com).

Dave Ulrich is a professor at the Ross School of Business, University of Michigan and a partner at the RBL Group (http://www.rbl.net), a consulting firm focused on helping organizations and leaders deliver value. He studies how organizations build capabilities of leadership, speed, learning, accountability, and talent through leveraging human resources. He has helped generate award-winning databases that assess alignment between strategies, organization capabilities, HR practices, HR competencies, and customer and investor results. Dave has published more than 200 articles and book chapters and more than 25 books. He edited *Human Resource Management* from 1990 to 1999, served on the editorial board of four journals, on the board of directors for Herman Miller, and on the board of trustees at Southern Virginia University. He is a Fellow in the National Academy of Human Resources.

Dave has received numerous honors. They include, in 2011, being ranked #1 most influential thought leader in HR by *HR Magazine*; being ranked #23 in Thinkers 50 as a management thought leader; and being ranked in the Top 100 Thought Leaders in Trustworthy Leadership Behavior. His book *Why of Work* (coauthored with Wendy Ulrich) was a #1 best-seller in 2010 in the *Wall Street Journal* and *USA Today*. He received an honorary doctorate from the University of Abertey in Dundee, Scotland. Dave has consulted and done research with more than half of the Fortune 200. He can be reached at dou@umich.edu.

Postlude

Dan L. Ward

BILL MAKI AND I met at an annual HRPS conference in 1980. While the conference had many great speakers, a dozen "hard-core" modeling and forecasting enthusiasts slipped away to meet in a suite one afternoon for a few hours to share comments on their approaches to what was then still called "manpower" planning. This original "data dozen" included Dick Niehaus, Jim Sheridan, Walt Garrett, and Tom Bechet, as well as Bill and me. Jim Walker made a brief appearance, but as the founder of HRPS, he had other obligations during the conference.

As the youngest and least experienced participant in the room that day, I was awed by the other attendees. I had been invited because of my proficiency with Bell Lab's Interactive Flow Simulator (IFS). A few of the attendees thought the kid might possibly have some potential for the future. IFS was a "comprehensive" manpower-modeling tool, originally developed in response to EEO class action litigation. It was used by several dozen Bell System planners to create workforce forecasts for individual companies. IFS generated detailed forecasts by individual positions (as required by the class action settlement) for the million-plus employees of AT&T. It killed a lot of trees with 100-page printouts, but many thought it was the future for all workforce forecasting and modeling.

We talked about current practices and future directions, but no one in the room predicted a migration away from the grandiose mainframe FORTRAN computer models like IFS to the more discrete special focus applications we see today. It was beyond the realm of our awareness.

ADVANCED PRACTITIONERS UNITE!

Tom Bechet, Bill Maki, and I were featured as speakers at HRPS workshops and conferences. We evangelized for our computer models and used emerging tools like IBM-PCs and Compaq and Apple computers to teach others how to build their own models and forecasts. Rob Tripp attended one of our workshops and was immediately drafted into the group for the work he was doing at General Motors and later at Ford. The four of us regularly shared thoughts about ways to advance our field until Tom passed away.

During the 1990s, we held annual *advanced practitioner colloquia* to advance the state of the art. HRPS hosted the initial two sessions, but HRPS needed to expand attendance to a broader audience so hosting costs could be recovered. The core group rebelled because we wanted to retain the "advanced practitioner" nature of the event. The group began holding private meetings, hosted by various employers such as CitiCorp, AT&T, Texaco, and General Mills. The host provided a meeting room and basic refreshments, and the attendees covered their own expenses. The only additional "cost" to attend was a requirement for a thirty-minute presentation on your current work and active participation in the group discussion. It was an invitation-only event, but participants could invite anyone they perceived as a "worthy" participant.

Unfortunately, by the late 1990s, we found it increasingly difficult to get sponsorship for these meetings. I am actually the last of the original dozen from the 1980 event who is still working in the field. Without a sustained, strong advocacy core, the number of forecasting and modeling papers also declined by the year 2000, and the practice of SWP slipped into a relatively quiet period.

SWP'S REAWAKENING

In autumn 2010, Bill, Rob, and I had a conversation about the resurgence of interest in the field. We were pleased to see recent work, led by a variety of groups such as the Human Capital Institute, Infohrm, SuccessFactors, the Institute for Corporate Productivity, the Institute for Human Resources, the Society for Workforce Planning Professionals, and a variety of LinkedIn and Facebook groups. The field did not die; it had only entered a temporarily quiet period and is now exploding into a wide variety of general and special interest groups.

We were enthusiastic to see the revival of interest in SWP. Better and more user-friendly tools were coming online. We believed the next generation of SWP would have very exciting prospects. We also, however, shared a concern that many of the recent advocates seemed unaware of the historical practices and progress.

Some very talented people were starting from scratch and consequently reinventing the wheel. We saw others making mistakes we had encountered and mostly solved, twenty years earlier. Lessons learned were not being shared. The field seemed largely stuck in covering old ground and generally unaware it was doing so. We hoped we could pass along some of our accumulated knowledge from our combined 100-plus years of SWP. This might save the current generation weeks, months, or even years of effort if these people could leverage the past experience and not repeat some of the hard-knocks lessons we endured.

THIS BOOK

Bill, Rob, and I quickly realized this was beyond the scope of an article, and this book began to take shape. We wanted it to be a book that we would enjoy reading—not just an academic treatise, but also not just a benchmarking compilation. The concept matured into a collective work, drawing on some of the best minds in and around the field, with four major subcollections of chapters.

The first section would briefly provide an overview of the evolution of the field to put things in context. The second would have practical experience chapters by people who are successfully practicing various aspects of the field within major organizations. The third section would focus specifically on analytics that form the central core of the field. The fourth section would have chapters from a few thought leaders on where the field will be going next.

We invited more than forty others who had established reputations for their impactful results within or on the edges of SWP to contribute to the four sections of the book. Most were happy to participate, and you are reading the result of these collective efforts.

CONTINUING DIALOGUE

Bill, Rob, and I also hoped this book could spark a continuing dialogue. The field is evolving quickly today. Tools are becoming more flexible, more sophisticated, and sometimes even simpler to use. We want the book to encourage more contemporary sharing events—not necessarily commercial conferences primarily focused on revenue generation, but more in line with the advanced practitioners' colloquia of twenty years ago. We believe social media and virtual meeting venues provide incredible opportunities for more real-time dialogue. Information when you need it, not stockpiled for a once-a-year event.

The LinkedIn discussion group, Strategic Workforce Planning, has invited readers of the book to share comments about ideas discussed in the book and to participate in discussions about future directions.

The LinkedIn SWP group is not associated with any vendor, but is a loose collection of people with shared passion for SWP topics. There are other groups with similar passion for SWP, but Rob and I wanted to stay with a grass roots approach that was not formally hosted by a specific association or vendor. We wanted a noncommercial venue where interested parties could share or test *non-proprietary* tools and techniques. We also welcome participation by emerging discussion groups who may not as of yet have achieved critical mass with their own efforts. We encourage you to drop in and connect with us.

If you are not already a LinkedIn member, you will need to register for access. Basic access is free and you can sign up at:

http://www.linkedin.com/

Once you are a registered LinkedIn user, you will need to apply to join the Strategic Workforce Planning members group. At the time this was written, the group had 2,400 members from around the world. Ms. Lacey All is the group manager and has agreed to approve membership for the readers of this book. There is no charge associated with membership, we only ask that you participate in the group discussion.

http://www.linkedin.com/groups?gid=77062

SEEDING SOME DIALOGUE: FLASH MOB SWP

Per the preceding comments about initiating a continuing dialogue, we hope to seed speculation about an initial scenario for the longer-term prospects of our field: a *flash mob* approach to SWP. Scenarios are valuable for stretching our thinking. These ruminations are not constructed as a classical scenario design but rather are along the lines of thinking out loud about what may be, with the hopes you will join in the fun.

Where We Are Today

In the future, we may not need a new version of this book. Strategic Workforce Planning may not exist in a form we would recognize today. It is not just that the definition will continue to evolve as it has in the past. Our current SWP tools were mostly designed and optimized for twentieth-century organizational constructs. Most of the SWP enhancements we have witnessed over the past forty years have been in the nature of faster, better, and cheaper ways of doing the same old things. Indeed, we truly can measure better, understand more, and make more improved and accurate forecasts. The concept has evolved to adopt a broader concept of "workforce" to include people who are not just company-badged "employees," but also temporary, contractual, or jointly aligned workers from multiple organizations. Despite these evolutions in organization scope, tools, techniques and jargon; the definition of the right person at the right place and time—where "right" refers to alignment with the organization's strategic interests—is still accurately used for SWP for most organizations. To quote Peter Howes, "it's all about the gap" between supply and demand for talent. Yet this definition may not fit in the future.

In *The Ghost in the Machine*, philosopher Arthur Koestler suggested that traditional human organizational structures are always doomed to failure as a result of the core nature of people.[1] He observed that people inevitably try to sustain organizations beyond their appropriate life span. Organizations are rigid and based on architectural concepts. He predicted that more adaptive biological models were needed. He envisioned semiautonomous groups that had no fixed structure, but rather would constantly align and realign on a temporary basis to engage in activities of mutual benefit or interest. He called these *holonic* organizations.

Where Will We Be Tomorrow?

While Koestler's *holonic* organizational metaphor did not evolve as he predicted, social media has spawned the incredibly fast growth of a phenomenon that resembles his concept, known as flash mobs.

▶ Could these flash mobs be the early signs of a future when all manner of human activity may be accomplished as a function of a real-time labor market for the identification, capability confirmation, and deployment of resources?

▶ Was the open source software concept that created products such as Linux a sign of things to come?

▶ Are traditional approaches to organization, structure, and planning about to be overwhelmed by a just-in-time approach to work?

The Arab Spring protests evolved from the real-time connectivity of people using social media on a scale never before witnessed. The revolutions occurred too quickly to be controlled by local governments using traditional approaches to maintaining the status quo. The next cycle may be even faster in some countries. Boycotts and social protests are conceived and executed literally overnight. More benign flash mob–like events have occurred for a variety of community service and charity events.

Disaster relief has already entered a new era where "unofficial" groups respond to emergencies long before traditional emergency services arrive. *Team Rubicon* is one example. (See http://teamrubiconusa.org/.) This informal network of military veterans began in the aftermath of events like the 2010 earthquake in Haiti and the 2011 earthquake and tsunami disaster in Japan. Rubicon volunteers connecting via social media have mobilized their chainsaws to clear roads of storm damage before the first of the official first responders have even loaded their trucks.

Some traditional emergency groups have warned that these "uncoordinated" efforts will result in the wrong supplies being collected and compounding the disaster instead of helping. However, advocates say these efforts use real-time supply chain management concepts. They suggest that these new groups are more adept at quickly responding to specific, actual needs than are the traditional organizations. Does this sound like a competitive turf war with the old school trying to snuff out the new, nontraditional competitors? Progress is inevitable, and those who resist it will eventually change or die. Change is hard but inevitable.

SWP exists because throughout human history, we have learned that it takes time to develop or identify special talents needed to preserve, maintain, or improve activities beneficial to a way of life. It takes time to develop the needed expertise. SWP improves our ability to anticipate demand and ensure an effective supply. As Dave Ulrich suggested in the last chapter of the book, the next challenge may be how to acquire *abilities* and *capabilities*, and the SWP challenge may be in how to strategize for this resource planning, not using "employees" but rather by effectively mobilizing temporarily aligned resources, organized under a yet to be defined concept of new "leadership." The next-gen SWP may involve time frames and recruiting processes that are hard for a twentieth-century thinker to imagine—not unlike the limited ability of nineteenth-century buggy whip manufacturers to conceive of the impact of new transportation breakthroughs.

How Do We Get There?

It is hard for this traditionally trained human capital economist to visualize exactly how the path might evolve from a flash mob to the real-time creation of a next-generation tablet alternative to iPads. I must, however, recognize that this failure of my imagination does not mean it will not happen. Not only is it possible; it may even be inevitable in a world where customer evaluations of performance could easily replace traditional certificates and degrees as primary credentials. If we could review the actual customer ratings of someone's work over the past five years, would we really care what degree or certificate he or she had from a twenty-year-old training program?

Frankly, I cannot yet visualize the go-forward path for next-generation SWP. I am asking for your help. The community of people who read this book is greater than just the sum of the individual readers. Share insights. It is better to be on the front end of the curve, thinking about what will happen, than to be dragged along at the back end, wondering what happened.

How about an SWP flash mob? *Embrace the possibilities!* Stay tuned for dates and times. . . . See you at:

http://www.linkedin.com/groups?gid=77062

Reference

1. Arthur Koestler, *The Ghost in the Machine* (New York: Penguin Books, 1967, 1990).

Index